Moral Spaces

Moral Spaces

Rethinking Ethics and World Politics

David Campbell and Michael J. Shapiro, editors

University of Minnesota Press

Minneapolis

London

Published by the University of Minnesota Press
111 Third Avenue South, Suite 290
Minneapolis, MN 55401-2520
http://www.upress.umn.edu

Library of Congress Cataloging-in-Publication Data

Moral spaces : rethinking ethics and world politics / David Campbell
    and Michael J. Shapiro, editors.
        p.   cm.
    Includes index.
    ISBN 0-8166-3275-8 (alk. paper). — ISBN 0-8166-3276-6 (pbk. :
alk. paper)
    1. Ethics.   2. World politics — Moral and ethical aspects.
I. Campbell, David, 1961–   II. Shapiro, Michael J.
BJ55.M57   1999
172 — dc21   99-13979

11 10 09 08 07 06 05 04 03 02 01 00 99   10 9 8 7 6 5 4 3 2 1

Contents

INTRODUCTION

From Ethical Theory to the Ethical Relation

David Campbell and Michael J. Shapiro

> The interests of the national society for which government has to
> concern itself are basically those of its military security, the integrity
> of its political life, and the well-being of its people. These needs have
> no moral quality.[1]

Space, Subjectivity, and Ethics

Written before the "official" end of the Cold War, George Kennan's
authoritative declaration encapsulates concisely the realist tradition's view
that moral concerns are largely inappropriate to international affairs.[2]
What enabled Kennan and others to claim the divorce of national interests and state security from morality is a spatial imaginary in which
the virtues of sovereignty are unproblematically affirmed.

However, this affirmation of sovereignty is itself insinuated with moral
considerations, for it is a stance that is enabled by faith in the notion of
raison d'état, an acceptance of the priority accorded the security of the
state. Far from being a principle that keeps morality at bay, reason of
state constitutes the realist problematic as a moral argument in which
the claim is that "the reasons for overriding the constraints of ordinary
morality in emergency situations are themselves moral."[3]

Kennan's problematization of the issue thus requires one to overlook
the way in which "the national" is itself a "moral" construction. Eliding
the ethical investments of "amoral" formulations is something that, because of the recent march of "normative theory" in international relations, is superficially at least increasingly difficult to sustain. Indeed, the

intellectual contestations of a discipline caught cold by the global transformations of the last decade have been marked by the resurgence of
moral questions and dilemmas, with "ethics and international affairs"
becoming something of a growth literature.[4]

This moral cartography of realism, manifest in Kennan's paradigmatic
claim about the amorality of sovereignty, has, however, done more than
legitimize the evacuation of ethical concerns from International Relations. It has also circumscribed the "ethics and international affairs" literature that seeks to redress the moral lacunae of the field. In this literature, the dilemmas of ethical theorizing are generally posed in terms
of ameliorating or overcoming, rather than contesting and problematizing, the parameters of anarchy and sovereignty.

As a result, the "ethics and international affairs" literature is based
on some questionable fundamentals. First there is the unsustainable assumption that "normative" concerns manifest issues and practices hitherto unknown or unrecognized, and that they can be distinguished from
a realm called "empirical theory." Second, having allegedly disentangled the normative from the empirical, the claim that problems can be
dealt with by the joining in intellectual marriage of an already established political theory literature of ethics and the untheorized domain
of international relations is open to serious question. All of which suggests that this literature is compromised by the orthodox frames of reference within which inquiry is largely contained.

These orthodox frames of reference — and the accounts of the
(im)probability of ethical action in international relations they license —
follow a familiar trajectory. They depend on the notion of a prior and
autonomous sovereign subjectivity (whether it be the individual, the
state, or some other corporate actor) deploying either a supposedly universal moral code (the deontological view) or muddling through their
situation in order to achieve what might be thought of as the best possible outcome (the consequentialist account).[5] In more specific terms,
these concerns are mostly articulated in the context of a debate between
communitarians and cosmopolitans, with both camps searching for a
singular ethical theory that could be devised in the abstract and applied in the concrete.[6] Judged from within these confines, where justice
is said to be about impartial rules, the impact of more critical approaches
is deemed to be insufficient.[7]

The approach to ethics and world politics that integrates the various contributions to this anthology involves a shift of focus from that which constitutes the familiar field of "ethics and international affairs." Indeed, Kennan's realist position, and the "ethics and international affairs" literature that claims to address realism's moral blindness, is representative of the thinking to which the contributions to this volume provide a critique. Rather than engaging in the traditional search for a grounding for supranational principles, the various contributions investigate the contingencies involved in specific, historically situated encounters. This is because responding effectively to the dilemmas that emerge from the spatial assumptions of the realist problematic, as well as the communitarian/cosmopolitan debate, requires a sustained consideration of the relationship between space, subjectivity, and ethics. Daniel Warner's chapter begins this process by revealing the links between community and responsibility, concluding with the thought that the search for communities in which responsibility can be grounded should itself be reconsidered.

The most general insight that integrates our studies is a recognition of the radical entanglement between moral discourses and spatial imaginaries. Accordingly, a primary emphasis of the investigations is on "moral spaces," the bounded locations whose inhabitants acquire the privileges deriving from practices of ethical inclusion, and on the need to intervene in the dominant practices of intelligibility that enable geopolitical imaginaries at the expense of an ethics of encounter. This is considered most obviously in Shapiro's chapter, where the focus is on narratives of collective identity, their spatial effects, and their implication in violence.

Against Theory, Ethics, and Justice

In constituting an alternative (not the *only* alternative, and not *the* alternative) to the increasingly familiar field of "ethics and international affairs" that has dominated recent thinking about ethics and world politics, the contributions to this volume together rethink the nature of "international" and "ethics," as well as the relationship between those terms. While this alternative — if we can speak of a singular position emerging from shared sensibilities of the contributors — does not stand in opposition to all that has gone before, it does distinguish itself from some common and central formulations that predominate in international relations literatures.

Most obviously this alternative is "against theory" insofar as it resists the desire for *a* theory of ethics that articulates abstracted principles in a systematized manner.[8] Struggling with the desire for systematic abstractions does not mean that these analyses engage in the simplistic rejection of the universal and its substitution by the particular. Indeed, especially given the attention paid to Levinas in the following arguments, there is a recognition of the way in which the concerns of the contributors embody a form of ethical transcendence. This form of ethical transcendence is not the transcendence of an ahistorical ego or principle. Instead, it is transcendence in the sense that alterity, being's other, is an inescapable condition produced by *differance* rather than ontology. The recognition of this results in a transcendence without presence, something that approaches a sense of universality without the fixed character of a universal foundation. In consequence, rather than being concerned with a *theory of ethics,* the contributors to this volume are motivated by *the ethical relation* in which our responsibility to the other is the basis for reflection. Eschewing hierarchical constructions of moral value, they focus instead on the always already ethical situation integral to the habitus of experience.

It is in this context that the arguments here might be thought of as being "against ethics." This position does not mean they wish to promote or be associated with the nonethical or the amoral. Instead it contests the idea that the development of a theory of ethics produces a body of thought called Ethics removed from the contexts that concern our authors. John Caputo's book *Against Ethics* offers the fullest account of this view.[9] In William Connolly's chapter, Caputo's focus on suffering and the experience of the flesh is endorsed insofar as it cuts through the abstractions of ethical theory. Caputo's concern is problematized and developed, however, so as to emphasize the political character of those most difficult ethical cases, and to formulate an ethos of critical engagement that drives an affirmative politics of becoming.

Being "against" theory, ethics, and justice is thus a matter of being against the orthodox renderings of those domains and the ethico-political effects of those renderings. Being "against" theory, ethics, and justice stems in large part from a suspicion that those preoccupied with theories of ethics end up eliding the ethical relation; that the concern with Ethics obscures the contingencies and complexities of the ethical; and that a striving for the rules and principles of justice, especially those that demand impartiality, effects injustice. In this context, being "against" theory, ethics, and justice is an affirmative position designed to foster the ethical relation.

It is for that reason that the work of Emmanuel Levinas assumes particular importance for many of the contributors to this volume. As John Caputo recognizes, "modern ethics is a species of the metaphysics of subjectivity."[10] We do not claim that Levinas provides unproblematic answers or satisfactory formulations, but when it comes to the inescapable connections between ethics and subjectivity, perhaps no thinker is more thought provoking than Levinas. Moreover, given the oft-made challenge to poststructuralist perspectives to articulate *an* ethics, working through the provocations of Levinas, Derrida, and others provides a reasoned response. And because the terms of the response are somewhat different from those of the challenge, they locate effectively the contingencies of rationalistic perspectives with universalistic aspirations.[11] This is the task undertaken in David Campbell's chapter, which takes up the unsettling of the link between community and responsibility prompted by Warner. The provocations and limitations of Levinas for a rethinking of ethics and subjectivity are explored in the context of an exchange with Derrida, the purpose of which is to outline some aspects of ethical thinking, given the need to deterritorialize responsibility. Aspects of the Levinasian problematic are further considered in Michael Shapiro's chapter and in Patricia Molloy's reading of the issues prompted by *Dead Man Walking*, where the issue of our obligation to an undesirable other is made prominent.

Although the poststructuralist problematic at work in this volume unsettles any fixed relationship between space, subjectivity, and ethics, something more than geopolitical imaginaries need to be disturbed. The imbrication of morality and cartography is historically evident, for example, in the way those who have employed the civilizational discourse treated those outside of their "civilizational" boundaries with less moral solicitude. While there have been variations in global projects, with the distinctions in moral callousness between those seeking wealth versus those collecting souls producing differing (Cortés trumps Las Casas in this regard), global ethics in general has been significantly inflected by a civilizational geographic imaginary. Since the displacement of the dynastic global structure with a state system, a "nation-state" geographic imaginary has been dominant in the production of moral spaces. As late as the nineteenth century, Alexis de Tocqueville justified French imperialism with resort to a civilization model of moral solicitude allied to reasons of state. Writing about Algeria in connection with his duties as a member of the French Chamber of Deputies, he articulated an imperialist cartography animated jointly by his identity as a French nationalist and a member of an "advanced" civilization.[12] While Tocqueville argued that slavery is immoral anywhere it can be found (it was immoral, he argued, for one [man] to own another), his text on Algeria makes it clear that he had no problem with one people owning another.[13] Tocqueville's report on the Algerian colony constitutes a rationale for repressive colonial rule on the basis of French nationalism *and* civilizational superiority: "For France works to create civilized societies, not hordes of savages."[14]

Nor are such rationalizations confined to the past. Contemporary strategic reflections on the grounds of (in)action in crises as varied as Bosnia and Rwanda have regularly emphasized axiological criteria. Civilizational discourses continue to affect practices of moral inclusion and exclusion and their attendant expressions of moral solicitude, but despite recent attempts to reinstall a civilizational model of global moral and strategic space,[15] the state model continues to dominate both moral spaces and the meta-ethical thinking of those who analyze global interactions.

A Kantian Prelude

Recognizing that ethics is inextricably tied to spatial practices, some reflections on the contributions of Immanuel Kant to a rethinking of ethics and politics are appropriate in situating our problematic. Indeed, Kant offers a productively ambiguous legacy. On the one hand, both his philosophical and political texts sought to promote a cosmopolitan, global hospitality. To this end, they encourage principles. In the case of the philosophical texts, those principles revolve around the development of a legal structure; in the political texts, the principles encourage solicitude to every citizen-subject, native born or not. On the other hand, however, Kantian thinking was locked into a state-oriented mode of global space, discouraging critical reflection of the extent to which global flows at a substantive level and symbolic forms of nomadism — that is, identity practices that do not fit within the citizen-subject model of personhood — challenge the very predicates of a state-oriented philosophy.[16]

An assessment of Kant's ambiguous legacy provides an effective threshold to the structure of the arguments about spaces and morals that this volume collects. Kant was sensitive to the spatial predicates of moral solicitude in both his philosophical and political writings. With respect to the latter, he was an early advocate of a cosmopolitan ethics of international relations. In his "Perpetual Peace," for example, he mapped a world of governmental states in a way that combined his commitment to a state sovereignty model of global geography with an ethic of hospitality toward those, such as immigrants or refugees, who cross state boundaries. Although his practical geography articulated a geopolitical, nation-state model of space, his prognosis for future global relations, based on his reading of events, envisioned a movement toward a peace-promoting cosmopolitan attitude, emphasizing an enlarged comprehension that would dispose all people favorably toward those existing or originating outside of their respective national spaces. At the same time, much of Kant's approach to global peace assumed a legalistic cast, which was in keeping with his philosophical imaginary. Kant submitted the clashes between reason and imagination to a harmony-producing judgment that operated as a "tribunal."[17] Similarly, at the level of practical policy, he argued that in order to end global violence, nations (i.e., governmental states) must produce laws that prohibit citizens of one nation from harming those of another who cross their borders. Questions flowing from the challenge of the foreigner and the stranger are taken up in Michael Dillon's and Bonnie Honig's chapters, where, in different ways, the émigré and the refugee function as subjects that unsettle prevailing accounts of subjectivity, and thus demand a more sophisticated response (which Honig terms a politically engaged, democratic cosmopolitanism). The analysis of both these chapters exceeds the legalistic discourse that normally predominates when such concerns are addressed, and thereby resists Kant's philosophical geography.

Kant's injunctions about such a universal hospitality stem from two different kinds of spatial commitments. First, his more general ethical universalism derives from a philosophical geography. On the basis of his insights into the aporias of experience, Kant recognizes that no morality can be derived from the world of phenomena. To overcome the absence of moral guidance in the phenomenal world (the world of necessity), he constructs a separate normative domain, the noumenal world, which is a domain of freely willed and universally aimed ethical injunctions. The insights with which persons derive norms of hospitality come from the exercise of a moral faculty, a productive understanding that legislates within this noumenal domain.

Kant's philosophical worlds, each of which corresponds to the exercise of separate faculties, are ultimately connected by the exercise of judgment, which makes coherent experience possible. Judgment can "effect a transition" from one domain to the other and thus stands as a middle term between reason and understanding.[18] Although this Kantian model of judgment has been subject to numerous critical commentaries, what has been less analyzed is the rhetoric with which Kant constructs the philosophical milieu within which the separate domains exist.[19]

Kant's philosophical geography is articulated through the same geopolitical metaphors that determine fiduciary aspects of the boundaries in his practical geography; it is dominated by a governmentally oriented, territorial metaphor. Concepts are referred to objects, but whether or not knowledge of them is possible, these concepts govern from within particular "fields":

> The part of the field in which knowledge is possible for us is a territory (*territorium*) for these concepts and the requisite cognitive faculty. The part of the territory over which they exercise legislative authority is the realm (*ditio*) of these concepts, and their appropriate cognitive faculty.[20]

Kant goes on to divide the realms into two, natural concepts and the concept of freedom, and philosophy, accordingly, is divided into the theoretical and the practical:

> But the territory upon which its realm is established and over which it *exercises* its legislative authority, is always confined to the complex of objects of all possible experience, taken as no more than mere phenomena, for otherwise legislation by the understanding in respect of them is unthinkable.[21]

A consideration of the homology between Kant's philosophical and practical geographies — both organized around the governmental and legal metaphors — makes it clear that his thought was significantly influenced by his historical location; he wrote during the rise of the territorial state and was very much taken with the displacement of monarchies by republican forms of governance. Doubtless reflecting the historical influences on his writing (Kant's three major critiques straddle the events of the French Revolution, and his reflections on the possibilities for an enduring global peace explicitly engage the events in France), Kant's response to his primarily philosophical query "what is Man" is to construct personhood not only as a set of a priori structures of apprehension, but also as something that emerges in a political milieu; Kant's subjects are cognizing moral citizens who are meant to displace the passive subjects of both monarchs and church hierarchies. His philosophical subject is therefore philosophico-political or, to use Balibar's contraction, "cosmopolitical."[22]

Kant's political subject is introduced to do more, however, than oppose religious and monarchical authority within the state. His citizen-subject contains a disposition extending beyond national borders; it is a global citizen, whose capacity for edification on the basis of publicity about political events disposes her/him away from a narrow nationalist partisanship and toward a cosmopolitan hospitality. However, despite his high-minded commitment to global citizenship, Kant's model of subjectivity, entangled rhetorically with the discourse of state governance, also participated in a radical nonhospitality. Indigenous peoples receive less than respectful presence in his world; although, given Kant's commitment to the universality of the germ of reason, they are eligible to participate in global exchanges of ideas, they lack a full citizen presence on their terms because Kant's philosophical and practical geography are dominated by legislative and legalistic figures. As a result, indigenous peoples, who were already within state boundaries, received none of Kant's moral solicitude; his remarks on nonstate peoples partook of the same dismissive and racist anthropology as others of his epoch.[23] Kate Manzo's paper draws attention to the racial sentiments of Kantian thought, and from there draws postcolonial writers into an engagement with the philosophical narratives of the West that are themselves shaped by geopolitical imaginaries.

Being unmapped as bodies, the only way indigenous peoples could achieve recognition as ethico-political agents in Kant's world would be through participation within a universal common sense. But they would not be able to participate in negotiating such a common sense because Kantian common sense does not comport well with encounters between incommensurate cultural practices. It is a sense that operates wholly within Kant's philosophical narrative. It begins at the level of cognitive faculties (figured in Euro-oriented governmental and legal terms) and works outward. To put it schematically, Kant's story of enlightenment begins with a subject who undergoes an enlargement of comprehension by imposing understanding on sense experience. However, because different faculties govern different domains of experience, another faculty, that of judgment, must function to integrate the disparate domains.

While a coherent and enlarged subjectivity emerges through the exercise of a faculty of judgment that integrates the various domains of cognition, the resulting subject is not rendered suitable for participating in a global world until the integrated faculties express themselves by engaging in publicity. In the final stage of its cognitive enlargement, Kant's subject is therefore ready for encounters. However, by the time there is space for ethical and political encounter in Kant's world, the dynamics of subjective enlargement and the social process of reading public signs and engaging in communicative exchanges has left no room for enigma. The signs of the times are read more or less homogeneously; there are no incommensurate interpretive practices, only mean-spirited selfishness, to inhibit the process of ethical accommodation. A universal subjectivity effectively swallows up oppositional practices and subjectivities that have incommensurate commitments to meaning and value, and a state-oriented geographic imaginary subsumes cultural difference. These issues arise in perhaps unlikely contexts, and Richard Maxwell's chapter demonstrates how the violence of representation is insinuated within the economic practices of global market research.

As a result, for indigenous peoples to achieve moral solicitude, in a Kantian world, they would have to have a coherent political culture that functions, interpretively, within the European state-oriented political imaginary. When Kant considered "culture," he thought not of dynamics of acculturation, in which continual encounters produce altered *practices* of identity, temporality, and space (space and time are imminent in subjectivity for Kant), but of distinct and static forms of "national character."[24]

Kant's map was wholly national rather than cultural, and his treatise on geography insulated him from considering the contingent historical events that created the boundaries to which he was so philosophically and politically committed. Indeed the radical separation he made between geography and history (he states that we learn about the world through *either* stories or descriptions—the former is history and the later is geography[25]) is part of a venerable yet particular European cultural practice. Philological comparison reveals that a geographer and a historian (and the knowledge to which they give rise) need only be necessarily distinguished by a culture in which writing and mapping have come to be regarded as different activities. In contrast, Meso-American cultures used terms for maps whose meanings included scribes and books as well as territorial descriptions, whereas for European languages the term *map* refers solely to "the material upon which graphic signs are inscribed."[26] Not surprisingly, therefore, Meso-American maps included historical emblems that indicated the ways in which various bounded territories had been acquired; unlike European maps, they depicted historical encounters as well as the boundaries of territorial control.[27]

The spatial limits of Kantian thought mean that while Kant's commitment to a cosmopolitan ethos and his resistance to ethical closure (through a rejection of the self-evidence of the world of experience) inspires the contributions in this volume such that they are all in one way or another post-Kantian in orientation, the papers collected here nonetheless want to problematize the cartographical parameters, and their political effects, found in Kantian thought. As a result, they draw initially on such thinkers as Derrida, Foucault, and Levinas (among others) to extend Kantian critique in ways that include subjects who are unfinished, ambiguously located, and enigmatic so as to resist the restriction of moral spaces to a state-oriented geographic imaginary.

The ethical models articulated in the contributions all seek to contest the ethical purview tied to state space and universalistic models of humanity. Accordingly, they contest a philosophical model of ethics based on what Jacques Derrida has called a "national philosophism": "the claim laid by one country or nation to the privilege of 'representing,' 'embodying,' 'identifying with,' the universal essence of man, the thought of which is supposedly produced in some way in the philosophy of that people of that nation."[28] And they contest the "fictional universalism" of those who seek to unite humanity by ascribing to everyone something "essential to human personality."[29]

Instead of an epistemologically oriented ethics of discovery, which presumes a preexisting commonality that must be discerned, our contributions promote an ethics of encounter without a commitment to resolution or closure. They resist a dream of conceptual mastery and allow various aspects of difference to remain dynamic rather than being definitively coded. They embrace contingency and enigma, assuming that problems are historically contingent, that subjectivities are unstable and never wholly coherent, and that spaces need to be continually negotiated rather than physically or symbolically secured.

Finally, because they regard the domain of the ethical as something other than an external epistemic space, our contributions resist seeking a single normative standard to justify ethical claims. The ethical relations advanced in our various investigations constitute a habitus within which we dwell. A hospitable recognition of alterity's worthiness of respect — irrespective of the national or global territorial practices through which it can be identified — is part of a condition that is immanent to being rather than argumentatively approachable through an externalized moral calculus.

Notes

1. Quoted in Robert W. McElroy, *Morality and American Foreign Policy: The Role of Ethics in International Affairs* (Princeton: Princeton University Press, 1992), 27.

2. Jack Donnelly, "Twentieth-Century Realism," in *Traditions of International Ethics,* edited by Terry Nardin and David R. Mapel (Cambridge: Cambridge University Press, 1992).

3. Terry Nardin, "Ethical Traditions in International Affairs," in *Traditions of International Ethics,* ed. Nardin and Mapel, 15. For a discussion of the divide between politics and morality, and the way it is mapped onto the division of domestic and international, see Kimberly Hutchings, "The Possibility of Judgment: Moralizing and Theorizing in International Relations," *Review of International Studies* 18 (1992): 51–62.

4. The majority of contributions to the journal *Ethics and International Affairs,* published by the Carnegie Council on Ethics and International Affairs, are representative of this outlook. For overviews, see Chris Brown, *International Relations Theory: New Normative Approaches* (New York: Columbia University Press, 1992); and Steve Smith, "The Forty Years Detour: The Resurgence of Normative Theory in International Relations," *Millennium* 21 (winter 1992): 489–506. This literature, specifically Brown's book, is critically reviewed in R. B. J. Walker, "Norms in a Teacup: Surveying the 'New Normative Approaches,'" *Mershon International Studies Review* 38 (October 1994): 265–70. This focus on normative concerns is more self-consciously evident in the United Kingdom and Europe, with those writing in North America addressing "normative" issues through other frames of reference, especially the renewed focus on culture and identity. See, for example, Yosef Lapid and Friedrich Kratochwil, eds., *The Return of Culture and Identity in IR Theory* (Boulder, Colo.: Lynne Rienner, 1995). Some of the problems associated with this focus on culture and identity are reviewed in the epilogue to David Campbell, *Writing Security: U.S. Foreign Policy and the Politics of Identity,* rev. ed. (Minneapolis: University of Minnesota Press, 1998).

5. This is what Jim George has referred to as the "egoism-anarchy thematic." See his " 'Realist Ethics,' International Relations, and Postmodernism: Thinking beyond the Egoism-Anarchy Thematic," *Millennium: Journal of International Studies* 24 (summer 1995): 195–223.

6. See *Traditions of International Ethics*, ed. Nardin and Mapel.

7. See Chris Brown, "Review Article: Theories of International Justice," *British Journal of Political Science* 27 (1997): 273–97; and Molly Cochran, "Postmodernism, Ethics, and International Political Theory," *Review of International Studies* 21 (1995): 237–50. One line of critical thought not explored by this volume in detail (although Michael Shapiro's chapter contains some observations) is that associated with Habermas's notion of discourse ethics. For an analysis that associates this perspective with the problematic term "postmodernism," see Neta C. Crawford, "Postmodern Ethical Conditions and a Critical Response," *Ethics and International Affairs* 12 (1998), especially 128–40. The fullest application of this approach can be found in Andrew Linklater, *The Transformation of Political Community: Ethical Foundations of the Post-Westphalian Era* (Columbia: University of South Carolina Press, 1998).

8. A position not dissimilar to that in Dwight Furrow, *Against Theory: Continental and Analytical Challenges in Moral Philosophy* (New York: Routledge, 1995).

9. John D. Caputo, *Against Ethics* (Bloomington: Indiana University Press, 1993).

10. John D. Caputo, "Disseminating Originary Ethics and the Ethics of Dissemination," in Arleen B. Dallery and Charles E. Scott, eds., *The Question of the Other* (Albany: State University of New York Press, 1989), 55.

11. In international relations, the mainstream challenge to poststructuralist thought is less a challenge and more an assertion that such positions eschew ethico-political concerns. For a discussion of the problems with the challenge, and a detailed response grounded in a particular political issue, see David Campbell, *National Deconstruction: Violence, Identity, and Justice in Bosnia* (Minneapolis: University of Minnesota Press, 1998). Nor should we assume that Levinas can be easily reconciled to a position called poststructuralism, or that Levinas, Derrida, and Foucault offer all there might be in something called poststructuralism. Levinas might be better considered in terms of the phenomenological tradition, while absent from this volume, for example, is any detailed consideration of the recent work of Lacan and Lyotard on ethical concerns. Both these issues are explored in Furrow, *Against Theory*.

12. See Alexis de Tocqueville, *Report on Abolition of Slavery in French Colonies* (Boston: James Monroe and Company, 1840).

13. This observation comes from Tzvetan Todorov's reading of Tocqueville's report on Algeria. See his "Tocqueville's Nationalism," *History and Anthropology* 4, 2 (April 1990): 357–71.

14. Tocqueville, *Report on Abolition of Slavery in French Colonies*, 360. Tocqueville would not have gone as far as Michelet's hypernationalist sentiment that "France is religion" (see Jules Michelet, *The People*, trans. John P. McKay [Urbana: University of Illinois Press, 1973], 190), but he and Michelet exchanged manuscripts and mutual praise (see, for example, Jules Michelet, *Correspondance Générale* Tome III [Paris: Libraire Honoré Champion, 1995], 232–33). Tocqueville, like Michelet, saw France as having an exemplary national culture, indeed as the cultural center of the globe, even though it might benefit from institutional developments elsewhere in the "civilized" world.

15. Samuel Huntington's controversial model is the best known. See *The Clash of Civilizations and the Remaking of World Order* (New York: Simon and Schuster, 1996).

16. Gilles Deleuze and Félix Guattari, who employ the concept of the nomad to challenge state-oriented models of space, indict this aspect of Kant vigorously. Ever since philosophy assigned itself the role of ground it has been giving established powers its blessing, and tracing its doctrine of faculties onto the organs of state power. Common sense, the unity of the faculties at the center constituted by the Cogito, is the state consensus raised to the level of the absolute. See Gilles Deleuze and Félix Guattari, *A Thousand Plateaus*, trans. Brian Massumi (Minneapolis: University of Minnesota Press, 1987), 376.

17. See Kant's *Critique of Judgment*, trans. James Creed Meredith (New York: Cambridge University Press, 1952).

18. Ibid., 17.

19. An exception is Willi Goetchli, *Constituting Critique: Kant's Writing as Critical Praxis*, trans. Eric Schwab (Durham, N.C.: Duke University Press, 1994).

20. Kant, *The Critique of Judgment*, 12.

21. Ibid.

22. Étienne Balibar, "Subjection and Subjectivation," in Joan Copjek, ed., *Supposing the Subject* (London: Verso, 1994), 6.

23. See Immanuel Kant, *Anthropology from a Pragmatic Point of View*, trans. Victor Lyle Dowdell (Carbondale: Southern Illinois University Press, 1978).

24. Ibid.

25. See the translation of Kant's *Physische Geographie* in J. A. May, *Kant's Concept of Geography and Its Relation to Recent Geographic Thought* (Toronto: University of Toronto Press, 1970), 255–64.

26. The quotations are from Walter Mignolo, *The Darker Side of the Renaissance* (Ann Arbor: University of Michigan Press, 1995), 10.

27. The Meso-American treatment of history and space in maps is treated in Gordon Brotherston, *Book of the Fourth World* (New York: Cambridge University Press, 1992).

28. Jacques Derrida, "Onto-Theology of National-Humanism (Prolegomena to a Hypothesis)," *Oxford Literary Review* 14 (1992): 17.

29. The quotations are from Étienne Balibar, "Ambiguous Universality," *differences* 7 (spring 1995): 58–59.

CHAPTER ONE

Searching for Responsibility/Community in International Relations

Daniel Warner

Let us laugh together, on principle.[1]

In his lecture on "Politics as a Vocation," Max Weber made the well-known distinction between an ethic of responsibility and an ethic of ultimate ends.[2] Although Weber's distinction has been called "a veritable leitmotif of realism,"[3] I am concerned here with its implications for international relations in general as well as the debate between liberals and communitarians in particular.[4] More specifically, an analysis of Weber's understanding of an ethic of responsibility and its relation to an ethic of ultimate ends allows us to appreciate its power as a basis for a politics of closure.

Weber's ethic of responsibility denies the importance of consequences and the possibility of objective norms because it is built on an image of an individual responsible only to himself and to his perception of his responsibility. Weber's use of Martin Luther as the paradigmatic "mature man" highlights the denial of otherness in Weber's understanding of responsibility. Through an analysis of the basis of the domestic analogy, we can see the importance of Weber's charismatic leader's being responsible only to himself. Just as Luther proclaimed himself outside societal norms, the realist/liberal nation-state is also responsible only to itself and remains outside international law.

In the final section, I discuss the limits of responsibility and community by questioning the very search for the limits through identity politics. After having argued against realist/liberal notions of autonomy and sovereignty, and after having followed much of the traditional communitarian criticisms of liberalism, I examine the very quest for responsibility and search for community and its implications for closure. Thus, while having followed a communitarian perspective in criticizing Weber's ethic of responsibility, I conclude by questioning the foundations of that communitarianism in the search for a new ethic of responsibility. The very search for responsibility/community may itself be part of a process of identity politics that denies new possibilities for openness. Understanding why we want to know who is responsible and the limits of that responsibility may be as important as, if not more important than, the process of determining responsibility that is so well developed in international law. Our understanding of the drive for knowing responsibility/community should be prior to knowing the limits of responsibility/community. It is only when we appreciate the politics of identity and closure that animate our desire to know that we can begin to glimpse new possibilities of responsibility/community outside of or beyond the limitations of that desire. And a reading of Weber's understanding of an ethic of responsibility is crucial to an understanding of that process.

Weber's Ethic of Responsibility

Weber made his distinction between an ethic of responsibility and an ethic of ultimate ends toward the end of his lecture. Much of Weber's speech dealt with the legitimation of domination, and, specifically, the charismatic leader. As Weber said:

> Here we are interested above all . . . in domination by virtue of the devotion of those who obey the purely personal "charisma" of the "leader." For this is the root of the idea of a calling in its highest expression. Devotion to the charisma of the prophet, or the leader in war, or to the great demagogue in the *ecclesia* or in parliament, means that the leader is personally recognized as the innerly "called" leader of men. Men do not obey him by virtue of tradition or statute, but because they believe in him . . . The devotion of his disciples, his followers, his personal party friends is oriented to his person and to its qualities.[5]

Weber's charismatic leader is not an active leader. He is inner directed, and those who choose to follow him do so by their own volition. The notion of passive leadership becomes evident when Weber discusses the responsibility of the charismatic leader; Weber emphasizes the personal responsibility of the leader to his cause, not to others. Mere passion, according to Weber, "does not make a politician, unless passion as devotion to a 'cause' also makes responsibility to this cause the guiding star of action."[6]

The inner calling of the charismatic leader is central in understanding Weber's distinction between an ethic of ultimate ends and an ethic of responsibility. When Weber makes this distinction, he says:

> We must be clear about the fact that all ethically oriented conduct may be guided by one or two fundamentally differing and irreconcilably opposite maxims: conduct can be oriented to an "ethic of ultimate ends" or to an "ethic of responsibility.". . . There is an abysmal contrast between conduct that follows the maxim of an ethic of ultimate ends — that is, in religious terms, "the Christian does rightly and leaves the results with the Lord" — and the conduct that follows the maxim of an ethic of responsibility, in which case one has to give an account of the foreseeable results of one's actions.[7]

The distinction hinges on the differentiation between leaving the results "with the Lord" and the charismatic leader's perception of his personal responsibility to his cause. The problem to be resolved is whether there is a difference between leaving the result with the Lord and the charismatic leader's own judgment of his personal responsibility. If the differentiation is meaningful, and there are indeed "two fundamentally differing and irreconcilably opposite maxims," there must be a difference between the Lord's judgment and the charismatic leader's judgment.

Weber's resolution of this difference occurs at the end of the speech:

> It is immensely moving when a *mature* man . . . is aware of a responsibility for the consequences of his conduct and really feels such responsibility with heart and soul. He then acts by following an ethic of responsibility and somehow he reaches the point where he says: "Here I stand I can do no other.". . . An ethic of ultimate ends and an ethic of responsibility are not absolute contrasts but rather supplements, which only in unison constitute a genuine man — a man who *can* have the "calling for politics."[8]

Weber uses Martin Luther as the archetype for the charismatic leader. For our discussion, it is important to emphasize that Luther nowhere saw himself as responsible for others or to others; he was responsible only to himself or through his perception of the Lord's will. For Luther, there was no visible sense of otherness in his decision-making process, no sense that "one has to give an account of the foreseeable results of one's actions" to anyone but oneself. Leszek Kolakowski, in describing Luther as "The Man Who Made Modernity," noted: "The radicals of the Reformation argued . . . that the visible church is useless or harmful, and that true Christianity is in the 'interior man,' in the conscience of every Christian separately."⁹ Through Luther and the radicals of the Reformation, the corruption of the Catholic Church became transformed into the rejection of institutions that are beyond the individual's control and ultimately to all that is outside the "interior man." As Habermas has said: "With Luther, religious faith became reflective; the world of the divine was changed in the solitude of subjectivity into something posited by ourselves. Against faith in the authority of preaching and tradition, Protestantism asserted the authority of the subject relying upon his own insight."¹⁰

The principle of subjectivity begun during the Reformation highlights that it is within the individual that there is ultimate reality and the ultimate determinant of validity. There are no outside or objective norms that can be applied. This is how Michael Oakeshott has described Luther:

> One who understands himself to be the messenger of a god, to be "illuminated" from above, or to be the voice of destiny, who denies having any thoughts of his own to give meaning to what he says or does, and thus absolves himself from all responsibility for his actions and utterances, is a character of a different sort; he has resigned the character of a human being and has contracted out of the conversation of mankind. He is either an angel or a lunatic.¹¹

This is the Luther at work in Weber's lecture, a "mature man" who resolves the contrast between an ethic of ultimate ends and an ethic of responsibility within his own subjectivity. This understanding of Luther is both exalting and disturbing. It is exalting from the historical perspective because we can see its force and utility at the end of the Middle Ages.¹² The charismatic leader represented by Luther becomes the man and citizen who by virtue of his birth has certain inalienable rights. The hierarchical religious and political systems come tumbling down when confronted with a society of individuals each possessing the strength and certainty associated with the inner conscience of Luther. As Charles Taylor said: "Disengagement from cosmic order meant that the human agent was no longer to be understood as an element in a larger, meaningful order. His paradigm purposes are to be discovered within. He is on his own . . . And this yields a picture of the sovereign individual who is 'by nature' not bound to any authority. The condition of being under authority is something which has to be *created*."[13] This is the ground-work for the Enlightenment, the Declaration of the Rights of Man, and the Napoleonic Code.

At the same time, it is disturbing because it leaves no basis on which to decide if the man and citizen is actually an angel or a lunatic. For the radical Protestant, there can be neither outside norms on which to judge, nor outside judges. Luther's declaration of "Here I stand" created a sit-uation in which only he could perceive the truth. "In Luther's 'ich kann nicht anders,' the emphasis is upon the ich, which is not feeling or mere 'conscience' but judgment springing from self-understanding."[14] If we imagine a society of Luthers, we can understand why there would be no objective norms; each individual would respond only to his or her self-understanding or inner conscience. To repeat Oakeshott's words: the We-berian subject "has resigned the character of a human being and has con-tracted out of the conversation of mankind." This is exactly how one can understand the statement of the assassin of Yitzhak Rabin, Yigal Amir, that: "I acted alone on God's orders, and I have no regrets,"[15] or the expla-nation by his fellow student: "Yigal Amir is not crazy which one might expect from such a crime. He acted out of profound conviction, after long reflection, as it is normal for an intelligent person to do. Even a long reflection can lead to a bad conclusion. Deliberation is the privi-lege of judges."[16] Amir himself had decided what he was to do through his reading and understanding of what God had ordered him to do.

Weber's choice of Luther as the archetypical charismatic leader shows the locus of the ultimate irresponsibility of his ethic of responsibility.[17] Luther was responsible to no one but himself. Even if one argues that he was ultimately responsible to a higher calling, we, the outsiders or others, can never be part of his calling. From the outsider's perspective, Luther was only responsible to himself. Those who followed Luther did so as an article of faith and not on the basis of a shared understanding or communication through language. To put it quite simply, Weber's charis-matic leader is asocial. He has no understanding of the consequences of his actions for others. In Weber's ethic of responsibility, judgment about action remains within the conscience or self-understanding of the charis-matic leader and is radically divorced from any consequences or others.[18] As a fellow student of Amir explained in language similar to Weber's: "Yigal Amir has nothing of a young, manipulated man. It is a mature person, responsible for his actions, who killed Prime Minister Yitzhak Rabin."[19]

The Basis of the Domestic Analogy

This reading of Luther is not confined to theology or political theory. It also has implications for international relations, especially in terms of an account of the relation between individual, state, and state system that is affirmed by the so-called "domestic analogy."[20] The domestic analogy suggests that as the individual is to the state, each state is to the society of states. The obvious difference between activities within states and among states is that states have some form of government and the international community of states does not. However, arguments against the domestic analogy fail to take into account the internal structure of the analogy. If we say that the individual is to the state as the state is to the society of states, instead of arguing about the differences between international and domestic jurisdiction, we should, to begin with, accept the analogy on its own terms and see what the consequences are for international relations.

That is, we should begin by accepting the terminology of the domestic analogy and ask about the image of the individual that is being used. If, for example, we use Weber's image of Luther as charismatic leader, by analogy we wind up with states that also consider themselves responsible only to themselves or to some higher authority based on their perception of their personal responsibility to a cause. The analogy, based on this atomistic vision of the individual, leads to a realist conception of a world of state interests, and a realpolitik with no objective norms and no international law.[21] R. B. J. Walker makes this very point concerning Weber's account of an ethic of responsibility:

> There is, in Weber's view, no rational way of deciding on criteria for judging what is responsible conduct, or to what and to whom one's responsibility should be directed. In effect, the meaning of responsibility is left hanging between a Kantian imperative to autonomous action in conformity with a universal moral law and an imperative to decide on the basis of one's own autonomous will (or in terms of international relations, on the non-rational will of one's own autonomous nation). Consequently, the sorry legacy of so much realist analysis of international relations has been either a constant relapse into the empty category of national interest or the amplification of personal judgment into appropriate criteria for state policy.[22]

On the other hand, if we change the image of the individual at the beginning, it is possible to conceive an intersubjective understanding of international relations, of states constantly interacting with other states and objective norms based on consequences of actions for that state *and* others. In other words, we move away from seeing states as separate geopolitical entities concerned only with their "inner conscience" or self-understanding to intersubjective states that are active members of a world community.

The realist understanding of the domestic analogy based on individual interest is obvious, but the liberal interpretation as expressed by Michael Walzer, although similar in its understanding of separated states, is more intriguing. The analogy says that "the individual is to the state as the society of states is to world society."[23] And, by extension, "the rules of international relations are derived from domestic morality by analogy; international society is understood as domestic society writ large, with states playing the roles occupied by persons in domestic society."[24] By virtue of the analogy, the state comes to incorporate the moral position of the individual. Whereas for liberal political theory the individual is the focus of concern, the analogy places the level-of-analysis with the liberal state in international relations. Thus, we find a reverence for state sovereignty in Vattel's international law similar to, for example, that which we find for individual rights in the Declaration of the Rights of Man and the U.S. Declaration of Independence. As a matter of fact, Albert de Lapradelle, in an introduction to Vattel, says that "Vattel's *Law of Nations* is international law based on the principles of 1789 — the complement of the Contract Social of Rousseau, the projection on the plane of the Law of Nations of the great principles of legal individualism."[25]

The analogy glorifies the state in the same way liberals glorify individuals. "Like persons in domestic society, states in international society are to be treated as autonomous sources of ends, morally immune from external interference and morally free to arrange their internal affairs as governments see fit."[26] The state, by virtue of its sovereignty, has both the freedoms and rights associated with the liberal individual. Berlin's positive and negative individual liberty[27] become projected onto the screen of international relations through the prism of sovereignty: the negative individual right of non-interference becomes the state's right of non-intervention, the positive right of self-expression becomes self-determination.

Walzer's Paradox and the Limits of Liberalism

It is within this liberal conception of the state that a controversy broke out over Michael Walzer's two books, *Spheres of Justice* and *Just and Unjust Wars*[28] — a controversy that was the theoretical predecessor to many of the practical debates concerning humanitarian intervention in Iraq and the former Yugoslavia. By implicitly using a liberal individual as the basis of the domestic analogy, Walzer wound up with a liberal state. However, the liberal state no longer protects the liberal individual, which was its initial function because of noninterference in the internal affairs of states. Thus, through the domestic analogy, Walzer's paradox shows the limits of liberalism for international relations as highlighted in debates over when and by whom humanitarian intervention is acceptable.

The core of Walzer's position is what he calls the legalist paradigm that prioritizes state sovereignty:

> The recognition of sovereignty is the only way we have of establishing an arena in which freedom can be fought for... It is this arena and the activities that can go on within it that we want to protect, and we protect them much as we protect individual integrity, by making out boundaries that cannot be crossed, rights that cannot be violated. As with individuals, so with sovereign states, there are things that we cannot do to them, even for their ostensible good.[29]

On what basis does Walzer allow the state to have these rights? Not on the basis of the activities of the state. The state does not earn its freedom and rights, just as fetuses do not earn their right to life. Walzer glorifies state sovereignty through his definition of the state by arguing that the state and the individual within the state are inseparable. He believes that there is a "historic fit" between the individual and community — that the community and state are mirror reflections. In this sense, the state can be said to reflect the individual through the homogeneous community. Because the individual is reflected in the community and the community reflected in the state, for Walzer the state comes to represent the individual and to encompass individual rights.

As a result, Walzer argues against outside intervention in the internal affairs of a state. According to Walzer, even if the "historic fit" is not perfect, it is within the nation-state that internal problems must be worked out. Even if the state is not democratic, the rights of noninterference and self-determination take precedence over any external notions of justice. As with Weber's description of Luther's personal responsibility and inner conscience, Walzer's hermetically sealed state is resistant to any external locus of authority. According to Walzer, outsiders have no moral standing by which to judge the state or those within the state.

Critics of Walzer have attacked him for his adherence to this conception of the nation-state.[30] Some have argued that Walzer confuses horizontal and vertical contracts, the contract between the people and the contract between the people and the state. Others have argued that Walzer is nostalgic for a unified, homogeneous political community that never existed, does not exist, or will not exist. My argument here is quite different (although I return to nostalgia about community later on). Walzer's improper use of the liberal individual in the analogy allows him to conceive of a state in which the protection of individual rights — the core of liberalism — is subsumed within the liberal state's rights. What I call Walzer's paradox, and what others have called "moral dissonance,"[31] is the situation in which a state maintains its rights and freedoms, but the individuals within that state are not protected by anything beyond the borders. States, for Walzer, possess rights and freedoms because they have sovereignty, just as individuals possess rights and freedoms because they are individuals.[32] Both the state's rights and individual's rights are noncontextual. For Walzer, moreover, the right of the state is more important than the right of the individual because he claims it is within the state that the individual can best be protected. If one tears down the walls of the state, Walzer argues, one winds up with a "thousand petty fortresses."[33]

This generalization of state's rights, incorporated into classical international law, blinds international law to specificity. International law, like legal individualism, remains oblivious to contextual behavior. States acquire certain rights once there is formal recognition, just as fetuses acquire certain rights once they have a certain age.[34] One could say that "states must earn their sovereignty through decent treatment of their people,"[35] but the international legal system doesn't, just as certain Western human rights activists speak of inalienable individual rights as moral absolutes divorced from specific behavior or situations.

The paradox of Walzer's liberalism is that whereas the state has as its primary obligation the protection of the individual, the isolated state through the domestic analogy only protects itself and appears from the outside to be similar to the realist state.[36] If, on the other hand, the individual from whom the analogy starts were not unencumbered,[37] then the state that emerges from the analogy would be situated and permeable and the individual within that state protected by institutions or a collective conscience outside the state. For communitarians, Walzer's paradox can be overcome by reexamining the image of the individual used as the basis of the domestic analogy. Thus, the situated state may become permeable and individual rights protected by those outside the state.

Responsible to Whom?

In our discussion of responsibility, I have so far argued against the personal responsibility of Luther and responsibility to or for a hermetically sealed, nation-state.[38] Both of these arguments have followed communitarian principles of context and embeddedness. After rejecting the two possibilities of isolated individuals and isolated nation-states, I could begin to talk of a global village in which we are all responsible for everyone else and we can all be held responsible for each other, the inverse of the closed system I have argued against. That is, instead of accepting Luther's image of the "mature man," I could posit an encumbered individual and a situated nation-state within a global community. This is not a viable solution, however, because the global village concept itself denies specificity; it is not situated. One cannot arbitrarily decide the parameters of the community of responsibility before deciding for what one is responsible. The concept of the global village is as univocal as that of the hermetically sealed nation-state or individual responsible only to inner conscience. The global village is as isolated a subject as Luther's individual and Walzer's nation-state.

In order to show how one might go about determining responsibility/community in an issue-specific manner, we will review the process used in international law for determining responsibility. What makes this process so helpful is that it is act-driven; it does not begin with an isolated subject, but starts from a specific act. The determination of responsibility in international law has several stages and indeed the first stage involves the observation that there has been a generating fact. It is the generating fact that begins the process of determining responsibility and eventually identifies the agent. The second stage involves the judgment that the generating act has been legal or illegal. Our analysis of Weber's ethic of responsibility and Walzer's paradox has tried to show

that for the charismatic leader or analogous state there can be no generating fact and outside judgment because the "goodness" of the leader/
state is incorporated in the persona itself and divorced from consequences
and outside judgment. There need be no relation between declaration/
self-perception and consequences/others because the agent/act schism
envelops the persona involved.[39]

Following from this observation, it is obvious that there can be no
outside judgment on the legality/illegality of the actions of the charismatic leader/state. The mere existence of norms presupposes some kind
of objective, outside judgment beyond the individual/state. To return
to Oakeshott's comment on Luther, we, the outsiders, have no way of
ascertaining whether or not the person/state in question is a lunatic or
an angel beyond an act of faith. When we are dealing with the "unencumbered" person/state, there can be no dialogue, conversation, or shared
understandings; there can be no norms. Just as Luther announced "Here
I stand," the liberal state, for example, can refuse to accept the decisions
of the International Court of Justice because it alone perceives a higher
truth. There is no conversation with the rest of mankind. The isolated
individual/state is only concerned with inner conscience and its perception of a higher truth.

The third stage in the determination of responsibility involves imputation. At a news conference in Geneva on April 12, 1991, U.S. Secretary of State James Baker, in a reply to a question about the responsibility of the United States for the situation of the Kurds, said: "The United
States certainly does not feel responsible in any way."[40] Almost a week
later, a U.S. official was quoted in the *Washington Post* as saying: "You
have to put aside the medium problems and the long-term problems
and deal with the fact that 1,000 people a day... are dying and we are
being held responsible."[41]

Although both quotations use responsibility in a nonlegal context,
they are strikingly different. On the one hand, the secretary of state referred to the feelings of the United States. Because the United States
did not feel responsible for the Kurds, it could not be held responsible.
Baker's statement is a form of self-judgment: the United States alone
decides when and how it is responsible. On the other hand, the statement by the unnamed official uses responsibility in terms of judgment
by others. According to the official, the United States was responding

to a collective conscience, something beyond the personal responsibility of the government, something beyond the inner conscience or self-understanding of the United States.

The statement by the official illustrates the power of non-legal imputation. But what are the implications of this process? The legal scholar Hans Kelsen made an important distinction between causality and imputation[42] when he said, "we connect acts of human feelings with one another and with other facts not only and exclusively according to the principle of causality, that is, as cause and effect, but according to another principle quite different from that of causality, a principle for which science has not yet established a generally recognized term."[43] According to Kelsen, this principle involves imputation. It is by imputing responsibility to someone for an act or situation that the agent/act schism can be overcome.

In causality we are searching for a simple connection between an action and what has caused the action. Causality applies to inanimate objects as well as to human behavior. On the other hand, imputation not only connects the act to an agent, but it also includes a judgment about whether the observed behavior deserves reward or punishment, praise or blame. By seeking to impute responsibility when we observe an act or situation, we not only want to know who has performed the act or caused the situation, we want to know who is responsible for the act or situation so that we can praise or blame, reward or punish that person. Imputation connects a person to an act based on a standard of behavior.

In terms of our critique of Weber and Walzer, there are three implications of this analysis of imputation that are worth highlighting. First, the process of imputing responsibility is a backward process. It does not begin with a fixed subject and then analyze its actions and their consequences. On the contrary, the process of imputation begins with consequences in order to define the subject. Thus, imputation is issue-specific and contextual. Second, following from this statement, it may be possible for the person judging to hold people responsible who were not directly involved in an action. Collective, indirect responsibility can arise beyond the immediate cause-and-effect actors. Third, it is obvious that the imputation of responsibility is not limited to the legal system. Indeed, the legal system usually focuses on individuals, and often corporate individuals.[44] The imputation system we have described means that both those imputing and those being held responsible are not limited by the legal system.

A variation on this theme appears in the writing of Haskell Fain and his "task-theoretic" normative politics.[45] This is a variation on the global village responsibility that is issue-specific and contextual. Fain has argued against legal conceptualism, the move from the state of nature to the contractarian political community, because he sees a normative imperative behind global problems. Fain's egalitarian, international political community has moral power because the tasks it confronts demand the cooperation of all. For Fain, it is the global nature of tasks that creates moral obligations and global responsibility. The imperative nature of the global tasks at hand in our modern world demands a common purpose and common responsibility. Because certain tasks cannot be solved by individuals or nation-states, Fain argues, we are morally responsible to each other in a larger community.[46] The parameter of Fain's normative community is formed around tasks; the global, responsible community is formed around global tasks; there is no a priori community. Complex interdependence provides the moral borders of responsibility/community.

Because Fain has argued that global tasks form a global, responsible community, one would assume that he would agree that nonglobal tasks would form different kinds of communities. The argument here is similar to the concept of subsidiarity used in reference to the European Union. Subsidiarity means that tasks are accorded to those political bodies that correspond to the task. Local problems should be left to local councils, and not to the national government or Brussels. On the other hand, tasks that should be solved in Brussels will be taken away from the local authorities. The parameters of the community to whom one is responsible, therefore, vary according to the issue. The advantage of the reverse procedure in imputation is that it allows the task to determine the community, which then determines the level of responsibility. The level of responsibility and community do not exist a priori, as they do, for instance, in Vernon Van Dyke's discussions of ethnic communities.[47]

Hence, the relationship between community and responsibility becomes crucial once we leave the liberal individual/state. If we assume that we are talking about more than personal responsibility and more than state responsibility, we must define the parameters of the community that can impute responsibility and to which responsibility can be imputed. To be issue-specific, following from the methodology of legal responsibility, allows a certain flexibility in our understanding of responsibility and community and gets us away from abstract discussions of individuals, states, and communities.

The Quest for Responsibility and the Search for Community

It may appear, therefore, that once the linkage has been established between tasks and responsibility and community, the obvious direction for one to proceed would be to investigate the different types of communities one could imagine from different tasks and the different types of understanding of responsibility they would entail.[48] Following my criticism of Weber and Walzer and my interest in Fain's task-theoretic normative community, I could now focus on the size of the community and the understanding of responsibility within that defined group for different tasks. I could, for example, analyze the specificity of the United States' responsibility for the situation of the Kurds, the European Union's responsibility in the former Yugoslavia, and the international community's responsibility in Somalia and Rwanda. I will, however, choose another road. Having looked at responsibility and community in rejecting certain liberal values and nonsituated communitarianism, I think it most important to investigate the reasons why responsibility and community are important. That is, instead of continuing on the path along which I started, I prefer to conclude with a discussion that questions the very enterprise in which I am involved. Rather than investigate what kinds of communities we can impute responsibility to and what kinds of persons/communities can impute responsibility, I conclude by questioning the very search for responsibility and community. Having rejected the noncontextual nature of Weber and Walzer and resisted the temptation of Fain's issue-specific responsibility, I think it crucial to discuss the basis of the enterprise itself.

My answer to the problem of defining responsibility/community is to reflect on why I want to know. While my argument has criticized Weber's isolation of the individual through the individual conscience and Walzer's insistence on hermetically sealed states, and while I have focused on the importance of defining the community through responsibility, we cannot move toward some kind of identification or delimitation without understanding the motivating force behind that search. To criticize individualism in certain interpretations of liberal theory and international relations need not be to fall into the lap of communitarianism. The notion of community itself is highly problematic and needs investigation in different ways. To say that one is a communitarian may be a necessary step in criticizing liberalism, but not a sufficient one, and has been made so, even in international relations, by a fair amount of recent literature.[49]

William Connolly has specifically called into question the quest for responsibility and the search for community. His criticisms add an important dimension to our previous discussion in that they raise the possibility that the quest for responsibility and the search for community are both firmly rooted in modernity and identity politics. Whereas I have previously located my discussion of responsibility and community within the context of international relations debates,[50] Connolly places the search for responsibility and community within a broader context (as indeed does Walker's discussion of Weber[51]). We will deal with each of Connolly's criticisms in turn before examining their importance in the larger context.

In his discussion of responsibility, Connolly notes: "The idea of 'responsibility' itself is a locus of persistent instability and contestation in late-modern discourse."[52] Connolly maintains that "established debates over the terms of responsibility and its proper range of application as a historically specific field of discourse [are] bound up with particular conceptions of self, nature, state, language, god, past and future."[53] While Sandel has argued that the self is situated, and I have argued that responsibility is situated in terms of specific actions and consequences, Connolly argues that debates over responsibility are also situated in time and place.

Connolly does not argue against the need to search for responsibility; he argues that the expression of that drive is articulated in different times and places because of a host of factors:

> Perhaps the insistence upon the truth of deep identity or singular
> responsibility simultaneously sets up these accusations and disarms the
> terms of response available to them ... Must we truly have a true
> identity? A Nietzschean perspective shares with the Augustinian
> tradition the conviction that this demand is rooted in an entire array of
> linguistic, psychological, epistemic, and political pressures built into the

human condition. The drive to strong identity and responsibility, to put
it briefly, is overdetermined as a disposition of life. What one must
refuse to do, one might say to modern Augustinianism and the heresies
it spawns, is to invest these dispositions with the blessings of
unambiguous truth. One must treat them as entrenchments installed in
the self and its world rather than depths that mirror the deepest truths
about the world and the self.[54]

Having shown the politicization of identity and responsibility, Connolly argues that the present drive to establish responsible agents is part
of an existential resentment:

> People tend to demand ... a world in which suffering is ultimately
> grounded in proportional responsibility. We resent a world in which it
> appears that this is not so. But resentment must locate an appropriate
> object if it is to be discharged as resentment. It thereby seeks a
> responsible agent that it can convince itself is worthy of receiving the
> load of incipient resentment it carries. Otherwise its existential rancor
> must be stored or translated into something else. So, part of the drive to
> insistent attributions of responsibility flows from existential
> resentment.[55]

The implications of Connolly's analysis threaten the algebraic equa-
tion between evil/illegality and responsibility/agent that is established
through imputation. "Idealizations of identity" serve a social, political
function for Connolly that exacerbates differences by codifying identities in stereotypes responding to the perceived need to localize agents
of responsibility. According to Connolly, responsibility "is both indispensable to life and acutely susceptible to inflation through existential
resentment."[56] Connolly tries to "challenge, contest, subvert, and abridge"
those discourses that lead to this inflation.

In Kelsen's terms, Connolly has taken the differentiation between
causality and imputation one step farther. Instead of imputation being
separated from natural cause and effect merely by the judgmental element of praise or blame, Connolly postulates this judgmental element
as part of a larger "existential resentment." Connolly does not seek to
negate that element of judgment to return us to some form of objective
cause and effect. Nor does he try to relativize the resentment by saying
that it is merely a human construct that has no grounding in some form
of objectivity. Connolly is arguing against the inflation of the discourses
that can lead to relativism.

For my purpose, Connolly has called into question Weber's idealization of the charismatic leader with his locus of authority/responsibility within the inner conscience, the analogous nation-state of Walzer with its locus of authority/responsibility firmly sealed within its borders, and our own quest for some outside norms and judgment through a "task-theoretic" normative community. Whether the ultimate judgment is within the charismatic leader or liberal nation-state or outside within a larger community, whether there is a differentiation between an ethic of responsibility or an ethic of ultimate ends is not Connolly's concern. In fact, the quest for responsible agent, the finality of the process of imputation, is just as specious in Connolly's reasoning as my criticism of the subject/persona that is separated from consequences. Where Connolly would agree with my criticism of the unencumbered self and analogous state and be tempted by the "task-theoretic" normative community, I believe he would question my insistence on defining the identity of the agent through searching for responsibility by imputation. Although Connolly's identity/difference is situated and may be seen as issue specific, it cannot be localized and defined in terms of responsibility. While I have defined agents in terms of responsibility, Connolly wants to "alert to the element of existential revenge lodged within idealizations of identity and responsibility."[57] Not only is the self or state situated, according to Connolly, so too is the quest for the determination of responsibility and the identity of agent. And it is the situated search that serves to deflate discourses about identity conceived of as responsibility through imputation.

Now, just as Connolly situates the search for the definition of the identity of agent through responsibility within a certain discourse of modernity, he also criticizes the search for community within a similar context.[58] Connolly states forthrightly that "[m]odern thinkers ... demand a solution to homesickness."[59] The problem that intrigues Connolly, and on which he focuses his discussion of Nietzsche, is the extent to which the posited basic urge to find a home in the world can be called into question. That is, the modern search for community may be a nostalgic search that has no solution. The criticism here is that the very notion of community as a final solution for responsibility may be wrong, as indeed may be the very notion of any ultimate solution and its search.[60] The implication is that while liberal responsibility incorrectly resides within the individual, communitarian responsibility is equally naive in that it seeks a response where none is possible. Connolly goes on to say:

> For if the human is the animal which requires social formation and coordination to fix itself and its conduct, it also encounters elements of resistance in itself to any specific form imposed upon it. It thus becomes the animal which requires reasons to live this way rather than that and then demands that these reasons too have their reasons. *Its sickness resides in its quest to reach the end of a trail which has no terminus.*"[61]

This lack of terminus for communitarians focuses on the home. According to Connolly, whereas we feel that we should have a home or be at home, the search for a home is infinitely more complex than a territorial integration; it is a more profound search, a search that is not necessarily tied to a specific place. Connolly quotes Nietzsche on the modern wish to find a home in the world and the separation of the physical sense of home from the feeling of being at home:

> *We who are homeless*—Among Europeans today there is no lack of those who are entitled to call themselves homeless in a distinctive and honorable sense: it is to them that I especially commend my secret wisdom and gaya scienza... We children of the future how could we be at home in this today? We feel disfavor for all ideals that might lead one to feel at home even in this fragile, broken time of transition... The ice that still supports people today has become very thin; the wind that brings the thaw is blowing; we ourselves who are homeless constitute a force that breaks open ice and other all too thin "realities."[62]

The homeless, therefore, are not necessarily those without territorial place, although the two can be easily confused. As Connolly stated elsewhere concerning this homesickness: "It is a homesickness that construes correspondence between the scope of troubles and a territorial place of action to form the essence of democratic politics. It is nostalgia for a politics of place."[63] In his essay on Nietzsche, Connolly further develops this nostalgia by redefining it in these terms: "The demand for self-knowledge presupposes a fit between inner life and the public resources of language, between the structure of desire and the logic of articulation."[64] The transposition of the territorial place occurs when the mind/body dualism is theoretically realized within one's own community. That is the nostalgia for community, a community wherein the desire for self-knowledge can be most easily integrated and fulfilled.

Connolly examines Nietzsche's position that this drive for integration/self-knowledge can never be fulfilled, whether by remaining in or returning to a specific place, or in some individual search for self-knowledge within a community. In Connolly's exegesis of Nietzsche, the situation of modernity is such that even if we were able to remain within the premodern understanding of community, we would still be strangers to ourselves. Connolly cites Nietzsche:

> "Self-knowledge" simultaneously lifts the self to a more complex level of social subtlety and subdues that which does not fit into the elevator: "So we are necessarily strangers to ourselves, we do not comprehend ourselves, we *have* to misunderstand ourselves, for us the law 'Each is furthest from himself' applies to all eternity—we are not 'men of knowledge' with respect to ourselves."[65]

In his criticism of responsibility, Connolly points to "existential resentment" as a driving force behind our search for identity/agent. In his criticism of community, Connolly points to an existential homesickness that can never be fulfilled. The criticism of responsibility situates the drive behind the search, the criticism of community points to the impossibility of attaining self-knowledge within community. While both criticisms are situated, they highlight different aspects of our modern dilemma. I highlighted the possibility of indirect, collective responsibility in the second point on the implications of imputation; Connolly's criticism of community leads us away from collectivity and community. If the search for responsibility is a form of rage against injustice, the search for community is forlorn nostalgia. The modern Luther had his inner conscience and self-understanding; according to Connolly, we postmoderns do not even have that.

In his criticisms of responsibility and community, Connolly questions the motivation behind our analysis of Weber and our attempt to construct responsible communities based on issue-specific problems. In a sense, he has situated our criticism of liberalism within a postliberal context. The question to ask is if he is helpful. I think the answer is yes on two levels. First, it is clear that the current international political situation calls into question all kinds of territorial relationships. The current integration in Western Europe may be held in opposition to the disintegration in the former Soviet Union and Yugoslavia.[66] In either case, as with the split in the former Czechoslovakia, rapid changes in borders/allegiances have raised significant issues involving sovereignty and identity. What has happened to those who have "refound" their "identities," such as the Balts? Is their "identity" merely something to be expressed in anti-Russian feelings?[67] How does one "create identity" in Belarus? In warning against plunging into these questions, Connolly allows us to reflect on the broader historical and philosophical background about why and how these problems are important. Before asking who I am, it may be helpful to ask why I want to know and why I am asking the question at this time.

Second, Connolly suggests that once we understand the reasons for wanting to know and the discourses out of which these desires have emerged, we should also understand the limits of our knowledge. His analysis of homesickness is terribly disturbing in that he posits a position wherein we will continue to search for something we will never be able to find. Should we stop searching? Can we stop searching? If we cannot go back to being premodern, why do we continue to try? Will we ever stop trying? How does being told that one's search is situated within a given context change the search itself? Can we self-deflate?

While I have taken one side in the liberal/communitarian debate, this last section has shown that I am aware that the communitarian position is as situated as the position it criticizes. The search for responsibility and community are fundamental elements in current discourse, and I have tried to explain the evolution from Weber's understanding of an ethic of responsibility to that ethic transposed onto current international relations. Weber's understanding was quite clear, although I am not sure that all those who cite Weber understand his implications for individuals and international relations. An ethic of responsibility in today's context is much more complex.

We are beginning to see discussions of a new understanding of an ethic of responsibility. Martti Koskenniemi speaks of an ideal of authentic commitment, a commitment that respects the conflictual character of social life by recognizing that normative commitment follows from context as well as consent:

> The ideal of authentic commitment directs normative conversation away from abstract principles of natural law, away from formal rules and the liberal ethic of consent and the market place. It recognizes that normative commitment may follow not only from whatever people might have consented to (although it does regard consent as important) but also by

virtue of the context in which they live. Authentic commitment means, in other words, respecting the conflictual character of social life. It tries to make life possible in conflict — indeed, it sees life in terms of constant coping with conflict, not in terms of assimilation into nostalgic utopia.[68]

In a similar vein, David Campbell refers to *an-arche* — being without first principle — and the constitution of subject in relation to Other through heteronomous and not autonomous responsibility:

In the move beyond metaphysics, ethics has been transformed from something independent of subjectivity — that is, from a set of rules and regulations adopted by autonomous agents — to something insinuated within and integral to that subjectivity. Accordingly, ethics is not ancillary to the existence of a subject (whether that subject be a person, a state, or some other figuration of identity); ethics is indispensable to the very being of that subject, because a subject's being is only possible once its *right to be* in relation to the Other is claimed. This recasting of the issue refigures the moral economy in which responsibility is assigned.[69]

We have become so accustomed to the assumptions associated with Weber's ethic of responsibility that we have difficulty imagining what a different ethic of responsibility might entail. Campbell makes some suggestions for future United States foreign policy, while recognizing that no single list of activities or specific agents will suffice. For Campbell, "Because engagement with the world is necessarily 'global' in its scope, but the world is characterized by a multiplicity of agents none of whom can singlehandedly bear the burden of global responsibility, the way in which our ethical responsibility is to be acted upon has to be contested and negotiated."[70]

The very processes of contestation and negotiation of an ethic of responsibility are crucial. In addition, given the restrictions I have mentioned in the quest for responsibility and the search for community, the results of that contestation and negotiation cannot be parsimonious. Therefore, just as Weber's ethic of responsibility was inappropriate because of its autonomous subjectivity, a communitarian ethic of responsibility may also be inadequate to our current situation. As Connolly notes in describing a new ethical sensibility, "Every moral economy also involves a certain forgetting, a forgetting of arbitrary impositions in the very pattern of equivalences it places under the star of morality.

The logic of forgetting built into the equivalences of morality needs to be engaged if we are to subject morality to critical ethical scrutiny."[71] By exposing the assumptions behind Weber's ethic of responsibility and the limits of responsibility/community, I have tried to engage in the process of subjecting morality to critical ethical scrutiny. What I am discovering through that engagement is that the liberal/communitarian debate does not lead us to a new understanding of an ethic of responsibility. For what I am proposing, in fact, is that a new ethic of responsibility may be postcommunitarian as well as postliberal, and that the liberal/communitarian debate may be two sides of the same coin.

To return to Max Weber and "Politics as a Vocation," the very basis of our initial observations and indeed an important foundation for understanding modern theories of international relations,[72] Bonnie Honig suggests that the two ethics described by Weber bear resemblance to virtue and virtu, and that they come together in the "mature man" in a way that is not dismissive of the other, nor dismissive of the contestations highlighted by Connolly. Honig states:

> The two ethics come together in a single person for whom politics is (therefore?) a vocation, but they do not produce a subject that is a unified, univocal whole. The miscegenation brings Weber's heroic figure to the point where he must say in proud torment: "Here I stand; I can do no other." The phrase unites freedom and necessity, performativity and contestation, existential choice and phenomenal determination. It attests to the beauty and impossibility of self-creation in a world already highly organized and disciplined. It echoes, in reverse order, Zarathustra's proclamation of the same impossible and enabling rift in subjectivity: "I am who I must be; I call myself Zarathustra."[73]

While Honig's point about the rift in subjectivity one can discern in Weber's analysis of politics as a vocation is important, my focus is on the contestations and rifts involved in the spaces between the individual and the Other. As Walker notes: "Weber's new personality requires the cultivation of a power over one's self and one's fate, an inner strength, a calling, a vocation, an integration of passion and perspective, a subjectivity that finds its specifically modern freedom among the determinations of inexorable rationalisation and warring gods."[74] We argued against Luther's position because outsiders have no place in his subjectivity beside blind faith and acceptance or rejection. The use of *I* in

Luther's statement should be differentiated from Emmanuel Levinas's Other and Martin Buber's I-Thou.[75] The etymological root of responsibility is *spondeo,* to promise solemnly; to bind, engage, pledge oneself; promise for another, become his security; promise sacredly, give assurance.[76] "The verb *respondeo* means to promise or offer in return, to answer, to return or repay."[77] It is in the working out of the dimensions of response to the Other that responsibility becomes meaningful and moral spaces opened. Luther's *I* is closure, as indeed is Walzer's nation-state and most of international relations based on the realist/liberal/modern understandings of subjectivity. It is only when that closure is contested from the outside that real spaces can be created.

Notes

1. William E. Connolly, *Identity\Difference: Democratic Negotiations of Political Paradox* (Ithaca, N.Y.: Cornell University Press, 1991), 120.

2. Max Weber, "Politics as a Vocation," in Hans Gerth and C. Wright Mills, eds., *From Max Weber: Essays in Sociology* (New York: Oxford University Press, 1946), 77–129.

3. Michael Joseph Smith, *Realist Thought from Weber to Kissinger* (Baton Rouge: Louisiana State University Press, 1986), 16. For an interesting discussion of the importance of Weber for realist theory, see R. B. J. Walker, *Inside/Outside: International Relations as Political Theory* (Cambridge: Cambridge University Press, 1993), 52–60.

4. See Charles Taylor, "Cross-Purposes: The Liberal-Communitarian Debate," in Nancy Rosenblaum, ed., *Liberalism and the Moral Life* (Cambridge: Harvard University Press, 1989), 159–82; Stephen A. Gardhaum, "Law, Politics, and the Claims of Community," 90 Michigan Law Review 685 (February 1992); Allen E. Buchanan, "Assessing the Communitarian Critique of Liberalism," *Ethics* 99 (July 1989): 852–82; Stephen Mulhall and Adam Swift, eds., *Liberals and Communitarians* (Oxford: Basil Blackwell, 1992); Shlomo Avineri and Avner de-Shalit, eds., *Communitarianism and Individualism* (Oxford: Oxford University Press, 1992).

5. Weber, "Politics as a Vocation," 79.

6. Ibid., 119.

7. Ibid., 120.

8. Ibid., 127.

9. Leszek Kolakowski, "The Man Who Made Modernity," *New Republic,* 6 May 1991, 40.

10. Jürgen Habermas, *The Philosophical Discourse of Modernity,* trans. Frederick G. Lawrence (Cambridge: The Massachusetts Institute of Technology Press, 1993), 17.

11. Michael Oakeshott, *On Human Conduct* (Oxford: Clarendon Press, 1975), 238.

12. See Michael Walzer, *The Revolution of the Saints: A Study in the Origins of Radical Politics* (Cambridge: Harvard University Press, 1965).

13. Charles Taylor, *Sources of the Self: The Making of the Modern Identity* (Cambridge: Harvard University Press, 1989), 193–94.

14. Oakeshott, *On Human Conduct*, 238.

15. *International Herald Tribune*, 6 November 1995.

16. *Le Nouveau Quotidien*, 7 November 1995 (my translation). The question of judgment concerning the assassin of Rabin is well reflected in this comment: "The 25-year-old assassin, who confessed in court, has been condemned by every religious leader in Israel. But he is neither a freak nor a misfit. Mr. Amir is something more disturbing to many Israelis: a young man of discipline and multiple gifts who thrived in the nation's mainstream and believed that he was serving Israel. His decision to kill reflected — perhaps as much as it distorted — the values he acquired in a journey through Israel's diverse establishments and some of their storied elite." *International Herald Tribune*, 13 November 1995.

17. See Jim George, "Realist Ethics, International Relations, and Postmodernism: Thinking beyond the Egoism-Anarchy Thematic," *Millennium: Journal of International Studies* 24, 2 (1995): 195–223, especially 198–207.

18. Obviously, this is not the only reading of Luther's statement. It is important to indicate this reading here since it is necessary to follow the realist/liberal understanding of the univocal individual/state. We will show another reading by Bonnie Honig at the end of the chapter in connection with reasons behind the search for responsibility/community.

19. *Le Nouveau Quotidien*, 7 November 1995.

20. See Hidemi Suganami, *The Domestic Analogy and World Order Proposals* (Cambridge: Cambridge University Press, 1989); "Reflecting on the Domestic Analogy: The Case of Bull, Beitz and Linklater," *Review of International Studies* 12:2 (1986): 145–58.

21. On this point, see Martti Koskenniemi, *From Apology to Utopia: The Structure of International Legal Argument* (Helsinki: Lakimiesliiton Kustannus, 1989), 200n.

22. Walker, *Inside/Outside*, 58.

23. R. J. Vincent, "Western Concepts of a Universal Moral Order," in Ralph Pettman, ed., *Moral Claims in World Affairs* (London: Croom Helm, 1979), 61.

24. Charles Beitz, "Bounded Morality," *International Organization* 33, 3 (1979): 408.

25. Emerich de Vattel, *The Law of Nations or the Principles of Natural Law*, vol. 3, trans. Charles Fenwick (Washington, D.C.: Carnegie Institution of Washington, 1916), 4. "The classic theories of international law themselves mirror the broader theory of liberal ethics. It is from liberalism that a 'domestic analogy' is drawn to create an image of world politics." Nigel Purvis, "Critical Legal Studies in Public International Law," *Harvard International Law Journal* 32, 1 (winter 1991): 93n.

26. Charles Beitz, *Political Theory and International Relations* (Princeton: Princeton University Press, 1979), 66.

27. Isaiah Berlin, *Two Concepts of Liberty* (Oxford: Clarendon Press, 1958).

28. Michael Walzer, *Just and Unjust Wars: A Moral Argument with Historical Illustrations* (New York: Basic Books, 1977); *Spheres of Justice: a Defence of Pluralism and Equality* (New York: Basic Books, 1983).

29. Walzer, *Just and Unjust Wars*, 89.

30. Gerald Doppelt, "Walzer's Theory of Morality in International Relations," *Philosophy and Public Affairs* 8, 1 (1978): 3–26; Richard Wasserstrom, review of *Just and Unjust Wars*, 92 Harvard Law Review 536 (1978); David Luban, "Just War and Human Rights," *Philosophy and Public Affairs* 9, 2 (1980): 161–81; Beitz, "Bounded Morality."

31. Gordon Christenson, "Jus Cogens: Guarding Interests Fundamental to International Society," 28 Virginia Journal of International Law 635 (1983).

32. For a criticism of individual rights in this sense, see Michael Sandel, "The Procedural Republic and the Unencumbered Self," *Political Theory* 12, 1 (1984): 81–96; Steven Lukes, *Individualism* (Oxford: Basil Blackwell, 1973); Charles Taylor, "Atomism," in Alkis Kantos, ed., *Powers, Possessions and Freedoms* (Toronto: University of Toronto Press, 1979), 39–61.

33. "To tear down the walls of the state is not, as Sidgwick worriedly suggested, to create a world without walls, but rather to create a thousand petty fortresses." Walzer, *Spheres of Justice*, 39.

34. There are analogous difficulties in arguments over state recognition and fetus rights. The international legal system has as much difficulty in determining when a state is a state with consequent rights as countries have in determining the age at which a fetus is a person with consequent rights.

35. Henry Shue, "The Geography of Justice: Beitz's Critique of Skepticism and Statism," *Ethics* 92, 4 (1982): 717.

36. Although realism and liberalism are obviously different, they both contain very strong statecentric models, an observation I owe to Cornelia Navari. See Mark Warren, "Max Weber's Liberalism for a Nietzschean World," *American Political Science Review* 82, 1 (1988): 31–50.

37. Sandel, "Procedural Republic."

38. See Henry Shue, *Basic Rights: Subsistence, Affluence, and U.S. Foreign Policy* (Princeton: Princeton University Press, 1980), chapter 6, where he focuses on "Nationality and Responsibility." See also David Miller, "The Ethical Significance of Nationality," *Ethics* 98, 4 (1988): 647–63.

39. A newspaper article indicated how during the 1992 presidential election Bill Clinton attacked George Bush on this very point: "Weaving various threads of his attack on George Bush into a newly coherent and more personal whole, the Democratic presidential nominee, Bill Clinton, has begun criticizing Mr. Bush for the most basic of shortcomings — the failure to take responsibility for his actions." The article goes on to note: "[I]n a speech at the University of New Orleans, Mr. Clinton returned to the attack on the administration as saying that none of the nation's economic problems are Mr. Bush's fault. 'He refused to assume a shred of responsibility,' Mr. Clinton said of his opponent. He added that Mr. Bush seemed to be saying, 'What do you expect me to do, I'm the president of the United States?'" "Clinton Theme for Bush: 'The Buck Stops Somewhere Else,'" *International Herald Tribune*, 31 July 1992.

40. Transcript of press conference, 12 April 1991, EUR503, 2.

41. "Quick Gulf Exit? Not So Fast," *International Herald Tribune*, 18 April 1991, 1.

42. Hans Kelsen, "Causality and Imputation," *Ethics* 61, 1 (1950): 1–11. For a relevant discussion of different types of causality, see Friedrich V. Kratochwil, *Rules, Norms and Decisions: On the Conditions of Practical and Legal Reasoning in Interna-*

tional Relations and Domestic Affairs (Cambridge: Cambridge University Press, 1989), 24–25.

43. Kelsen, "Causality and Imputation," 1.

44. For a discussion of legal individualism from this point of view, see Robin West, "Taking Freedom Seriously," 104 Harvard Law Review 403 (1990).

45. Haskell Fain, *Normative Politics and the Community of Nations* (Philadelphia: Temple University Press, 1987).

46. See also Hans Jonas, *The Imperative of Responsibility: In Search of an Ethics for the Technological Age,* trans. Hans Jonas with David Kerr (Chicago: University of Chicago Press, 1984).

47. Vernon Van Dyke has written extensively on ethnic groups in this sense. See especially "The Individual, the State, and Ethnic Communities in Political Theory," *World Politics* 29, 3 (1977): 343–69; "Collective Entities and Moral Rights: Problems in Liberal-Democratic Thought," *Journal of Politics* 44 (1982): 21–40.

48. One could, for example, enter into the debate over Habermas's Ideal Speech Community. See Seyla Benhabib and Fred Dallmayr, eds., *The Communicative Ethics Controversy* (Cambridge: Massachusetts Institute of Technology Press, 1990).

49. Daniel Warner, "The Community of the Refugee," *International Journal of Refugee Law* 3:4 (1991), 731–34. See the excellent article by Jim George summarizing much of the recent literature: "Of Incarceration and Closure: NeoRealism and the New/Old World Order," *Millennium: Journal of International Studies* 22, 2 (1993): 197–234.

50. Daniel Warner, *An Ethic of Responsibility in International Relations* (Boulder, Colo.: Lynne Rienner, 1991), 125–29.

51. See Walker, *Inside/Outside,* and Walker, "Violence, Modernity, Silence: From Max Weber to International Relations," in David Campbell and Michael Dillon, eds., *The Political Subject of Violence* (Manchester: Manchester University Press, 1993).

52. Connolly, *Identity\Difference,* 111.

53. Ibid., 96.

54. Ibid., 118.

55. Ibid., 121. While we will focus on Connolly's emphasis on the relationship between attributing responsibility and existential resentment, Richard Rorty enlarges this resentment when he suggests that the entire drive for identity is close to the drive to seek vengeance. For Rorty, both drives are cruel and against solidarity. Richard Rorty, *Contingency, Irony, and Solidarity* (Cambridge: Cambridge University Press, 1989), especially 141–98.

56. Connolly, *Identity\Difference,* 118.

57. Ibid.

58. William E. Connolly, *Political Theory and Modernity* (Oxford: Basil Blackwell, 1989), chapter 5.

59. Ibid., 137.

60. In a reply to a formulation I have used elsewhere ("Responsibility as responsiveness means piercing the veil of the state and piercing the hermetic seal around its borders . . . [O]ne could imagine borders being like permeable cell walls allowing people to move in and out freely until an equilibrium — homeostasis — is achieved," *An Ethic of Responsibility in International Relations,* 128n), James C. Hathaway commented that "[l]iberal absolutism of this kind, with its implied advocacy of con-

stant social flux and volatility of community, may simply not be consistent with the human need for meaningful solidarity." "Reply to Warner," *Journal of Refugee Studies* 6, 2 (1992): 169–71. However, Hathaway has misconstrued the human need for community and the ability of the individual today to fulfill that need. My description of mobile, issue-specific communities points to the difficulty of finding a final, permanent, stable community. Connolly's invocation of Nietzsche's homesickness is one step further away from the kind of stability expressions like durable solutions and right to community." Daniel Warner, "We Are All Refugees," *International Journal of Refugee Law* 4, 3 (1992): 368n–69n.

61. Connolly, *Political Theory and Modernity*, 138 (emphasis added).

62. Friedrich Nietzsche, *The Gay Science*, quoted in ibid., 141.

63. Connolly, "Democracy and Territoriality," *Millennium: Journal of International Studies* 20, 3 (1991): 464.

64. Connolly, *Political Theory and Modernity*, 148.

65. Nietzsche, *On the Geneology of Morals*, quoted in ibid., 149.

66. "Coming Together, Coming Apart," *The Economist*, 7 December 1991.

67. "Baltic Identity: Russians Wonder if They Belong," *New York Times*, 22 November 1992.

68. Koskenniemi, *From Apology to Utopia*, 488.

69. David Campbell, *Politics without Principle: Sovereignty, Ethics, and the Narratives of the Gulf War* (Boulder, Colo.: Lynne Rienner, 1993), 92. Campbell extends this discussion in *National Deconstruction: Violence, Identity and Justice in Bosnia* (Minneapolis: University of Minnesota Press, 1998).

70. Campbell, *Politics without Principle*, 99.

71. William E. Connolly, *The Augustinian Imperative: A Reflection on the Politics of Morality* (Newbury Park, Calif.: Sage Publications, 1993), 132.

72. As Rob Walker correctly notes in his discussion of violence and modernity, "the most important name . . . is that of Max Weber . . . Weber the quintessentially political theorist of a century of both reason and violence, of the double-edged reason of capitalist modernity that issues in renewed demands upon the autonomous identities of state and individual, demands implicated in a knowing violence since Machiavelli and Hobbes first calculated the price of liberty amidst the collapsing hierarchies of Christendom . . . Weber, then, is interesting as a political theorist because he both assumes and problematises the possibility of autonomy—of the self-identical subject capable of acting on the basis of some inner 'freedom.' As an initial assumption, autonomy is read into both his preoccupation with the constitution of the modern individual and his definition of the state." Walker, "Violence, Modernity, Silence," 140, 150.

73. Bonnie Honig, *Political Theory and the Displacement of Politics* (Ithaca: Cornell University Press, 1993), 205–6.

74. Walker, "Violence, Modernity, Silence," 148–49. Walker goes on to discuss the implications of Weber's understanding of individual subjectivity for his famous definition of the state.

75. See Daniel Warner, "Buber, Levinas and the Concept of Otherness in International Relations: A Reply to David Campbell," *Millennium: Journal of International Studies* 25 (spring 1996): 111–28. This article deals principally with Campbell's "The Deterritorialization of Responsibility: Levinas, Derrida, and Ethics after the

End of Philosophy," this volume. Campbell's response can be found in "The Politics of Radical Interdependence: A Rejoinder to Daniel Warner," *Millennium: Journal of International Studies* 25 (spring 1996): 129–41.

76. Warner, *An Ethic of Responsibility in International Relations*, 96–100.

77. Moorhead Wright, "An Ethic of Responsibility," in J. Mayall, ed., *The Community of States* (London: George Allen and Unwin, 1982), 161–62.

CHAPTER TWO

The Deterritorialization of Responsibility: Levinas, Derrida, and Ethics after the End of Philosophy

David Campbell

The Problem of Responsibility

The orthodox foundations for ethical consideration in international relations — sovereign states in an anarchic realm — have been increasingly
subject to both theoretical critique and political violence. If we accept,
following Daniel Warner's argument, that this problematization of community puts the question of responsibility into doubt, we need to develop an approach to responsibility that is cognizant of the way in
which the reterritorialization of states necessitates a deterritorialization of theory.[1]

Getting to grips with such a challenge requires a sustained reflection
on the interrelationships between the problematic of subjectivity and the
question of ethics. To that end, especially given his radical refiguration
of responsibility, the thought of Emmanuel Levinas stands as a provocation. Insufficient in itself, largely because of its often unacknowledged
spatial predicates, Levinas's thought can be considered in relationship
to Derrida's overt attentiveness to ethico-political dilemmas (especially
as mediated through Simon Critchley's *Ethics of Deconstruction*). Bringing these strands together, this chapter seeks to make Levinas's thought
more "Levinasian." That is, after an exegesis of the Levinasian problematic that sets the stage for some of the subsequent chapters, it seeks to
go beyond the limits of Levinas's statist cartography by exploring and
deploying Derrida's arguments in a manner different from Critchley's
account. The purpose is to deterritorialize responsibility and articulate

the parameters of a critical, political ethos that can be appreciated as central to poststructuralist theorizing.

Ethics after the End of Philosophy

The "end of philosophy"—the problematic term that signifies, among other developments, the Heideggerian critique of metaphysics and its many offspring—appears to pose something of a hurdle for thinking through the ethical challenges of our era.[2] Not the least of these obstacles is the view that in the wake of the Heideggerean critique, the ground for moral theory has been removed, because the *ethos* of moral philosophy cannot remain once the *logos* of metaphysics has gone.[3] At the same time, and equally in the wake of Heidegger, is a range of concerns—the German *Historikerstreit*, the wartime writings of Paul de Man, and various attempts at Holocaust revisionism, along with Heidegger's own Nazi affiliations—that many take to be proof of the dangers that postmetaphysical thinking portends.

In this contemporary milieu, a 1934 essay by Emmanuel Levinas ("Reflections on the Philosophy of Hitlerism") has been republished with a preface offering a different account of danger. In that short note, Levinas argued that the origins of National Socialism's "bloody barbarism" were not to be found in an aberration of reasoning or an accident of ideology, but rather in "the essential possibility of *elemental Evil* into which we can be led by logic and against which Western philosophy had not sufficiently insured itself."[4] Moreover, the possibility of evil as a product of reason, something against which Western philosophy had no guard, was "inscribed within the ontology of a being concerned with being." As such, this possibility remains a risk: it "still threatens the subject correlative with being as gathering together and as dominating," even though this subject (the subject of liberalism and humanism) is "the famous subject of transcendental idealism that before all else wishes to be free and thinks itself free."[5]

In this statement, Levinas offered the core of a thought developed over the last six decades, a thought with the potential to chart an ethical course for subjects implicated in deconstruction but who want to resist destruction. Levinas's philosophy—that of ethics as first philosophy—is "dominated by the presentiment and the memory of the Nazi horror,"[6] and from under the shadow of Auschwitz seeks to install a disposition that will prevent its repetition.[7] Yet this summons is not answered by the admonition to return to the dominant moral-philosophical discourse of modernity with its traditional concept of responsibility, where ethics is most often understood in terms of the moral codes and commands pertaining to autonomous agents (whether they be individuals or states).[8] For Levinas, being beholden by reason to elements of that tradition was the basis upon which the Holocaust (among other related atrocities) was possible.[9] Instead, Levinas argues that in order to confront evil it is the totalities of that moral-philosophical discourse that must be contested, for "political totalitarianism rests on an ontological totalitarianism."[10]

The critique of "ontological totalitarianism" puts Levinas in tension with the legacies of (Greek) philosophy, at least insofar as Levinas understands that philosophy to have been dominated by a way of thinking in which truth is equivalent to presence. "By this I mean an intelligibility that considers truth to be that which is present or copresent, that which can be gathered or synchronized into a totality that we would call the world or *cosmos*."[11] That which is Other is thereby reduced to the Same. This transformation is considered by Levinas to be an "alchemy that is performed with the philosopher's stone of the knowing ego," a being concerned with being.[12] "Political totalitarianism" originates in this privilege granted to presence because it disenables and resists an understanding of that which cannot be thematized, the "otherwise than Being."[13] In this context, antisemitism — as one of the bases for the Nazi horror — is more than "the hostility felt by a majority towards a minority, nor only xenophobia, nor any ordinary racism." Instead, it can be understood as "a repugnance felt for the unknown within the psyche of the Other, for the mystery of its interiority or . . . a repugnance felt for the pure proximity of the other man, for sociality itself."[14]

However, there is for Levinas another tradition of thought that takes us in this otherwise direction: the Hebraic (as opposed to Hellenic) tradition.[15] Although Levinas does not discount the Greek tradition's capacity to understand the interhuman realm as presence, he argues that this realm "can also be considered from another perspective — the ethical or biblical perspective that transcends the Greek language of intelligibility — as a theme of justice and concern for the other as other, as a theme of love and desire, which carries us beyond the infinite being of the world as presence."[16] Levinas cannot therefore be understood as being bound by an either/or logic through which one tradition is rejected in favor of another. Instead, he argues that "the interhuman is thus an interface: a double axis where what is 'of the world' qua *phenomenological intelligibility* is juxtaposed with what is 'not of the world' qua *ethical responsibility*."[17]

This double axis of presence and absence, identity and alterity, "essence and essence's other," stands as "the ultimate relationship in Being," the "irreducible structure upon which all the other structures rest."[18] It is that which constitutes, or reterritorializes, the space — the "null-site," a nonplace of a place — of responsibility, subjectivity, and ethics in the location deterritorialized by Heidegger (and others).[19]

Responsibility, Subjectivity, Ethics

Levinas's thought radically refigures our understanding of responsibility, subjectivity, and ethics, for the meaning of each is implicated in the other: "[R]esponsibility [is] the essential, primary and fundamental structure of subjectivity. For I describe subjectivity in ethical terms. Ethics . . . does not supplement a preceding existential base; the very node of the subjective is knotted in ethics understood as responsibility."[20] Of these concepts, responsibility is perhaps the most important because, for Levinas, being is a radically interdependent condition, a condition made possible only because of my responsibility to the Other:

> Responsibility for the Other, for the naked face of the first individual to come along. A responsibility that goes beyond what I may or may not have done to the Other or whatever acts I may or may not have committed, as if I were devoted to the other man before being devoted to myself. Or more exactly, as if I had to answer for the other's death even before being. A guiltless responsibility, whereby I am none the less open to an accusation of which no alibi, spatial or temporal, could clear me. It is as if the Other established a relationship or a relationship were established whose whole intensity consists in not presupposing the idea of community.[21]

This responsibility is unlike that associated with the autonomous moral agents of traditional conceptions. It is "a responsibility without limits, and so necessarily excessive, incalculable, before memory . . . a responsibility before the very concept of responsibility."[22] It is a responsibility that is pre-original, an-archic, and devolved from an "infrastructural alterity,"[23] and thus reworks our understanding of both subjectivity and ethics.

Responsibility understood as such refigures subjectivity because the very origin of the subject is to be found in its subjection to the Other, a subjection that precedes consciousness, identity, and freedom, does not therefore originate in a vow or decision, and — ergo — cannot be made possible by a command or imperative.[24] In other words, subjects are constituted by their relationship with the Other. Their being is called into question by the prior existence of the Other, which has an unremitting and even accusative hold on the subject. Moreover, and this is what re-articulates ethics, this relationship with the Other means that one's being has to be affirmed in terms of *a right to be* in relation to the Other:

> One has to respond to one's right to be, not by referring to some abstract and anonymous law, or judicial entity, but because of one's fear for the Other. My being-in-the-world or my "place in the sun," my being at home, have these not also been the usurpation of spaces belonging to the other man whom I have already oppressed or starved, or driven out into a third world; are they not acts of repulsing, excluding, exiling, stripping, killing?[25]

Having decentered subjectivity by making it an effect of the relationship with the Other, Levinas's thought recasts ethics in terms of a primary responsibility that stakes our being on the assertion of our right to be. As Levinas declares, "We name this calling into question of my spontaneity by the presence of the Other ethics."[26] In turn, the recasting of ethics reinforces the decentering of subjectivity:

> Ethical subjectivity dispenses with the idealizing subjectivity of ontology, which reduces everything to itself. The ethical "I" is subjectivity precisely insofar as it kneels before the other, sacrificing its own liberty to the more primordial call of the other. The heteronomy of our response to the human other, or to God as the absolutely other, precedes the autonomy of our subjective freedom. As soon as I acknowledge that it is "I" who am responsible, I accept that my freedom is anteceded by an obligation to the other. Ethics redefines subjectivity as this heteronomous responsibility, in contrast to autonomous freedom.[27]

Levinas's philosophy of ethics as first philosophy is clearly in accord with the demise of universality as signalled by "the end of philosophy," especially as his enterprise has been animated by a concern for the political consequences of Being, ontology, and totality. At the same time, and partly because its truly radical nature goes beyond the confines of either/or logic, it can be argued that there remains an important moment of universality in Levinas's thought. It is to be found — paradoxically — in "the very particularity" of the obligation to the Other.[28] We are all in that circumstance, and it is thus universal, a form of transcendence. Not the transcendence of an ahistorical ego or principle, but transcendence in the sense that alterity, being's other, is a necessity structured by *differance* rather than ontology, which effects a transcendence without presence.[29] As Levinas observes, "The fundamental experience which objective experience itself presupposes is the experience of the Other."[30]

The ethical transcendence of alterity that marks the moment of universality in Levinas's thought also fundamentally problematizes liberal humanism, an oft-considered alternate ground for ethics. In the prefatory note to "The Philosophy of Hitlerism," Levinas posed a radical question: "We must ask ourselves if liberalism is all we need to achieve an authentic dignity for the human subject. Does this subject arrive at the human condition prior to assuming responsibility for the other man in the act of election that raises him up to this height?"[31] The answer could only be no. In *Otherwise Than Being*, Levinas wondered "if anything in the world is less conditioned than man, in whom the ultimate security a foundation would offer is absent. Is there then anything less unjustified than the contestation of the human condition?"[32] But this concern for justification abounds only if one requires sovereign grounds in advance of the Other. If that hope, driven by the perceived security such a foundation would offer, is expunged — and expunged it need be, otherwise ressentiment derived from the elusiveness of a foundation will thrive — the human condition will be understood as stemming from the relationship of alterity, and will be seen as without warrant prior to the responsibility the relationship with the Other entails. Accordingly, subjectivity is "imposed as an absolute" not through any interior value, but because it "is sacred in its alterity with respect to which, in an unexceptionable responsibility, I posit myself deposed of my sovereignty. Paradoxically it is qua *alienus* — foreigner and other — that man is not alienated."[33]

Liberalism is thus insufficient for human dignity because the election that justifies man "comes from a god — or God — who beholds him in the *face* of the other man, his neighbor, the original 'site' of the Revelation."[34] Similarly, humanism is insufficient, and "modern antihumanism . . . is true over and beyond the reasons it gives itself." What Levinas finds laudable in antihumanism is that it "abandoned the idea of person, goal and origin of itself, in which the ego is still a thing because it is still a being." As such, antihumanism does not eradicate the human, but "clears the place for subjectivity positing itself in abnegation, in sacrifice, in a substitution which precedes the will." It would therefore be a grave error to conclude in haste that Levinas's antihumanism is either inhuman or inhumane. To the contrary. Levinas declares that "humanism has to be denounced only *because it is not sufficiently human*,"[35] because it is insufficiently attuned to alterity. If one understood "humanism" to mean a "humanism of the Other," then there would be no greater humanist than Levinas.[36]

The Politics of Responsibility

Levinas's thought is appealing for rethinking the question of responsibility, especially with respect to situations like the Balkan crisis, because it maintains that there is no circumstance under which we could declare that it was not our concern. As Levinas notes, people can (and obviously do) conduct their relationship to the Other in terms of exploitation, oppression, and violence. But no matter how allergic to the other is the self, "the relation to the other, as a relation of responsibility, cannot be totally suppressed, even when it takes the form of politics or warfare." In consequence, no self can ever opt out of a relationship with the other: "[I]t is impossible to free myself by saying, 'It's not my concern.' There is no choice, for it is always and inescapably my concern. This is a unique 'no choice,' one that is not slavery."[37]

This unique lack of choice comes about because in Levinas's thought ethics has been transformed from something independent of subjectivity—that is, from a set of rules and regulations adopted by pregiven, autonomous agents—to something insinuated within and integral to that subjectivity. Accordingly, ethics can be understood as something not ancillary to the existence of a subject; instead, ethics can be appreciated for its indispensability to the very being of the subject. This argument leads us to the recognition that "we" are always already ethically situated, so making judgments about conduct depends less on what sort of rules are invoked as regulations and more on how the interdependencies of our relations with others are appreciated. To repeat one of Levinas's key points: "Ethics redefines subjectivity as this heteronomous responsibility, in contrast to autonomous freedom."[38]

Suggestive though it is for the domain of international relations—
where the bulk of the work on ethics can be located within a conventional
perspective on responsibility[39]— Levinas's formulation of responsibility, subjectivity, and ethics nonetheless possesses some problems when
it comes to the implications of this thought for politics. What requires
particular attention is the means by which the elemental and omni-
present status of responsibility, which is founded in the one-to-one or
face-to-face relationship, can function in circumstances marked by a
multiplicity of others. Although the reading of Levinas here agrees that
"the ethical exigency to be responsible to the other undermines the ontological primacy of the meaning of being," and embraces the idea that
this demand "unsettles the natural and political positions we have taken
up in the world and predisposes us to a meaning that is other than being, that is otherwise than being,"[40] how those disturbances are negotiated so as to foster the maximum responsibility in a world populated
by others in struggle remains to be argued. To examine what is a problem of considerable import given the context of this essay, I want to
consider Levinas's discussion of "the third person," the distinction he
makes between the ethical and the moral, and—of particular importance in a consideration of the politics of international action—the role
of the state in Levinas's thought.

Levinas's philosophy, although clearly nonindividualist and antihumanist in its rendering of subjectivity, is nonetheless located within the
logic of an individual, one-to-one relationship with the Other. Which
is not to say that it is asocial. Aside from the fact that the basic premise
of the one-to-one relationship is the interdependent character of subjectivity, Levinas clearly recognizes that the world does not simply comprise one-to-one relationships. "In the real world there are many others,"
he writes.[41] But can Levinas's articulation of ethics as first philosophy,
and of responsibility as the primary structure of subjectivity, be ex-
panded from the one-to-one to the one-and-the-many? And if so, how
is this expansion achieved? While some have argued it cannot, Levinas's
discussions of "the third person," the state, and morality indicate that
transference is considered within his thought.[42] The question is, then,
whether the means by which that transference is possible fulfill the radical promise of Levinas's argument.

If ethics is "a responsible, non-totalizing relation with the Other," then
politics for Levinas is "conceived of as a relation to the third party (*le*

tiers), to all others, to the plurality of beings that make up the community."[43] There is thus a distinction derived from the existence of the third party in Levinas's thought concerning others, which contrasts the Other as neighbor, the participant in the one-to-one relationship, with all others, those with whom my neighbor is the third party.[44] Additionally, the neighbor appears to exercise the primary demand of responsibility, and then serves as the basis for my relationship with all others: "My relationship with the other as neighbor gives meaning to my relations with all the others."[45]

Levinas recognizes that the (inevitable) entry of the third party poses a dilemma: "The responsibility for the other is an immediacy antecedent to questions, it is proximity. It is troubled and becomes a problem when a third party enters."[46] The concern arises because the third party dissolves the uniqueness of the one-to-one relationship, not just because it presses the numerical claim that the world comprises many others, but because it establishes that "the third party is simultaneously other than the other, and makes me one among others."[47] However, as Lingis observes, "[T]o find that the one before whom and for whom I am responsible is responsible in his turn before and for another is not to find his order put on me relativized or cancelled."[48]

Nonetheless, the entry of the third party does raise questions that potentially put in doubt the universality of responsibility to the Other. As Levinas remarks, "[W]hen others enter, each of them external to myself, problems arise. Who is closest to me? Who is the Other?"[49] These questions suggest the need for a calculation as to the nature of responsibility. Because there are always three people in the world, Levinas says, "this means that we are obliged to ask who the other is, to try to define the undefinable, to compare the incomparable, in an effort to juridically hold different positions together."[50]

It appears, particularly when Levinas asks "Who is closest?" that this calculation of the order of responsibility has a spatial dimension. Yet in his discussion of the concept of "proximity," the term that deals with this issue of closeness, the spatial implications of the concept are sometimes denied. Proximity, argues Levinas, is "not an 'experience of proximity,' not a cognition which a subject has of an object. Nor is it the representation of the spatial environment, nor even the 'objective' fact of this spatial environment observable by a third party or deducible by me."[51] Levinas also maintains that "the proximity of beings of flesh and blood is not their presence 'in flesh and bone.'"⁵² In formulations of this kind, it seems that proximity is the condition of possibility for the inter-human relationship of the one-to-one, the basis on which one cannot escape the universal demand of particular responsibility. Proximity is understood to be the relationship with the other, which "cannot be reduced to any modality of distance or geometrical contiguity, nor to the simple 'representation' of a neighbor; it is already an assignation, an extremely urgent assignation — an obligation, anachronously prior to any commitment."⁵³

In these terms, proximity could also signify the closeness of culture, the priority of time over space. But on other occasions the spatial dimension is there, notably when the third party enters. "In proximity a subject is implicated in a way not reducible to *the spatial sense which proximity takes on* when the third party troubles it by demanding justice."⁵⁴ Indeed, the major problem with the entry of the third party is that the disturbance of responsibility in the one-to-one relationship it creates requires justice. As Levinas argues, "[I]f there were only two people in the world, there would be no need for law courts because I would always be responsible for and before, the other."⁵⁵ The justice required is, according to Levinas, a justice of laws, and courts, and institutions, which means that as soon as the third party enters, "the ethical relationship with the other becomes political and enters into a totalizing discourse of ontology."⁵⁶

Moreover, the spatial dimension foregrounded by the third party's disturbance and the resultant need for justice is associated with the state. "Who is closest to me? Who is the Other? . . . We must investigate carefully. Legal justice is required. There is need for a state."⁵⁷ Equally, in *Otherwise Than Being,* Levinas writes that "a problem is posited by proximity itself, which, as the immediate itself, is without problems. The extraordinary commitment of the other to the third party calls for control, a search for justice, society and the State."⁵⁸ Indeed, Levinas has an approving view of the state, regarding it as "the highest achievement in the lives of western peoples,"⁵⁹ something perhaps attributable to his contestable interpretation of the legitimacy of the state of Israel.⁶⁰

This view needs to be contrasted with Levinas's belief, cited above, that not even in politics or warfare can the relationship with the other, the relationship of primary responsibility and the demand it imposes, be eradicated. Levinas's faith in the state as the sovereign domain in which freedom can be exercised has the capacity to overlook the restrictions on the freedom of others the state's security requires. This potential was, disturbingly, most evident in an interview Levinas gave on the topic of the massacre of Palestinians in the Sabra and Chatila refugee camps, which occurred during the 1982 Israeli invasion of Lebanon, after Israeli forces knowingly let Lebanese Christian soldiers into the camps to pursue suspected "Arab infiltrators." Although Levinas spoke of those events as a "catastrophe" and as events "which we would rather hadn't happened," and although he sees profound need for the "honor of responsibility," he concludes that there is a "lack of guilt."[61] The following exchange ensued:

> [Q.] Emmanuel Levinas, you are the philosopher of the "other." Isn't history, isn't politics the very site of the encounter with the "other," and for the Israeli, isn't the "other" above all the Palestinian?
>
> [A.] My definition of the other is completely different. The other is the neighbour, who is not necessarily kin, but who can be. And in that sense, if you're for the other, you're for the neighbour. But if your neighbour attacks another neighbour or treats him unjustly, what can you do? Then alterity takes on another character, in alterity we can find an enemy, or at least then we are faced with the problem of knowing who is right and who is wrong, who is just and who is unjust. There are people who are wrong.[62]

In this answer the notion of the Other is restricted to the neighbor in such a way as to keep the Palestinians outside of the reach of those to whom the "I" is responsible. Although Levinas elsewhere argues that "justice remains justice only, *in* a society where there is no distinction between those close and those far off,"[63] it seems that the border *between* societies, the state border that is enabled by the transformation of alterity into enmity (and especially those borders that separate Israel from its neighbors), permits the responsibility for the Other as neighbor to be diminished. Indeed, while Levinas argued in the 1982 interview that he rejected the idea that responsibility had limits — "my *self*, I repeat, is never absolved from responsibility towards the Other" — in *Otherwise Than Being* he remarked almost in passing that "my responsibility *for all* can and has to manifest itself also in limiting itself."[64]

This potential limiting of responsibility, which takes place on the passage from ethics to politics, can also be identified in the transition from ethics to morality. For Levinas, the distinction between the ethical and the moral is one that is important to maintain, even though they are intimately intertwined. Ethics does not decree rules for society; it is morality that governs society. But it is ethics — as "the extreme sensitivity of one subjectivity to another," the heteronomous responsibility of our subjectivity — that governs morality. "The norm that must continue to inspire and direct the moral order is the ethical norm of the interhuman."[65]

Notwithstanding the interrelated nature of the norm of the interhuman and the rules of governance, in the shift to morality Levinas argues that ethics "hardens its skin as soon as we move into the political world or the impersonal 'third' — the world of government, institutions, tribunals, prisons, schools, committees, and so on."[66] This "hardening of the skin" is a manifestation of the way in which Levinas understands politics to involve "a totalizing discourse of ontology,"[67] a discourse most evident in arguments enunciated by and for the state. Nonetheless, in his discussion of the shift from ethics to morality, Levinas exhibits a less sanguine attitude to the state than noted above:

> If the moral-political order totally relinquishes its ethical foundation, it must accept all forms of society, including the fascist or totalitarian, for it can no longer evaluate or discriminate between them. The state is usually better than anarchy — but not always. In some instances — fascism or totalitarianism, for example — the political order of the state may have to be challenged in the name of our ethical responsibility to the other. That is why ethics must remain the first philosophy.[68]

Even though Levinas's limited reservations about the state are here restricted to the nature of (domestic) political order, the idea that "the state may have to be challenged in the name of our ethical responsibility to the other" at least allows for the possibility of extending political action in terms of the ethical relation beyond the bounds suggested by Levinas's previous reflections on the third party and the state. There is no doubt, however, that to fulfill the promise of Levinas's ethics with respect to international politics, this possibility for challenge has to be carried a good deal further. Moreover, I would argue, this possibility for challenge has to be pursued in order to maintain fidelity with Levinas's conviction that neither politics nor warfare can obliterate the relationship of the self to the other as a relation of responsibility. Indeed, this endeavor might be thought of in terms of making Levinas's thought more "Levinasian," for pursuing this possibility of challenge flows from the recognition that "injustice—not to mention racism, nationalism, and imperialism—begins when one loses sight of the transcendence of the Other and forgets that the State, with its institutions, is informed by the proximity of my relation to the Other."[69]

Supplementing Levinas

Augmenting Levinas's thought so that when it comes to the question of politics and the state it is more "Levinasian" is a twofold process. It involves the retention of those aspects that suggested how an ethical attitude could be fashioned in a manner consistent with (and perhaps enabled by) the questioning of the metaphysics of presence, especially the idea that heteronomous responsibility is our raison d'être, which cannot be escaped. And it involves a ceaseless effort of folding the ethical relation into the social effects of the ontologies of politics that harden skin and feign presence, so that the relationship with the Other which makes those effects possible, the state among them, is never elided.[70] In particular, this means the heteronomous responsibility that is our raison d'être must be made to intervene in the claims to autonomous freedom associated with raison d'état. This possibility can be thought, I want to argue, if we turn to Derrida.

The affinities between "Levinasian ethics" and "Derridean deconstruction" are considerable. Most notably, alterity incites ethics and responsibility for each, as both depend on the recognition of a structural condition of alterity prior to subjectivity and thought. As Derrida argues in defense of the proposition that deconstruction entails an affirmation, "[D]econstruction is, in itself, a positive response to an alterity which necessarily calls, summons or motivates it. Deconstruction is therefore vocation—a response to a call . . . The other precedes philosophy and necessarily invokes and provokes the subject before any genuine questioning can begin. It is in this rapport with the other that affirmation expresses itself."[71] As such, "Deconstruction is not an enclosure in nothingness, but an openness towards the other."[72]

Deconstruction's unconditional affirmation has enabled Simon Critchley to argue that the question of ethics and deconstruction is not one of deriving an ethics from deconstruction, but of recognizing that deconstruction has a basic ethicality, that it takes place ethically, because of its orientation to the call of the other. But, for Critchley, deconstruction alone "fails to navigate the treacherous passage from ethics to politics,"[73] and requires the supplement of Levinas's unconditional responsibility to traverse this passage. The Levinasian fortification is effective because "for Levinas *ethics is ethical for the sake of politics*—that is, for the sake of a new conception of the organization of political space." In consequence, Critchley's argument (although it is not specifically intended as a critique of Derrida) is that "politics provides the continual horizon of Levinasian ethics, and that the problem of politics is that of delineating a form of political life that will repeatedly interrupt all attempts at totalization."[74]

That this is the problem of politics certainly brooks no disagreement from the argument being made here. However, the discussion above of Levinas's reflections on politics and the state suggested that while his critique of "ontological totalitarianism" unsettled "political totalitarianism" *within* states, it did not carry through to the dangers of "political totalitarianism" that inhere in the strategies necessary to secure (even liberal-democratic) states, or to the question of "political totalitarianism" *between* states. Thus, while Critchley supplements Derrida with Levinas in pursuit of the political goal this argument shares, I would suggest that in order to establish the grounds for "a form of political life that will repeatedly interrupt all attempts at totalization," his argument requires a resupplementation in the form of Derridean deconstruction.

This move connects to Derrida's provocative and suggestive statement that deconstruction can be considered "a stroke of luck for politics, for all historical progress."[75] Part of the reason for this is that deconstruction can be regarded as the "at least necessary condition for identifying and combatting the totalitarian risk."[76] To see how this is so, recall that the containers of politics are indispensably deconstructible because their foundations of authority are "mystical." At the same time, remember that such structures exist and exercise power because the interpretive and performative *coup de force* that brings them into being occludes the mystery within that unfounded process. Consider also that the greatest acts of violence in history have been made possible by the apparent naturalness of their practices, by the appearance that those carrying them out are doing no more than following commands necessitated by the order of things, and how that order has often been understood in terms of the survival of a (supposedly pregiven) state, people, or culture. Then it is possible to appreciate that only if we examine, through strategies of deconstruction (among others), the *coup de force* that encloses this logic in a timeless quality can we resist such violence.[77] Indeed, we can say that without deconstruction there might be no questions of ethics, politics, or responsibility. Were there in fact secure foundations, privileged epistemological grounds, and unquestionable ontological bases "somehow removed from the strife, investments, and contamination regularly associated with them,"[78] then social action would be no more than the automatic operation of a knowledge, and ethics and politics would be no more than technology.[79]

To say, however, that without deconstruction there would not be politics is not to argue that deconstruction gives us a politics. Nor is it to diminish the importance of the question of the impasse Critchley identifies within deconstruction when it comes to the question of politics. While agreeing that deconstruction's understanding of the social as forever without closure was "a crucial step in the subversion of dominant conceptions of society and the development of new political strategies," Critchley identified the political problem within deconstruction in these terms: "[H]ow is one to account for the move from undecidability to the political *decision* to combat that domination?"[80]

"Undecidability" is one of the Derridean concepts that most attracts criticism. Often (mis)understood as licensing an anarchical irresponsibility, it is taken to be the very negation of politics, understood in terms of the decision, and a concomitant denial of responsibility. However, as Derrida makes clear, he has never "proposed a kind of 'all or nothing' choice between pure realization of self-presence and complete freeplay or undecidability."[81] Indeed, the very notion of undecidability is the condition of possibility for a decision. If the realm of thought was preordained such that there were no options, no competing alternatives, and no difficult choices to make, there would be no need for a decision. Instead, the very existence of a decision is itself a manifestation of undecidability, so that we can comprehend undecidability "as an opening of the field of decision and decidability." As Derrida argues, "even if a decision seems to take only a second and not to be preceded by any deliberation, it is structured by this *experience and experiment of the undecidable*."[82] It is for this reason that Derrida has talked in terms of undecidability rather than indeterminacy: the former signifies the context of the decision, a context in which there is "always a *determinate* oscillation between possibilities," whereas the latter suggests a relativism or indeterminism absent from deconstruction.[83] Moreover, just as deconstruction is necessary for politics, undecidability is a prerequisite for responsibility. Were there no decisions to be made, were all choices eradicated by the preordination of one and only one path, responsibility — the ability to respond to differing criteria and concerns — would be absent. Rather than being its abnegation, the possibility of decision ensured by undecidability is the necessary precondition for the existence and exercise of responsibility. Which leads Derrida to state: "There can be no moral or political responsibility without this trial and this passage by way of the undecidable."[84]

The Politics of the Decision

The theme of undecidability gives us the context of the decision, but in and of itself undecidability does not provide an account of the decision that would satisfy the concern raised by Critchley. "Decisions have to be taken. But how? And in virtue of what? How does one make a decision in an undecidable terrain?"[85] These questions point to the nub of the problem, for sure, but they are issues that do not go unnoticed in Derrida's work. They are of particular concern for Derrida in "Force of Law."

In that essay, subsequent to making the case for the intrinsic deconstructibility of the law and noting how this is good news for politics and historical progress, Derrida argues that the law's deconstructibility is made possible by the *un*deconstructibility of justice. Justice is outside and beyond the law. "Justice is the experience of the impossible."[86] Justice is not a principle, or a foundation, or a guiding tradition. Justice is infinite, and — in a favorable comparison to Levinas's notion of justice — "the heteronomic relation to others, to the faces of otherness that govern me, whose infinity I cannot thematize and whose hostage I remain."[87] In these terms, justice is like the pre-original, an-archic relation to the other, and akin to the undecidable. It represents the domain of the impossible and the unrepresentable that lies outside and beyond the limit of the possible and the representable. But it cannot be understood as "utopian," at least insofar as that means the opposite of "realistic." It is not indeterminate. It is undecidable. It is that which marks the limit of the possible; indeed, it is that which brings the domain of the possible into being and gives it the ongoing chance for transformation and refiguration, that which is one of the conditions of possibility for ethics and politics.

In this context, justice enables the law, but the law is that which "is never exercised without a decision that *cuts,* that divides."[88] The law works from the unrepresentable and seeks to represent; it takes from the impossible and conceives the possible; it is embedded in the undecidable but nevertheless decides. Nonetheless, "the undecidable remains caught, lodged, at least as a ghost — but an essential ghost — in every decision, in every event of decision. Its ghostliness deconstructs from within any assurance of presence, any certitude or any supposed criteriology that would assure us of the justice of the decision, in truth of the very event of a decision."[89]

The undecidable within the decision does not, however, prevent the decision or avoid its urgency. As Derrida observes, "a just decision is always required *immediately,* 'right away.'" This necessary haste has unavoidable consequences because the pursuit of "infinite information and the unlimited knowledge of conditions, rules or hypothetical imperatives that could justify it" are unavailable in the crush of time. Nor can the crush of time be avoided, even by unlimited time, "because the moment of *decision, as such,* always remains a finite moment of urgency and precipitation." The decision is always "structurally finite," it "always marks the interruption of the juridico- or ethico- or politico-cognitive deliberation that precedes it, that *must* precede it." This is why, invoking Kierkegaard, Derrida declares that "the instant of decision is a madness."[90]

The finite nature of the decision may be a "madness" in the way it renders possible the impossible, the infinite character of justice, but Derrida argues for the necessity of this madness. Most importantly, although Derrida's argument concerning the decision has, to this point, been concerned with an account of the *procedure* by which a decision is possible, it is with respect to the necessity of the decision that Derrida begins to formulate an account of the decision that bears upon the *content* of the decision. In so doing, Derrida's argument addresses more directly — more directly, I would argue, than is acknowledged by Critchley — the concern that for politics (at least for a progressive politics) one must provide an account of the decision to combat domination.

That undecidability resides within the decision, Derrida argues, "that justice exceeds law and calculation, that the unpresentable exceeds the determinable *cannot* and *should not* serve as alibi for staying out of juridico-political battles, within an institution or a state, or between institutions or states and others."[91] Indeed, "incalculable justice *requires* us to calculate." From where does this insistence come? What is behind, what is animating, these imperatives? It is both the character of infinite justice as a heteronomic relationship to the other, a relationship that because of its undecidability multiplies responsibility, and the fact that "left to itself, the incalculable and giving (*donatrice*) idea of justice is always very close to the bad, even to the worst, for it can always be reappropriated by the most perverse calculation."[92] The necessity of calculating the incalculable thus responds to a duty, a duty that inhabits the instant of madness and compels the decision to avoid "the bad," the "perverse calculation," even "the worst." This is the duty that also dwells with deconstruction and makes it the starting point, the "at least necessary condition," for the organization of resistance to totalitarianism in all its forms. And it is a duty that responds to practical political concerns when we recognize that Derrida names the bad, the perverse, and the worst as those violences "we recognize all too well without yet having thought them through, the crimes of xenophobia, racism, anti-Semitism, religious or nationalist fanaticism."[93]

Furthermore, the duty within the decision, the obligation that recognizes the necessity of negotiating the possibilities provided by the impossibilities of justice, is not content with simply avoiding, containing, combating, or negating the worst violence—though it could certainly begin with those strategies. Instead, this responsibility, which is the responsibility of responsibility, commissions a "utopian" strategy. Not a strategy that is beyond all bounds of possibility so as to be considered "unrealistic," but one which in respecting the necessity of calculation, takes the possibility summoned by the calculation as far as possible, "*must* take it as far as possible, beyond the place we find ourselves and beyond the already identifiable zones of morality or politics or law, beyond the distinction between national and international, public and private, and so on."[94] As Derrida declares, "The condition of possibility of this thing called responsibility is a certain *experience and experiment of the possibility of the impossible: the testing of the aporia* from which one may invent the only *possible invention, the impossible invention.*"[95] This leads Derrida to enunciate a proposition that many, not the least of whom are his Habermasian critics, could hardly have expected: "Nothing seems to me *less* outdated than the classical emancipatory ideal. We cannot attempt to disqualify it today, whether crudely or with sophistication, at least not without treating it too lightly and forming the worst complicities."[96]

Residing within — and not far below the surface — of Derrida's account of the experience of the undecidable as the context for the decision is the duty of deconstruction, the responsibility for the other, and the opposition to totalitarianism it entails. The Levinasian supplement that Critchley argues deconstruction requires with respect to politics thus draws out that which is already present. It is, though, perhaps an element that needs to be drawn out, for Derrida has been candid about, and often criticized for, his political hesitancy. In answer to a question about the potential for translating the "theoretical radicality of deconstruction" into a "radical political praxis," Derrida confessed (his term) "that I have never succeeded in directly relating deconstruction to *existing* political codes and programmes."[97] This "failure" is derived not from any apolitical sentiment within deconstruction, but from the "fundamentally metaphysical" nature of the political codes within which both the right and the left presently operate. The problem for politics that this disjuncture creates is, according to Derrida, that one has "to gesture in opposite directions at the same time: on the one hand to preserve a distance and suspicion with regard to the official political codes governing reality; on the other, to intervene here and now in a practical and *engagé* manner whenever the necessity arises." This, Derrida laments, results in a "dual allegiance" and "perpetual uneasiness" whereby the logic of an argument structured in terms of "on the one hand" and "on the other hand" may mean that political action, which follows from a decision between the competing hands, is in the end insufficient to the intellectual promise of deconstruction.[98] But in *The Other Heading*, Derrida's reflection on the question and politics of European identity, the difficulty of simultaneously gesturing in different directions is posed in an affirmative political manner.

The title of Derrida's essay calls attention to the sense of (Levinasian) responsibility that motivates it, the necessary recognition "that there is another heading . . . the *heading of the other*, before which we must respond, and which we must *remember*, *of which* we must *remind ourselves*, the heading of the other being perhaps the first condition of an identity or identification that is not an ego-centrism destructive of oneself and the other."[99] These differing headings have given rise to paradoxes within European identity (the way in which "European" has been made possible by the "non-European"), and continue to pose dilemmas for the prospect of European identity. Moreover, these paradoxes and dilemmas are understandable in terms of a "double injunction":

> *on the one hand,* European cultural identity cannot be dispersed (and when I say "cannot," this should also be taken as "must not" — and this double state of affairs is at the heart of the difficulty). It cannot and must not be dispersed into a myriad of provinces, into a multiplicity of self-enclosed idioms or petty little nationalisms, each one jealous and untranslatable. It cannot and must not renounce places of great circulation or heavy traffic, the great avenues or thoroughfares of translation and communication, and thus, of mediatization. But, *on the other hand,* it cannot and must not accept the capital of a centralizing authority that, by means of trans-European cultural mechanisms . . . be they state-run or not, would control and standardize.[100]

"Neither monopoly nor dispersion," that is the condition for European identity Derrida identifies as the consequence of the double injunction. With neither of the two available options being desirable, one confronts an aporia, an undecidable and ungrounded political space, where no path is "clear and given," where no "certain knowledge opens up the way in advance," where no "decision is already made." Moreover, one confronts an aporia that, even if "we must not hide it from ourselves," embodies a political hesitation: "I will even venture to say that ethics, politics, and responsibility, *if there are any,* will only ever have begun with the experience and experiment of aporia." But — and here we must recall the ghost of undecidability within each and every decision — were there no aporia there could be no politics, for in the absence of the aporia every decision would have been preordained, such that "irresponsibly, and in good conscience, one simply applies or implements a program."[101]

How then does one remain faithful to the double injunction yet traverse the aporia? Derrida takes a step forward, a step of increasing specificity, by articulating the double injunction in terms related to the question of gesturing in different directions drawn from the political issue at hand, European identity:

> if it is necessary to make sure that a centralizing hegemony (the capital) not be reconstituted, it is also necessary, for all that, not to multiply the borders, i.e., the movements [*marches*] and margins [*marges*]. It is necessary not to cultivate for their own sake minority differences, untranslatable idiolects, national antagonisms, or the chauvinisms of

idiom. Responsibility seems to consist today in renouncing neither of these two contradictory imperatives. One must therefore try to *invent* new gestures, discourses, politico-institutional practices that inscribe the alliance of these two imperatives, of these two promises or contracts: the capital and the a-capital, the other of the capital.[102]

Increasing though the specificity may be, it remains not very specific. As Derrida observes, it "is not easy" to imagine of what such inventions might consist. Indeed, "it is even impossible to conceive of a responsibility that consists in being responsible *for* two laws, or that consists in responding *to* two contradictory injunctions." Of course, says Derrida. Without question. "No doubt." But then — and here we return again to the relationship of the decision and undecidability, the law and infinite justice — "there is no responsibility that is not the experience and experiment of the impossible."[103] And although Derrida remains faithful to "the perpetual uneasiness" inherent in the "dual allegiance" these impossible political inventions must respect, he ventures that there are duties dictated by responding to the demands of the other heard within the call of European memory. These duties include "welcoming foreigners in order not only to integrate them but to recognize and accept their alterity"; "*criticizing*... a totalitarian dogmatism [fascism] that ... destroyed democracy and the European heritage"; criticizing also "a religion of capital that institutes its [fascism's totalitarian] dogmatism under new guises, which we must also learn to identify"; "cultivating the virtue of such *critique, of the critical idea, the critical tradition,* but also submitting it, beyond critique and questioning, to a deconstructive genealogy that thinks and exceeds it without yet compromising it"; assuming the idea of European democracy, but not as an idea that is given or functions as a regulative ideal, but as something "that remains to be thought and *to come*... not something that is certain to happen tomorrow, not the democracy (national or international, state or trans-state) of the *future,* but a democracy that must have the structure of a promise"; "respecting differences, idioms, minorities, singularities, but also the universality of formal law, the desire for translation, agreement and univocity, the law of the majority, opposition to racism, nationalism, and xenophobia"; and, with regard to certain faiths and certain thoughts, "tolerating and respecting all that is not placed under the authority of reason ... [which] may in fact also try to remain faithful to the ideal of the Enlightenment ... while yet acknowledging its limits, in order to work on the Enlightenment of this time, this time that is ours — *today.*" Above all else, maintaining fidelity to the other heading and the heading of the other "surely calls for responsibility, for the responsibility to think, speak, and act in compliance with this double contradictory imperative — a contradiction that must not be only an apparent or illusory antimony… but must be effective and, *with experience, through experiment,* interminable."[104]

Concluding Reflections

In pursuing Derrida on the question of the decision, a pursuit that ends up in the supplementing of Derridean deconstruction with Levinasian ethics, Critchley was concerned to ground political decisions in something other than the "madness" of a decision, and worried that there could be a "refusal of politics in Derrida's work" because the emphasis upon undecidability as the condition of responsibility contained an implicit rejection of politics as "the field of antagonism, decision, dissension, and struggle," the "domain of questioning."[105] Yet from the above discussion, I would argue that Derrida's account of the procedure of the decision also contains within it an account of the duty, obligation, and responsibility of the decision within deconstruction. Moreover, the undecidable and infinite character of justice that fosters that duty is precisely what guarantees that the domain of politics bears the characteristics of contestation rightly prized by Critchley. Were everything to be within the purview of the decidable, and devoid of the undecidable, then (as Derrida constantly reminds us) there would be no ethics, politics, or responsibility, only a program, technology, and its irresponsible application. Of course, for many (though Critchley is clearly *not* among them), the certainties of the program are synonymous with the desires of politics. But if we seek to encourage recognition of the radical interdependence of being that flows from our responsibility to the other, then the provocations give rise to *a different figuration of politics,* one in which *its purpose is the struggle for — or on behalf of — alterity, and not a struggle to efface, erase, or eradicate alterity.* Such a principle — one that is ethically transcendent if not classically universal — is a powerful starting point for rethinking, for example, the question of responsibility vis-à-vis "ethnic" and "nationalist" conflicts.[106]

But the concern about politics in Derrida articulated by Critchley is not about politics per se, nor about the possibilities of political analysis, but about the prospects for a progressive, radical politics, one that will demand — and thus do more than simply permit — the decision to resist domination, exploitation, oppression, and all other conditions that seek to contain or eliminate alterity. Yet, again, I would argue that the above discussion demonstrates that not only does Derridean deconstruction address the question of politics, especially when Levinasian ethics draws out its political qualities, it does so in an affirmative antitotalitarian manner that gives its politics a particular quality, which is what Critchley and others like him most want (and rightly so, in my view). We may still be dissatisfied with the prospect that Derrida's account cannot *rule out forever* perverse calculations and unjust laws. But to aspire to such a guarantee would be to wish for the demise of politics, for it would install a new technology, even if it was a technology that began life with the markings of progressivism and radicalism. Such dissatisfaction, then, is not with a Derridean politics, but with the necessities of politics per se, necessities that can be contested and negotiated, but not escaped or transcended.

It is in this context that the limits of the Levinasian supplement proposed by Critchley as necessary for deconstruction become evident. While it is the case that Levinas's thought is antagonistic to all totalizing forms of politics, recognizing the way that ontological totalitarianism gives rise to political totalitarianism, I argued above that the limit of its critical potential is exposed by the question of the state. In this regard, insofar as Derridean deconstruction requires the Levinasian supplement, that supplement itself needs to be supplemented, and supplemented with recognition of the manner in which deconstruction's affirmation of alterity deterritorializes responsibility, and pluralizes the possibilities for ethics and politics over and beyond (yet still including) the state.[107]

Notes

1. For some reflections on the latter concept, see James Der Derian, *Antidiplomacy: Spies, Terror, Speed, and War* (Cambridge, Mass.: Blackwell, 1992), 198–99.

2. For a discussion of this thesis, see David Campbell and Michael Dillon, "The End of Philosophy and the End of International Relations," in David Campbell and Michael Dillon, eds., *The Political Subject of Violence* (Manchester: Manchester University Press, 1993).

3. Edith Wyschogrod, *Saints and Postmodernism: Revisioning Moral Philosophy* (Chicago: University of Chicago Press, 1990), 191. As Levinas has argued, "Like

the categorical imperative, axiology belongs to Logos." Emmanuel Levinas, "Ideology and Idealism," in Emmanuel Levinas, *The Levinas Reader*, edited by Sean Hand (Oxford: Basil Blackwell, 1989), 237.

4. Emmanuel Levinas, "Reflections on the Philosophy of Hitlerism," trans. Sean Hand, *Critical Inquiry* 17 (autumn 1990): 63.

5. Ibid.

6. Levinas, "Signature," in Emmanuel Levinas, *Difficult Freedom: Essays on Judaism*, trans. Sean Hand (Baltimore: Johns Hopkins University Press, 1990), 291.

7. Simon Critchley, *The Ethics of Deconstruction: Derrida and Levinas* (Oxford: Basil Blackwell, 1992), 221.

8. See the discussion of "the Augustinian imperative," the belief that there is an intrinsic moral order, of either "high command" or "intrinsic pattern," in William E. Connolly, *The Augustinian Imperative: A Reflection on the Politics of Morality* (Newbury Park, Calif.: Sage, 1993).

9. For a similar argument, see Zygmunt Bauman, *Modernity and the Holocaust* (Ithaca: Cornell University Press, 1990). As Bauman argues, with its plan rationally to order Europe through the elimination of an internal other, its bureaucratized administration of death, and its employment of the technology of a modern state, the Holocaust "was not an irrational outflow of the not-yet-fully-eradicated residence of pre-modern barbarity. It was a legitimate resident in the house of modernity; indeed, one who would not be at home in any other house." Ibid., 17.

10. Levinas, "Freedom of Speech," in Levinas, *Difficult Freedom*, 206. In an interview Levinas observed that his "critique of the totality has come in fact after a political experience that we have not yet forgotten." Emmanuel Levinas, *Ethics and Infinity: Conversations with Philippe Nemo*, trans. Richard Cohen (Pittsburgh: Duquesne University Press, 1985), 78–79.

11. Emmanuel Levinas and Richard Kearney, "Dialogue with Emmanuel Levinas," in Richard A. Cohen, ed., *Face to Face with Levinas* (Albany: State University of New York Press, 1986), 18–19.

12. Simon Critchley, "The Chiasmus: Levinas, Derrida, and the Ethical Demand for Deconstruction," *Textual Practice* 3, 1 (April 1989): 100.

13. Critchley, *The Ethics of Deconstruction*, 113–14.

14. Levinas, "Politics After!" in *The Levinas Reader*, ed. Hand, 279.

15. See Michael J. MacDonald, " 'Jewgreek and Greekjew': The Concept of the Trace in Derrida and Levinas," *Philosophy Today* 35 (fall 1991): 215–27.

16. Levinas and Kearney, "Dialogue with Emmanuel Levinas," 20.

17. Ibid.

18. Emmanuel Levinas, *Otherwise Than Being: Or Beyond Essence*, trans. Alphonso Lingis (The Hague: Martinus Nijhoff Publishers, 1981), 10; and Emmanuel Levinas, *Totality and Infinity*, trans. Alphonso Lingis (Pittsburgh: Duquesne University Press, 1969), 48, 79.

19. Levinas, *Otherwise Than Being: Or Beyond Essence*, 10. To speak of Levinas's thought operating in the space opened by Heidegger raises the difficult issue of the intellectual relationship between Levinas and Heidegger. Although it is commonly understood to be antagonistic, and a question is often raised about Levinas's understanding of Heidegger's ontology, it is possible to interpret the relationship in more complex terms. See Robert John Sheffler Manning, *Interpreting Otherwise Than Heidegger: Emmanuel Levinas's Ethics as First Philosophy* (Pittsburgh: Duquesne

University Press, 1993). The most important analysis of Levinas's representation of Heidegger's philosophy is Jacques Derrida, "Violence and Metaphysics: An Essay on the Thought of Emmanuel Levinas," in Derrida, *Writing and Difference*, trans. Alan Bass (Chicago: University of Chicago Press, 1978).

20. Levinas, *Ethics and Infinity*, 95. It is important to acknowledge, even if it is not explored here in the necessary depth, that Levinas's rendering of the subject and alterity embodies a specific and problematic gendered positioning. See Critchley, *The Ethics of Deconstruction*, 129–41.

21. Emmanuel Levinas, "Ethics as First Philosophy," in *The Levinas Reader*, ed. Hand, 83–84.

22. Jacques Derrida, "Force of Law: The 'Mystical Foundations of Authority,'" in Drucilla Cornell, Michel Rosenfeld, and David Gray Carlson, eds., *Deconstruction and the Possibility of Justice* (New York: Routledge, 1992), 19.

23. Critchley, "The Chiasmus," 96.

24. Fabio Ciaramelli, "Levinas's Ethical Discourse: Between Individuation and Universality," in Robert Bernasconi and Simon Critchley, eds., *Re-Reading Levinas* (Bloomington: Indiana University Press, 1991), 87. See also Levinas, "Ideology and Idealism," 245; Levinas, *Otherwise Than Being: Or Beyond Essence*, 10.

25. Levinas, "Ethics as First Philosophy," 82.

26. Levinas, *Totality and Infinity*, 43.

27. Levinas and Kearney, "Dialogue with Emmanuel Levinas," 27.

28. Ciaramelli, "Levinas's Ethical Discourse," 85.

29. "Transcendence is passing over to being's *other*, otherwise than being." Levinas, *Otherwise Than Being: Or Beyond Essence*, 3. Critchley speaks of the insights, interruptions, and alterity uncovered by a *clotural* reading as "moments of *ethical transcendence*, in which a necessity other than that of ontology announces itself within the reading." Critchley, *The Ethics of Deconstruction*, 30.

30. Levinas, "Signature," in *Difficult Freedom*, 293.

31. Levinas, "The Philosophy of Hitlerism," 63.

32. Levinas, *Otherwise Than Being: Or Beyond Essence*, 59.

33. Ibid.

34. Ibid. "God" is an important figure and site in Levinas's discourse that, according to Lingis, is located in the ethical relation as "the very nonphenomenal force of the other." As such, Levinas neither reinscribes "god's" ontotheological status nor avoids agreement with Nietzsche's account of the death of God. Alphonso Lingis, "Translator's Introduction," in Levinas, *Otherwise Than Being: Or Beyond Essence*, xxxiii; and Critchley, *The Ethics of Deconstruction*, 113–14.

35. Levinas, *Otherwise Than Being: Or Beyond Essence*, 127.

36. According to Derrida, Levinas does talk in terms of a "'Jewish humanism,' whose basis is not 'the concept of man,' but rather the other; 'the extent of the right of the other.'" Levinas, "Un droit infini," in *Du Sacre au Saint: Cinq Nouvelles Lectures Talmudiques*, 17–18, quoted in Derrida, "Force of Law," 22. See also Critchley, *The Ethics of Deconstruction*, 221.

37. Levinas, "Ideology and Idealism," 247.

38. Levinas and Kearney, "Dialogue with Emmanuel Levinas," 27.

39. For a guide, see *Traditions of International Ethics*, edited by Terry Nardin and David Mapel (Cambridge: Cambridge University Press, 1992). Only the work of Daniel Warner goes some way toward the position being argued here, at least in-

sofar as it invokes Martin Buber's I-Thou relationship to articulate a form of social morality in the ethics of international relations. See Warner, *An Ethic of Responsibility in International Relations* (Boulder, Colo.: Lynne Reinner, 1991). However, although Buber's argument moves us toward Levinas, it leaves us some distance from him. See Levinas, "Martin Buber and the Theory of Knowledge," in *The Levinas Reader*, ed. Hand. However, Daniel Warner has contested this in "Levinas, Buber and the Concept of Otherness: A Reply to David Campbell," *Millennium* 25 (spring 1996): 111–28. My detailed response is in "The Politics of Radical Interdependence: A Rejoinder to Daniel Warner," *Millennium* 25 (spring 1996): 129–41.

40. Levinas and Kearney, "Dialogue with Emmanuel Levinas," 23.

41. Levinas, "Ideology and Idealism," 247.

42. For the view that Levinas's thought is good only for the individuated relationship with the Other, see George Salemohamed, "Of an Ethics That Cannot Be Used," *Economy and Society* 20 (February 1991): 120–29.

43. Critchley, *The Ethics of Deconstruction*, 220.

44. Levinas, *Otherwise Than Being: Or Beyond Essence*, 11, 87, 88, 128.

45. Ibid., 159.

46. Ibid., 157.

47. Lingis, "Translator's Introduction," in Levinas, *Otherwise Than Being: Or Beyond Essence*, xxxv.

48. Ibid.

49. Levinas, "Ideology and Idealism," 247.

50. Kearney and Levinas, "Dialogue with Emmanuel Levinas," 21.

51. Levinas, *Otherwise Than Being: Or Beyond Essence*, 76.

52. Ibid., 78.

53. Ibid., 100–101.

54. Ibid., 81–82. Emphasis added.

55. Kearney and Levinas, "Dialogue with Emmanuel Levinas," 21.

56. Ibid.

57. Levinas, "Ideology and Idealism," 247.

58. Levinas, *Otherwise Than Being: Or Beyond Essence*, 161.

59. Levinas, "The State of Israel and the Religion of Israel," in *The Levinas Reader*, ed. Hand, 260.

60. This is not to suggest that the state of Israel is illegitimate. Instead, it is to draw attention to the particular ethical and historical claims through which Levinas attempts to secure that legitimacy. For his views, see "The State of Israel and the Religion of Israel," "The State of Caesar and the State of David," and "Politics After!" in *The Levinas Reader*, ed. Hand; and "From the Rise of Nihilism to the Carnal Jew," and "Exclusive Rights," in Levinas, *Difficult Freedom*.

61. "Ethics and Politics," in *The Levinas Reader*, ed. Hand, 290, 293.

62. Ibid., 294.

63. Levinas, *Otherwise Than Being: Or Beyond Essence*, 159. Emphasis added.

64. "Ethics and Politics," 291; and Levinas, *Otherwise Than Being: Or Beyond Essence*, 128. Second emphasis added. Although a number of commentators have rightly remarked that the epithet to *Otherwise Than Being* is addressed to all victims of anti-Semitism broadly understood it contains within it a limit. It reads: "To the memory of *those who were closest* among the six million assassinated by the National Socialists, and of the millions on millions of all confessions and all nations,

victims of the same hatred of the other man, the same anti-semitism." However, that limit could mark a personal reflection, for nearly all of Levinas's family in Lithuania were put to death in concentration camps. See Manning, *Interpreting Otherwise Than Heidegger*, 11.

65. Kearney and Levinas, "Dialogue with Emmanuel Levinas," 29.

66. Ibid.

67. Ibid., 21.

68. Ibid., 29–30.

69. Critchley, *The Ethics of Deconstruction*, 233.

70. This bears considerable affinities to William Connolly's articulation of a "post-Nietzschean ethical sensibility," which seeks (among other things) to "expose artifice in hegemonic identities, and the definitions of otherness (evil) through which they propel their self-certainty... [and] to contest moral visions that suppress the constructed, contingent, relational character of identity with a positive alternative that goes some distance in specifying the ideal of political life inspiring it." See Connolly, *The Augustinian Imperative*, 143–44.

71. Richard Kearney and Jacques Derrida, "Dialogue with Jacques Derrida," in Richard Kearney, *Dialogues with Contemporary Continental Thinkers: The Phenomenological Heritage* (Manchester: Manchester University Press, 1984), 117–18.

72. Ibid., 123–24.

73. Critchley, *The Ethics of Deconstruction*, 189.

74. Ibid., 223.

75. Derrida, "Force of Law," 14.

76. Jacques Derrida, "Like the Sound of the Sea Deep within a Shell: Paul de Man's War," trans. Peggy Kamuf, in Werner Hamacher, Neil Hertz, and Thomas Keenan, eds., *Responses: On Paul de Man's Wartime Journalism* (Lincoln: University of Nebraska Press, 1989), 155.

77. As Derrida observes, "[W]ithout deconstructive procedures, a vigilant political practice could not even get very far in the analysis of all these political discourses, philosophemes, ideologemes, events, or structures... what I have practiced under that name [deconstruction] has always seemed to me favorable, indeed destined (it is no doubt my principal motivation) to the analysis of the conditions of totalitarianism in all its forms." Derrida, "Like the Sound of the Sea Deep within a Shell," 155.

78. Thomas Keenan, "Deconstruction and the Impossibility of Justice," 11 Cardozo Law Review 1681 (July/August 1990).

79. Jacques Derrida, *The Other Heading: Reflections on Today's Europe*, trans. Pascale-Anne Brault and Michael B. Naas (Bloomington: Indiana University Press, 1992), 44–45.

80. Critchley, *The Ethics of Deconstruction*, 199.

81. Jacques Derrida, "Afterword: Toward an Ethic of Discussion," in Derrida, *Limited Inc.* (Evanston: Northwestern University Press, 1988), 115.

82. Ibid., 116.

83. Ibid., 148.

84. Ibid., 116. See the discussion in John Llewelyn, "Responsibility with Indecidability," in David Wood, ed., *Derrida: A Critical Reader* (Oxford: Blackwell, 1992), especially 93–94.

85. Critchley, *The Ethics of Deconstruction*, 199.

86. Derrida, "Force of Law," 14–15.

87. Ibid., 22.

88. Derrida, "Force of Law," 24.

89. Ibid., 24–25.

90. Ibid., 26.

91. Ibid., 28. Emphasis added.

92. Ibid.

93. Derrida, *The Other Heading,* 6.

94. Derrida, "Force of Law," 28.

95. Derrida, *The Other Heading,* 41.

96. Derrida, "Force of Law," 28. Emphasis added.

97. Kearney and Derrida, "Dialogue with Jacques Derrida," 119. Emphasis added.

98. Ibid., 120.

99. Derrida, *The Other Heading,* 15.

100. Ibid., 38–39.

101. Ibid., 41. Emphasis added.

102. Ibid., 44.

103. Ibid.

104. Ibid., 76–79. Levinas has also argued for a politics that respects a double injunction. When asked "Is not ethical obligation to the other a purely negative ideal, impossible to realize in our everyday being-in-the-world," which is governed by "ontological drives and practices"; and "Is ethics practicable in human society as we know it? Or is it merely an invitation to apolitical acquiescence?" Levinas's response was that "of course we inhabit an ontological world of technological mastery and political self-preservation. Indeed, without these political and technological structures of organization we would not be able to feed mankind. This is the greatest paradox of human existence: we must use the ontological *for the sake of the other,* to ensure the survival of the other we must resort to the technico-political systems of means and ends." Kearney and Levinas, "Dialogue with Emmanuel Levinas," 28.

105. Critchley, *The Ethics of Deconstruction,* 199, 200.

106. It is from this basis that I address some of the many questions prompted by the Bosnian war in *National Deconstruction: Violence, Identity, and Justice in Bosnia* (Minneapolis: University of Minnesota Press, 1998).

107. As Derrida observes, in pursuing what is possible to its impossible limits, we must recognize that "beyond these identified territories of juridico-politicization on the grand geopolitical scale, beyond all self-serving interpretations, beyond all determined and particular reappropriations of law, other areas must constantly open up that at first seem like secondary or marginal areas." Derrida, "Force of Law," 28. These marginal areas could be thought of in terms of civil society and its networks of power. For a discussion concerning the way in which these features could aid humanitarian relief efforts, see Alex Rondos, "The Collapsing State and International Security," in *Global Engagement: Cooperation and Security in the Twenty-First Century* (Washington, D.C.: Brookings Institution, 1994).

CHAPTER THREE

The Ethics of Encounter:
Unreading, Unmapping the Imperium

Michael J. Shapiro

Sovereignty's Moral Cartography

Beginning with the modest statement, "What I shall have to say here is neither difficult nor contentious; the only merit I should like to claim for it is that of being true, at least in parts," John Austin went on to disrupt the authority of the referential view of language with an elaboration of speech acts.[1] However, Austin's analysis of performative utterances (what one does *in* saying something) has proven to be quite contentious, for it has tended to reinstate two stabilities even as it destabilizes notions of the force or meaning of utterances. In the process of showing that both performatives (e.g., I now pronounce you man and wife) and descriptively oriented statements ("constatives") are equally context dependent, Austin proceeded to make his case as if both the contexts of utterances and the identities of speaking subjects, which are essential predicates to their rhetorical force, are stable or noncontestable.[2]

Years later, in a contentious encounter with an Austin-inspired speech-act theorist, Jacques Derrida pointed to some of the instabilities in the "system of predicates" that Austin had neglected.[3] He argued that Austin had not heeded the dependence of speech on writing, on prior "graphemic structures," the plays of difference, presence, and absence from which intelligibility emerges. Most significantly, after an inquiry into the Austinian elaboration of speech acts, Derrida showed that "the finiteness of context is never secured or simple," that there is always an "irreducible violence" involved in "the attempt to fix the context of utterances."[4]

Derrida's critique helps me to position my argument in this chapter. His point that intelligibility is a historically evolving practice, closely tied to spatio-temporal sites of enunciation, locates meaning as function of the historically constructed stage upon which speakers perform, not simply as a characteristic of the immediate speaking context. Recognizable speech acts draw from the archive of the already said, from that which is already inscribed. A recognition of the extraordinary lengths to which one must go to challenge a given structure of intelligibility, to intervene in resident meanings, opens up possibilities for a spatio-temporally situated politics and ethics of discourse.

Alasdair MacIntyre achieved a similar recognition. He formulated a view of ethics with a temporally dynamic rather than static view of the self. Acts, for MacIntyre, must be located within a narrative structure of performances. They take on their meanings with reference to specific, historically evolving personae. His approach to ethics is constructed around two important insights. The first and more general is treated in his commentary on the relationship between ethics and social life. Seeking to overcome the estrangement between ethical thinking, history, and anthropology, he shows, for example, how such contemporary ethical traditions as emotivism developed to fit particular modern "characters," such as the manager, bureaucrat, and therapist.[5]

The second and more specific insight derives from MacIntyre's various demonstrations that the intelligibility of action is dependent on its location within a narrative with historical depth. Using the metaphor of the theatrical character engaged in performances, he argues that as individual agents we are, at best, only coauthors of our narratives: "[W]e enter upon a stage which we did not design. . . . we find ourselves part of an action that was not of our making."[6] MacIntyre's recognition of the centrality of narrative goes a long way toward avoiding the empty abstractions that analytic philosophy's model of the self produces in its commitment to universal, contextless bases for judgment. However, he fails to treat adequately the depth and contentiousness of the narrative aspect of identity. Seeking to restore an Aristotelian basis for virtue, MacIntyre treats narratives in terms of their forward aims, their projections toward a future world. This teleological structure is insensitive to what is more basic and contestable in the narrative context of the actor. While, at the level of immediate public intelligibility, people's actions take on much of their significance through the extension of stories into an imagined future, which justifies actions by connecting them instrumentally to "ends," actions also derive their significance through the identity affirmation they supply; they are connected to stories that locate people in time and space. They belong to people in the sense that they reaffirm who they are.

The identity stories that construct actors as one or another type of person — man versus woman, national citizen versus nomad, one versus another ethnicity, and so on — provide the foundations for historical and contemporary forms of antagonism, violence, and interpretive contention over the meaning of actions. For example, to be a member of a particular tribe, ethnicity, or nation, a person must be located in a particular genealogical and spatial story. Such stories precede any particular action aimed at a future and provoke much of the contestation over claims to territory and entitlement to collective recognition. They are part of the reigning structure of intelligibility and tend to escape explicit contentiousness within ongoing political and ethical discourses. To produce an ethics responsive to contestations over identity and the spatial stories upon which structures of recognition rest, it is necessary to disrupt the dominant practices of intelligibility.

Michel Foucault was calling for such a disruption when he noted that the purpose of critical analysis is to question, not deepen, existing structures of intelligibility. Intelligibility results from an aggressive practice. It does not make *the* world intelligible but rather excludes alternative worlds. "We must," Foucault urged, "make the intelligible appear against a background of emptiness, and deny its necessity. We must think that what exists is far from filling all possible spaces."[7]

Accordingly, by heeding the contingency of intelligibility, I will be analyzing two particular kinds of contextual commitments, which have been silent and often unreflective predicates of ethical discourses. Specifically, I want to show how fixations on particular narratives of collective identity — the stories through which "peoples" enact their identities and collective coherences (and on particular geographic imaginaries) and the spatial models allocating global proprietary control — participate in violence and inhibit ethical modes of mutual recognition at a global level.

"Violence" here refers primarily to the violence of representation, the domination of narratives of space and identity: "The power to narrate, or to block other narratives from forming and emerging," as Edward

Said has noted, constitutes one of the primary mechanisms of the imperialist violence involved in monological cultural encounters.[8] In accord with Said's observation, I argue that a major dimension of an ethics of encounter involves providing space for peoples who claim a collective coherence to tell an effective identity story, to locate the temporal and spatial bases for their claim to recognition.

At present, one particular spatial story is blocking alternatives. A geopolitical imaginary, the map of nation-states, dominates ethical discourse at a global level. Despite an increasing instability in the state-oriented, geopolitical map, the discourses of "international affairs" and "international relations" continue to dominate both ethical and political problematics. Analyses of global violence tend to be constructed within a statecentric, geostrategic cartography, which organizes the interpretation of enmities on the basis of an individual and collective national subject and cross-boundary antagonisms. Ethical approaches aimed at a normative inhibition of these antagonisms continue to presume this same geopolitical cartography.[9]

Although the interpretation of maps is usually subsumed within a scientific imagination, "the cartographer's categories," as J. B. Harley has put it, "are the basis of the morality of the map."[10] "Morality" here emerges from the boundary-drawing and place-naming practices that construct the map. The self-other relations embedded in maps arise from the representations of desire-driven imaginaries: proprietary ideologies and commitments to nationhood with accompanying territorial fantasies. Moreover, the practice of drawing a boundary around a collective self constitutes, at the same time, a practice of exclusion. Thus, the contemporary geopolitical map of states is also a construction of an "unchosen" alterity.[11] The map of states represents the production of others: "As a necessary counterpart to delimiting its own space, to fashioning a domestic self-image, the nation simultaneously projects libidinal images of other spaces and other nations against which to define itself and its own frontiers."[12]

But the geopolitical map's moral cartography is more than spatial; it contains a temporal depth. Its "topographical amnesia,"[13] the effacements of older maps in its namings and configurations, constitutes a nonrecognition of older, often violently displaced practices of identity and space. The history of maps is a history in which the place names and spatial practices of some peoples have been overcoded or effaced by those

of others. Among the consequences of this neglected dimension of cartography—a morality-delegating spatial unconscious and a historical
amnesia with respect to alternatives—has been a radical circumspection of the kinds of persons and groups recognized as worthy subjects
of moral solicitude. State citizenship has tended to remain the primary
basis for the identities recognized in discourses such as the "ethics of
international affairs."[14]

For example, a recent analysis in this discursive genre, one that is both
critical of the ethical limitations of the sovereignty system and aware
that "conflict has increasingly moved away from interstate territorial disputes,"[15] nevertheless has reinstalled the dominance of geopolitical thinking by remaining within its cartography and conceptual legacy. Arguing for a humanitarianism that avoids interstate partisanship, the writers
reproduce the geopolitical discourse on war, which grants recognition
only to state subjects. Even as they criticize the language of "intervention" as a reaffirmation of a sovereignty discourse, they refer to "the
Persian Gulf War" on the one hand and "insurgencies" on the other.

As Bernard Nietschmann has shown, the map of global warfare
changes dramatically when one departs from the language of sovereignty. Challenging the state-oriented language of war and unmapping
the geostrategic cartography of "international relations," Nietschmann
refers to "the Third World War," which is "hidden from view because
the fighting is against peoples and countries that are often not even on
the map," a war in which "only one side of the fighting has a name."[16]
Focusing on struggles involving indigenous peoples, Nietschmann maps
120 armed struggles as part of the "war." Only four of his wars involve
confrontations between states; seventy-seven involve states against nations.[17] In order to think beyond the moral boundaries constituted by a
state sovereignty commitment, it is necessary to turn to ethical orientations that challenge the spatial predicates of traditional moral thinking
and thereby grant recognition outside of modernity's dominant political identities. This must necessarily also take us outside the primary
approach that contemporary philosophy has lent to (Anglo-American)
ethical theory.

As applied at any level of human interaction, the familiar neo-Kantian
ethical injunction is to seek transcendent values. Applied to the interstate, or sovereignty model of global space more specifically, this approach seeks to achieve a set of universal moral imperatives based on

shared values and regulative norms. This dominant tradition has failed to provide guidance for specific global encounters because it does not acknowledge the historical depth of the identities involved in confrontations or collisions of difference — incommensurate practices of space and narratives of identity. It depends instead on two highly abstract assumptions. The first is that morality springs from what humanity holds in common, which is thought to yield the possibility of a shared intuition of what is good. The second is that the values to be apprehended are instantiated in the world and are capable of being grasped by a human consciousness, wherever it exists. But, as Hegel pointed out in one of his earliest remarks on Kantian moral reasoning, Kant's system involves "a conversion of the absoluteness of pure identity . . . into the absoluteness of content."[18] Because, for Kant, the form of a concept is what determines its rightness, there remains in his perspective "no way to treat conflicts among specific matters."[19]

A brief account of an encounter between alternative spatial imaginaries helps both to exemplify the problem of spatially insensitive models of cognition and to situate the alternative ethical frame I elaborate below. It is provided by the writer Carlos Fuentes and describes an unanticipated encounter with a Mexican peasant. Lost while driving with friends in the state of Mirelos in Mexico, Fuentes stopped in a village and asked an old peasant the name of the village. "Well, that depends," answered the peasant. "We call the village Santa Maria in times of peace. We call it Zapata in times of war."[20] Fuentes's meditation on this answer discloses the historical depth of forms of otherness existing relatively unrecognized within modernity. He recognizes that the peasant has existed within a narrative trace that tends to be uncoded in the contemporary institutionalized discourses on space.

That old campesino knew what most people in the West have ignored since the seventeenth century: that there is more than one time in the world, that there is another time existing alongside, above, underneath the linear time calendars of the West. This man who could live in the time of Zapata or the time of Santa Maria, depending, was a living heir to a complex culture of many strata in creative tension.[21]

Fuentes's reaction constitutes an ethical moment. Provoked by another, he engages in ethnographic self-reflection rather than reasserting the dominant temporal and spatial imaginaries within which he has resided. His reaction cannot therefore be contained solely within what constitutes the discursively enclosed ethical life of his community. By encountering an alterity that is at once inside and wholly outside of the particular narrative within which his social and cultural self-understanding has been elaborated, he is able to step back from the modernity that is continually recycled within the West's reigning discourses on time and space: "What we call 'modernity' is more often than not this process whereby the rising industrial and mercantile classes of Europe gave unto themselves the role of universal protagonists of history."[22]

Face-to-face with an otherness that these "protagonists," those who have managed to perform the dominant structures of meaning, have suppressed, Fuentes is able to recover the historical trace of that otherness, and on reflection, to recognize that the encounter reveals that his way of life contains aspects of this otherness: "To discover the other is to discover our forgotten self."[23] Most significantly, the encounter produces a disruption of the totalizing conceptions that have governed contemporary state societies. In order to elaborate the ethical possibilities toward which Fuentes's story points, it is necessary to consider an approach that assails such totalizations with the aim of providing an ethics of encounter.

Levinas and the Ethics of the Face-to-Face

The Fuentes experience and the conclusions he draws from it — the ethical epiphany he expresses — is elaborately prescripted in the ethical writings of Emmanuel Levinas, for whom the face-to-face encounter and the experience of the Other as a historical trace are crucial dimensions of an ethical responsibility. To confront Levinas is to be faced with a wholly different ethical tradition. In Levinas's ethical thinking/writing, morality is not an experience of value (as it is in the Kantian tradition and in Alasdair MacIntyre's post-Kantian application of an anthropology of ethics) but a recognition of and vulnerability to alterity.

Levinas's idea of a vulnerability to alterity is not a moral psychology, as is the case with Adam Smith's notion of interpersonal sympathy.[24] It is a fundamentally ethical condition attached to human subjectivity; it is an acceptance of the Other's absolute exteriority, a recognition that "the other is in no way another myself, participating with me in a common existence."[25] For Levinas, we are responsible to alterity as absolute alterity, as a difference that cannot be subsumed into the same, into a totalizing conceptual system that comprehends self and other. Rejecting totalizing ontologies that homogenize humanity in such a way that self-recognition is sufficient to constitute the significance of others, Levinas locates the ethical regard as one that treats others as enigmatically and irreducibly other, as prior to any ontological aim of locating oneself at home in the world: "The relation with the other... does not arise within a totality nor does it establish a totality, integrating me and the other.[26]

Ontologies of integration are egoistically aimed at domesticating alterity to a frame of understanding that allows for the violent appropriation of the space of the other:

> My being in the world or my "place in the sun," my being at home, have
> not also been the usurpation of spaces belonging to the other man
> whom I have already oppressed or starved, or driven out into a third
> world; are they not acts of repulsing, excluding, exiling, stripping,
> killing?[27]

To be regarded ethically, the Other must remain a stranger "who disturbs the being at home with oneself,"[28] who remains infinitely other. The ethical for Levinas is, finally, "a nonviolent relationship to the other as infinitely other."[29]

As one follows Levinas's argumentation, however, a number of problems and inconsistencies present themselves. At this juncture, though, it is important to recognize that Levinas's ethical practice is not something he simply writes about; it emerges as well in his struggle to distance himself in his writing from the very philosophical tradition that has enabled his ethical thinking. An ethics of responsibility for Levinas takes the form of agonistic relationships with key figures in his philosophical patrimony, most significantly, Hegel and Heidegger.

The primary Levinasian struggle with philosophical discourse is conducted within Heideggerian language because the philosophical depth of Levinas's ethics of infinite responsibility to alterity is revealed in both his debts *to* and departures *from* Heidegger. Prepositions are crucial here for while Levinas accepts Heidegger's notion of the individual's intimate connection with alterity, he rejects the Heideggerian grammar of the self-other relationship. The rejection takes the form of two grammatical shifts enacted in Levinas's writing, beginning with the change from "with" to "in front of."

Whereas for Heidegger the relationship to the other "appears in the essential situation of *Miteinandersein*, reciprocally being with another,"[30]

Levinas expresses resistance to the "association of side-by-side" that Heidegger's *Mit* suggests: "[I]t is not the preposition *mit* that should describe the original relationship with the other."[31] It is instead the in front of, the face-to-face that locates the ethical relation to the other. This grammatical shift to the face-to-face acknowledges the fundamental separation of the self from the Other. To maintain an ethical bond with the Other, to maintain the infinity of the Other, is to see the self in its relation to something "it cannot absorb."[32]

The second important grammatical shift expresses Levinas's rejection of the Heideggerian ontology of Being and being with. Having swung the other around to a position in front of the self, in order to create an ethics of encounter with an alterity that cannot be subsumed within totalizing conceptions, and having recognized that instead of self-confirmation the Other provides a disruption of the self's abiding, leaving one never at home, Levinas adds a grammatical change at the level of discursive interaction: he shifts the case of enunciation. Standing in front of the other, in a conversation with which one greets the other, the conversational summons to alterity is in the vocative, not the nominative:

> To speak, at the same time as knowing the Other, is making onself known to him. The Other is not merely known, he is *greeted* [*salué*]. He is not only named, but also invoked. To put it in grammatical terms, the Other does not appear in the nominative, but in the vocative.[33] This vocative summons is an important part of the non-violence that Levinas ascribes to authentic conversation, a speaking which performs a "moral relationship of equality."[34]

Levinas's struggle against philosophy within the language of philosophy is also manifested in his debts to and departures from Hegel. His indebtedness to Hegel is reflected in the dialectical frame with which he locates selves in a relationship with alterity. However, rejecting Hegel's narrative of overcoming contradiction and achieving reconciliation, the mechanisms with which the dialect moves, Levinas suggests a different journey: "It is not a matter of traversing a series of contradictions, or of reconciling them while stopping History. On the contrary, it is toward a pluralism that does not merge into a unity that I should like to make my way."[35]

While Levinas's struggle with Heideggerian language was effected grammatically, his linguistic encounter with Hegel involves attention to narrative structure. To represent the self's journey toward alterity, Levinas juxtaposes Abraham's journey to Odysseus's, which is the basis for Hegel's narrative of the self's encounters with alterity: "To the myth of Odysseus returning to Ithaca, we wish to oppose the story of Abraham, leaving his fatherland forever for a land yet unknown."[36] The biblical Abraham's journey, in response to Jehovah's summons, represents an infinite responsibility to God. However, in Levinas's treatment, this is an allegory of a more general responsibility to alterity. Alterity must remain infinitely other, hence the encounter with alterity is not to be domesticated; it must be allowed to serve as a disruption of the self. The narrative of the Odyssey, in which Odysseus returns home, is a Hegelian dialectical journey in which alterity simply serves the enhancement of the self.

Levinas's struggle with Hegel represents more than a philosophical encounter. In rejecting the circular journey of Odysseus as an allegory of the self's encounters with alterity, Levinas is rejecting philosophy (in the Hegelian sense of self-reflection) in favor of religion. The novelist Lars Gustafsson seems to affirm this Levinasian insight in a meditation one of his male characters has on the difference between homo- and heterosexual encounters:

> I was amused by the funny mirror effect that appears when you go to bed with someone of the same sex. You return to your own world so to speak, although from a different direction; you see the world you just left in a new light. Women always retain their mystery. I can understand why philosophers have always been more interested in boys than girls. Girls are theology, boys are philosophy.[37]

We arrive at Levinas's position by replacing sexuality with ethics and Gustafsson's "girls" with Others more generally. (Indeed, Levinas seems to wholly subordinate sexuality to ethical relations—a point taken up below.) What is important to note at this juncture is that Levinas treats "the ethical relation as religious relation," and rejects, for example, Plotinus's proto-Hegelian conception that "the soul will not go toward any other thing, but towards itself."[38] He sees the relationship with the Other as being like a consciousness of God as irredeemably other, as a being whom one has a duty to recognize as separate.

It is clear from Levinas's textual practice that he depended heavily on those whose positions he rejected. His efforts to extract himself from those traditions are an important part of his ethics of language; they constitute much of the performative aspect of his attempt to use the "saying" to avoid the traps of the already "said." Indeed, Levinas's notion of the way the ethical is performed in conversation, in a "saying" that disrupts the "said," is central to his ethical sensibility as well as the performative aspect of his writing. This accords with his more general opposition to philosophical systems as totalizing structures that reduce to the same, e.g., those like Hegel's, which posit a universalizing consciousness that reconciles difference and overcomes opposition.

The "said" for Levinas is constituted by the reigning philosophical discourse within which interpersonal encounters are conceptually contained. It is the domain of obtuse consciousness, a consciousness that elides the past and present, closing off history. Consciousness thematizes the past, depluralizing it and inhibiting the effects of encounters.[39] In contrast, the proximity of the Other in conversation is a saying that disrupts the incorporation of the other's past into a thematized said. The saying allows the other to be face-to-face as a "trace," which is a mark of the other's being there in a way that disturbs preconceived orders of the world.[40] This Levinasian notion of the trace — "a face signifies as a trace . . . a face is in the trace of the utterly bygone, utterly past absent"[41] — accords with the experience of Carlos Fuentes, who, as though for the first time, became attuned to a bygone order of temporality and space in his face-to-face conversation with a Mexican peasant.

Yet Levinas's resistance to the already inscribed discourses the "said" is, of necessity, only partially successful. While he manages to twist and turn Heideggerian and Hegelian language with his grammatical innovations and alternative narrative structures, ultimately, as Derrida has effectively shown, Levinas's attempt to draw himself out of Heideggerian ontology with an ethico-metaphysical transcendence presupposes Heideggerian ontological transcendence.[42]

That Levinas's language is profoundly Heideggerian is not so much a criticism as it is the recognition of a more general dilemma. Any war against a form of language must come from within. While speech can counter the violence of language by disrupting language's pretension to conceptual mastery, it must inevitably, to remain intelligible, do some violence and thereby affirm aspects of what it resists. It is for this reason that Derrida argues that an ethical regard requires one to acknowledge this dilemma. By avowing the continuing violence of one's own discourse, one commits the least possible violence. The most violent position, he asserts, is precisely the commitment to total nonviolence.[43]

Despite the paradoxes afflicting it, Levinas's linguistic struggle was aimed at minimizing that violence, at resisting the anticipatory conceptualizations through which alterity is denied an independent existence and thereby a worthiness of ethical solicitude. For Levinas, the encounter with the Other must be resistant to all conceptualizations because "concepts suppose an anticipation, a horizon within which alterity is amortized as soon as it is announced precisely because it has let itself be foreseen."[44]

As many recent analyses of the European voyages of "discovery" have shown, it was in part the conceptually proleptic construction of the alterity of the "New World" that encouraged a violent rather than an ethical apprehension of the Amerindian Other. In the case of Christopher Columbus, the anticipatory regard with which he constructed the indigenous peoples of the Americas as "Indians" derived in part from a fantastic medieval cartography, various *mappemondes* (world maps mentioned in Columbus's journal from his first voyage) that owed more to biblically inspired fantasy than to geographic hypothesizing.[45] The violent encounters associated with the initial European contacts with the "New World" were therefore not merely the result of philosophical conceptualizations. They emerged from a "said" that had already existed in narratives on peoples, e.g., the discourse on savagery and world-constructing cartographies, which preempted an ethical form of encounter.

To approach this supplement to the history of philosophical discourse it is useful to consider two of Levinas's more egregious blind spots, in which he gives in wholly to the already "said." One of these emerges in his understanding of Israel's relationship with Palestinians. When the question of Palestinians as Other was posed bluntly to Levinas ("[I]sn't the 'other' above all the Palestinian?") Levinas's response was to refer to the Palestinians as aggressors and enemies, concluding that "there are people who are wrong."[46]

What makes Palestinians wrong? It becomes evident in Levinas's understanding of what "Israel" is: a "coincidence of the political and spiritual."[47] Israel provides the "opportunity to carry out the social law of Judaism."[48] This is astounding partisanship from one committed to wholly non-anticipatory ethics of encounter, one who grants rights to

the "neighbor" that are "prior to all entitlement," rights based on "absolute identity."[49] Levinas attempts to take Israel beyond partisanship
by interpreting "Jewish life" as it is represented through Israel past and
present as a model for all humanity. Jewish doctrine — the rabbinic tradition as Levinas reads it — is "a doctrine that is none the less offered
to everyone . . . this is the sovereignty of Israel."[50]

Ironically, the same thinker who has charged ontological commitments
to space with a "usurpation of spaces belonging to the Other,"[51] who has
argued that "the defense of the rights of man corresponds to a vocation
outside the state,"[52] can say that the "sovereignty of the state incorporates the universe," that "in the sovereign state, the citizen will finally
exercise a will," and that "man recognizes his spiritual nature in the
agency he achieves as a citizen, or even more so, when acting in the service of the state."[53] It is clear that Levinas's attachment to the venerable
story of state sovereignty, and even to a Hegelian spiritualization of states
as instruments of spiritual reconciliation, makes him veer away from
his commitment to an ethical bond that precedes all such ontological/
spatial attachments. In his perspective on Israel, his model of alterity
seems ultimately not to heed the Other's stories of self and space.

This neglect of competing narratives is even more evident when one
examines Levinas's other blind spot, his neglect of the feminine aspect
of alterity. Apart from his use of pronouns (his statements about sovereignty invariably construct the ethical subject as masculine) and apart
from his more general indifference to gender difference,[54] Levinas's treatment of Jewish women in the Hebrew Bible is wholly inattentive to
women's effective public roles and to their victimization. In the case of
Jewish women, Levinas, the Talmudic scholar and exemplar of the close
reader, offers a bleary-eyed celebration of women as "charming" and
woman as "genius of the hearth." "[T]he house is woman the Talmud
tells us,"[55] he writes, adding that "Jewish women are mothers, wives and
daughters" whose "silent footsteps in the depths and opacity of reality"
make "the world precisely inhabitable."[56]

How could such an assiduous, hermeneutically oriented reader miss,
for example, what Mieke Bal has called to our attention, the home of the
Hebrew Bible as a place of danger for women? Focusing on the murder
of women in the Book of Judges, for example, Bal notes that "[t]he house
is a place where daughters [who are murdered by fathers] meet their
undoing."[57] Levinas's Hebrew Bible achieves its intelligibility in relation

to what Bal refers to as a "political coherence" concerned with "the geography of the land to be conquered."[58] "Stories about women have been subordinated," she asserts, "to the major historiographical project, which is nationalistic and religious."[59] This is certainly Levinas's project, which both directs his reading of Israel and is implicated in his failure to politicize Jewish women in the Hebrew Bible.[60]

What does Levinas's project necessarily miss, aside from the murder of women (by heroic "Judges" among others)? It misses the way in which women are active in the public sphere, not simply, as in Levinas's characterization, acting as keepers of the hearth. Delilah, Yael, and Deborah, for example, kill men in behalf of their tribal factions and thereby create significant political results.[61] By producing a reading that constitutes what she calls a "counter coherence," Bal resists the pious religious nationalism that Levinas's reading recirculates. What is especially significant about Bal's reading is that the identities of Jewish women in the Hebrew Bible are wholly different when one heeds a different narrative and is more attentive to spatial imagery. "Daughters who live in their father's houses are the least safe," she notes.[62] Most important, this recognition arises from a different kind of spatial story: instead of being about the land of Israel to be conquered, the story of space "becomes meaningful on a smaller scale of individual houses to be conquered."[63]

Despite Levinas's lack of sensitivity to such other stories, his more general position, centered on the self in its performance of a respectful relationship with alterity, provides an important frame for thinking about an ethics of encounter. Ultimately, Levinas's reading of the Talmud, as contrasted with his legitimation of the state of Israel and his casual treatment of "Jewish women in the Hebrew Bible," is not aimed at recovering a genealogical claim to specific territory. In his Talmudic readings, rather than enacting a narrative of identity, Levinas enacts an encounter between Jewish thought and the philosophy of ethics. To be Jewish, for Levinas, is to accept what he calls "a difficult freedom."[64] He sees the significance of Judaism as a performance of the ethical, as a doing before hearing or knowing; it is an acceptance of the Torah as something prior to the choice between good and evil, a "consent prior to freedom and non-freedom."[65] For Levinas, this aspect of Judaism migrates out of its containment in the scriptures and becomes an allegory of the ethical in general. The acceptance of the Torah (of God and the law of God) is the condition of possibility for beginning the history of the Jewish people, and more generally, doing before hearing translates as an injunction to regard ethical responsibility as prior to conceptualization.[66]

Levinas's reversal of sequence as the essence of Jewish thought supplies the model for his rejection of ontological thinking, in which a universalizing concept of being precedes the significance of action. For Levinas, one makes a pact with the good; one rejects violence before one seeks to understand good and evil. Responsibility to alterity as infinite simply is.[67] The Talmudic Levinas is thus complementary to the philosophical Levinas. This is not the Levinas seeking a fixed narrative to legitimate Israeli nationalism, but the Levinas seeking a permanent disengagement of the self from conceptualization, from what he calls "the temptation of knowledge,"[68] which appropriates the Other to a preexisting understanding and thereby negates the possibility of an ethical encounter.

What is important at this juncture, however, is to further explore the trap into which Levinas (on two occasions) and others have fallen prey in their failure to practice an ethics of encounter, more specifically in their lack of attention to others' stories and practices of space. I turn therefore to the narratives through which specific kinds of persons and locations emerge as significant, paying special attention to spatial narratives, for they are proto-ethical: they provide the frames through which persons and groups gain or elude significant recognition. To treat this aspect of the ethical, which largely escapes Levinas's circumspection, we can return to one of his most important texts, the Hebrew Bible, and engage yet another reading of it, one that bears not only on the fates and roles of Jewish women, but also on the ambiguities of their identities as "Jews."

Narrative Encounters

"And I will give unto thee, and to thy seed after thee, the land wherein thou art a stranger, all the land of Canaan, for an everlasting possession" (Genesis 17:8). In addition to the historical and contemporary violence that has sprung from the consequences of this divine land grant, the biblical promise by Jehovah to Abraham resulted in a paradox in the midst of the primary identity story of the Jewish people. This paradox is at the center of an Old Testament reading by Edmund Leach, an elaborate exercise of Lévi-Strauss's method of structural interpretation.[69]

Resisting the ordinary theological/hermeneutic model for reading, Leach's analysis is anthropological; it is focused on "a patterning of arguments about endogamy and exogamy."[70] He begins with a contradiction that has plagued Jewish history "from the earliest times right down to the present day":

> On the one hand the practice of sectarian endogamy is essential to maintain the purity of the faith, on the other hand exogamous marriages may be politically expedient if peaceful relations are to be maintained with hostile neighbors.[71]

This tension is revealed in the biblical texts, which "consistently affirm the righteousness of endogamy and the sinfulness of exogamy,"[72] but nevertheless have those in the main genealogical line, from Judah onward, taking foreign wives. However, because of the pressure on the text to conform to "the doctrine of the unique legitimacy of the royal house of Judah and the unitary ascendency of Solomon and Jerusalem,"[73] the marriages are treated as within-tribe, legitimate ones. Thus, for example, although Tamar and Ruth are not Israelites, and their approaches to the members of the Israelite lineage (Judah and Boaz, respectively) are those of harlots (the former explicitly and the latter implicitly), the descendants are treated as pure-blooded.[74]

What emerges from Leach's reading is a treatise on land and politics. The Old Testament is cast as a story that has been arranged both to legitimate Jewish title to the "land of Canaan" and to affirm the historical coherence of the Jewish people. By paying close attention to the paradoxes brought about by the contradictions between the rules of endogamy and exogamy, Leach shows how the text has turned the arbitrary into the coherent and unitary. The most significant implications for the discussion here derive from the connections between narrative, space, and collective identity, exemplified in Leach's analysis. What constitutes Jewish identity through the centuries is commitment to a continuous genealogical and spatial story.

This, of course, does not distinguish the Jewish collective identity from many others; collective identities are always a combination of narrative depth and spatial extension. A "people" maintains and reproduces its unity and coherence by performing its identity, by telling a story that legitimates its model of who is inside and who is outside, as well as by territorializing that exclusiveness. Therefore, for purposes of understanding a people's encounters with other peoples, their self-affirmations and challenges to those outside are constructed through the repetitions of their identity stories.

Two aspects of narrative identity performances require special attention if one is to appreciate them as socio-political practices. The first relates to their persistence and the second to their encounter with other, sometimes opposing, stories. Persistence is demonstrated in the way that any group maintains its coherence in the process of engaging in social action or inter-society (inter)action. Individuals and peoples maintain their identity coherence and social significance by repetition, by continually performing their identities. In the case of individuals, the performances are usually reflected in the various signifying practices through which they reproduce themselves as gendered, as adult, as professional or skilled, and so on. Once we pay attention to how identity emerges in performance, we can appreciate that it is an achievement rather than a fact or essence.[75] In the case of an entire people, identity renewal performances are often embodied in the retelling of primary identity stories, such as those in the Hebrew Bible, the Icelandic sagas, the *Coetzala Codex,* and so on.

A return to the Hebrew Bible is useful here, because in addition to its historical role in persistent identity practices, it has been drawn into contemporary encounters. Both of these modalities are evident in an exemplary exchange between Michael Walzer and Edward Said over Walzer's contribution to the Jewish people's identity renewal in *Exodus and Revolution.*[76]

Unlike Leach's reading, Walzer's is identified as hermeneutic; he sought not to look at the repetitive structure of the various fragments but rather to assemble them in order "to grasp the deepest meaning of the interpretations."[77] Walzer's reading bridges his roles as a "connected critic" and political theorist. As a connected critic, he reads as a Jew who is sympathetic to Israeli nationalism but critical of some Israeli domestic policy. As a political theorist, he constructs the Exodus as an exemplary liberation story that has influenced subsequent liberationist radicals. However, apart from his concern with political theory and despite his recognition that "every reading is a construction, a reinvention of the past for the sake of the present,"[78] Walzer's *Exodus and Revolution* stands as a reaffirmation of both the coherence of the Jewish people and Israeli nationalism. Unlike Leach, Walzer represents the narrative as untroubled and noncontradictory; it is a linear story, "a journey forward—not only in time and space. It is a march toward a goal, a moral progress, a transformation."[79] While this is how Walzer represents the view of the authors of the Hebrew Bible, his characterization displays no ambivalence about the coherence of the people in the story; it is the march of the "people of Israel"[80] and how they have territorialized their identity. For Walzer, as for the biblical scribes, "the promised land" and similarly the conquest of Canaan—both during the time of the Exodus and now, in terms of the institutionalized conquest that the state of Israel represents—constitute not a mere land grab, not a merely "territoralist"[81] story, but a moral tale. The land can be held only in righteousness, i.e., in obedience to the law (as interpreted within the Jewish tradition), and in juxtaposition to the practices, such as idolatry, of non-Jewish others.

Moving from Leach's story to Walzer's, one finds a dramatic reversal of the identity economy of ancient and modern Israel. In both stories, what is taken by force of arms is overcoded by a story of legitimate title, but here the similarity ends. Leach is clear about the administration of silences and the management of contradiction. He shows that ancient Israelite identity requires the suppression of alterity within, a set of stories that deny the tribal hybridization of the "children of Israel." And he shows how the domesticated otherness within is expunged so it can be expelled as otherness without. The "other tribes" remain in the story only as territorial and moral adversaries.

By contrast, Walzer's reading operates from this foundation based on erasure. He assumes an unproblematic identity coherence and tells a simple boundary story. Presuming a single identity for the Jewish people, he must at once exclude the other (Canaanite), and recognize both its need to constitute the same (the Jew as non-Canaanite) and its disruption (its claim to the same territorial identity). A Jew as an individual is not a Canaanite, and Israel, which Walzer identifies unproblematically as a "Jewish State," must expel disruptive elements, or, in his more benign imagery, "help[ing] people to leave."[82] In short, Walzer employs a representational economy to do violence.[83] He allows the Jews an unproblematic presence by denying their debts to alterity, but this labor of preservation or maintenance, begun in ancient texts and repeated in his retelling, requires a negation of otherness.

In his review of *Exodus and Revolution*, Edward Said reminds us of this violence by providing what he calls a "Canaanite view" of the Exodus.[84] Said's representational economy is also debt-denying, for his "Canaanites" are just as consolidated as Walzer's "Jews." Nevertheless, Said effectively identifies the scarcity of the moral solicitude in Walzer's story, which is not only a moral tale — specifically a redemption story — but also a nationalist one. Canaanites cannot ultimately be objects of moral concern because Walzer's affirmation of a nationalist political geography is also a moral geography. Jewish control over the state of Israel is part of the redemption story, and Walzer "minimizes . . . a sense of responsibility for what a people undergoing Redemption does to other less fortunate people, unredeemed, strange, displaced and outside moral concern."[85]

In effect, "Canaanites" are not legitimately on the map of Israel in Walzer's story. One could tell more contentious stories that reveal the narrative twists and turns by which peoples and their identities are gathered and dispersed and boundaries are drawn. But Walzer is an advocate of unambiguous identity and spatial boundaries. In his response to Said, as elsewhere, he draws them tightly around identities for persons and peoples, and he wants spatial separations between peoples rigorously policed: "Good borders make good neighbors. And a good border, in time of growing national antagonisms, is a line so drawn that different people are on different sides."[86] At the level of explicit policy, Walzer is opting, as Said notes, for partition, but much of the spatial contribution to his rigorous identity economy is textual. Because Walzer identifies Israel as a Jewish state, state violence is merely "policy" (some of which he condemns as overly messianic) while Palestinian violence is "terrorism." This is, of course, the category of all nonstate violence in discourses that sanctify existing state boundaries and otherwise fail to treat them as contentious.

The Walzer-Said encounter therefore replays an ancient one. Two incompatible identity narratives are involved; two different identity performances collide as "Jew" and "Canaanite" contest both the past and present with incommensurate claims to space and identity practices. Here, as in the past, the antagonists question each other's moral eligibility. Although their clash is textual, a certain violence of representation is involved, for there are antagonistic sites of enunciation involved.

Their discourses depend on incompatible territorial imaginaries. In Walzer's case, the interpretive practice is inseparable from his aim of legitimating a "Jewish State."[87] His "Jewish people" are headed toward a moral destiny that has already been contracted.

This forward heading of Walzer's story fails to take cognizance of what Jacques Derrida has called (in a play on words) the *heading of the other* and the *other of the heading.* Insofar as the aims (headings) of the other, as well as of the otherness of one's own heading (contradictions, ambiguities, paradoxes) are ignored, an encounter with an-other cannot avoid the egocentrism or moral exclusivity that exemplifies Walzer's Exodus story. More generally, with respect to encounters with alterity, Derrida cautions that "there is another heading, the heading not being only ours." Before embarking, then, "we must remember . . . we must *remind ourselves,* the heading of the other being perhaps the first condition of an identity or identification that is not an egocentrism destructive of oneself and the other."[88]

Pursuing identity politics in the context of contemporary Europe, Derrida discerns a paradox (a "double injunction") not unlike the one Leach discloses in the Old Testament:

> *On the one hand,* European cultural identity cannot (. . . "must not") . . . be dispersed . . . into a myriad of provinces, into a multiplicity of self-enclosed idioms or petty little nationalisms . . . It cannot and must not renounce places of great circulation or heavy traffic, the great avenues or thoroughfares of translation and communication and thus of mediatization. But, *on the other hand,* it cannot and must not accept the capital of a centralizing authority that, by means of trans-European cultural mechanisms . . . would control and standardize, subjecting artistic discourses and practices to a grid of intelligibility.[89]

Most pertinent for the discussion here is the ethical sensibility that Derrida derives from this aporia in the midst of the European identity. He asserts that the lack of a clear "path" in the encounter with alterity (within and without) is precisely what opens the way to an ethics and politics: "[W]hen the path is clear, when a certain knowledge opens the way in advance . . . one simply applies or implements a program." Whereas, "ethics, politics, and responsibility, *if there are any,* will only ever have begun with the experience and experiment of the aporia."[90] Derrida goes on to elaborate the senses in which the dominant European self-understanding has led to a failure in ethical discernment precipitated by its moral geography. Having taken itself "to be a promontory, an advance — the avant-garde of geography and history," it has (and "will have") "never ceased to make advances on the other."[91]

Writing an Ethics of Community

The analysis thus far has dwelled on the performative aspect of an ethical regard. As understood by both Levinas and Derrida, the ethical is the enactment of a response to the summons of alterity beyond or prior to any institutionalized normativity and foundational conceptuality. Among what is required to heed this summons of the Other is a distancing from the prolepses through which others are already inscribed. The ethical apprehension or regard of alterity outside of institutionalized inscriptions, as practiced by Levinas and Derrida for example, is achieved with performances immanent in their writing practices. Because the obverse of the ethical regard, a violent one, consists in appropriating alterity to an already inscribed set of conceptualizations, which, given my specific concern with "peoples," I have allocated to temporal (e.g., genealogical narratives of ethnicity) and spatial (e.g., global cartographies) prolepses, ethical practices realized as writing performances require a degree of unreading, unmapping, and rewriting.

This requirement of undoing was evident in Levinas's struggle to extract an ethics from a philosophical tradition in which it had been suppressed. He had not only to struggle within the language of philosophy by redirecting many of its dominant tropes (twisting and turning that which already twists and turns) but also to confront a philosophy suffused with Greek conceptualizations with an even more venerable tradition, Jewish thought as he understands it. However, inasmuch as "Jewish thought" is also available to us in a form mediated by the Greek philosophical tradition, Levinas's Talmudic readings involve an unreading of a long tradition of Greek-influenced commentary.[92] Thus on every front, Levinas's enactments of the ethical have demanded a strenuous unreading, a resistance, expressed ultimately as a form of writing, to the institutionalized "said" of philosophy. Accordingly, in his reading of Levinas, Derrida has emphasized that *an* ethics cannot be explicated precisely because the institutionalized said, resident in discourse, reproduces a violence toward alterity; it can only be enacted through "the perpetual undoing of the said."[93] Derrida prefers the imagery of writing to "saying," suggesting that it is perhaps a better mode for "escaping empirical urgencies" and that "the writer more effectively renounces violence."[94] And the deconstructive enactments in Derrida's writings are precisely constitutive of his ethical practice. Thus, for example, his deconstructive reading of Levinas is manifestly ethical, for rather than being a critique in the traditional sense, it is an appreciation of Levinas's struggle to push against the limits of philosophy.

Recognizing the limits that Levinas's struggle displayed, Derrida challenges the confinements of the already said, seeking to think what has thus far been unthinkable, to push toward what has remained unthinkable or unthought. Derrida's deconstructive writing is therefore aimed at pointing to a remainder, that which is excluded or unrecognized in the established system of intelligibility, the prevailing condition of possibility for recognition. Inasmuch as any system of thought will always produce its remainder, any final recovery of what is remaindered is impossible, but an ethics, embodied in Derrida's deconstructive practice, recognizes the necessity of pursuing that remainder nevertheless. It accepts both the impossibility and the necessity of pursuing it at the same time. Derrida's practice therefore recognizes that the responsibility to alterity amounts to a permanent excursion, and it takes the form of writing practices that disrupt the totalities within which identity spaces and domains are shaped and confined.

Before pursuing more specifically an ethics of writing, however, it is necessary to address how what may seem like a solitary struggle participates in an ethics in the more familiar sense of being communitarian in its implications. Not surprisingly, to do this it is necessary to "unread" a traditional way that the individual-community relationship has been inscribed in contemporary social theory. Jürgen Habermas, for whom both encounters and the communitarian pull in discourse are paramount, provides a convenient point of departure for this purpose. He constructs the individual as an independent mode of consciousness and then asserts that an ethical orientation requires that individual to engage in self-reflection when confronted with an other who pursues a different "interest." Habermas therefore reverses the Levinasian order of ethical understanding by starting the individual off with a reflection on the question "what should I do" understood in the context of that individual's "strong preferences."[95] In the next step that individual's "preferences" are forced into a reflective encounter, undergoing a "transformation" with the recognition that one's preferences affect the interests of others.

Alterity thus enters Habermas's picture rather late, in the context of Levinasian time. Alterity becomes significant for Habermas well after conceptualizations are brought to the public market. But apart from the way that Habermas's temporal ordering produces a mediated rather than an absolute responsibility to alterity, his perspective effectively denies the dimension of alterity that is always already there in the mobilization of the discourses of action and preference, i.e., the "said" within which individuals construe who they are, what they might do, and who else is out there with conflicting preferences. To build community, in short, Habermas begins by denying it in favor of a scattering of isolated, independent forms of consciousness.[96]

In effect, Habermas divorces individuals from collective relations to effect a marriage ceremony later, one that was already consummated in the linguistic resources mobilized by individuals in their reflective consciousness. He seeks to build an intersubjectivity after having removed an intersubjectivity that is already there in intelligible modes of subjectivity. Denying the subject's preexisting debts to alterity, Habermas constructs a community of impartial communication that is precisely one that cannot become ethical.[97] Because it exists only in the public discourses mobilized in confrontations of preferences, it supplies no mechanism for pushing beyond the limits of the already inscribed normativities. Habermassian consensuality is therefore limited to the domain of the "said." In stark contrast, the force of Levinasian and Derridian thought-as-writing is disruptive rather than consensual. It is aimed toward overcoming the limits of the possible resident in the "said."

Where, then, is community in the deconstructive project? Derrida sees community as precisely the aim of his version of a deconstructive questioning of philosophical and other discourse's pretensions to totality or mastery. Community for Derrida is that which is constituted by questioning the possibility of community in the face of its ultimate impossibility, the impossibility of a definitive answer. Derrida's community is thus based on the ethical injunction to continually question the limits of conceptions of community. It is "a community of the question about the possibility of the question."[98] This view of community provides the possibility for an ethics of encounter, for it seeks to go beyond community as already enclosed within the self-understandings of a given collectivity. It is community always open to unforeseeable encounter.

An ethics that exceeds the institutionalized spaces of the sovereignty system, and various other institutionalized narrations of space and time that vindicate peoples as well as their territorial claims, can only be performed at the moment of encounter. An ethics of encounter amounts to an encounter between two different identity performances. Given that whatever may be shared in the encounter lies only in the respect the performances can engender, the performers must of necessity be ready to be afflicted by the performance of the other; they must be prepared to recognize the radical contingency of their own spatial claims and identity narratives. Ethics, on this understanding, can only be practiced. Rather than the violence of identity politics, which seeks to make names stick, the ethical sensibility takes the form of loosening and attenuating what has already been named, thereby allowing various forms of alterity with contending modes of denotation and meaning to enter into the negotiation of space and identity.

Conclusion: Two Exemplary Writing Performances

There are two specific writing performances that have exemplified an ethics of openness to encounters with alterity while, at the same time, recognizing the radical contingencies of space and identity. One is located in the ethnographic discourse of Michael Taussig and the other in a novel by Peter Handke. Ethnographic and literary discourses suggest themselves as ways into the ethical because both, in their more critical modes, achieve distance from reigning structures of representation, but they do so with radically different strategies.

In the case of ethnography, we find a practice that is close to a constituent element in Levinas's idea of ethics, the need for a proximity beyond distancing modes of representation. Investigators with both a philosophical and ethnographic interest have noted that in contrast to modern industrialized societies, various tribal peoples have practiced a radically nonrepresentational mode of encounter with alterity. For example, speaking of the Hurons of the seventeenth century, as represented in the writings of the French Jesuits, Michael Pomedli has discerned what he calls an excursive rather than a discursive relation practiced toward alterity.[99] Instead of appropriating alterity to a prexisting discursive system, the Huron closed the distance through practices of incorporation/ adopting, consuming/eating, and so on. While the Hurons certainly practiced extreme violence — cruel tortures and killings of enemy/others — at the same time they resisted a certain violence of representation (as noted in the example of encounter above), thereby perhaps avoiding the more totalizing or genocidal forms of violence that more representationally oriented cultures have practiced on others they have located in disparaged and diminished frames of thought.

Taussig also focuses more on the excursive, rather than the discursive dimension of encounter. In a provocative analysis of the role of a particular nonrepresentational practice, mimesis, he offers some very particular instances of a nonappropriating mode of relation to alterity. In his version of Levinasian "proximity," Taussig's aim is to resist a "context-free reason" and to reinstate what he deems crucial to the way thought can arrive at its object, through "its sensuousness, its mimetricity."[100] Also like Levinas, Taussig is engaged in a war with language. In his case, it is not the discourse of philosophy, but ethnographic modes of representation, favoring instead an ethnography that does what various mimetically oriented peoples do: move toward objects, embodying alterity through mimicry or replication. Pursuing this mode of approaching alterity, Taussig explores how various uses of magic — e.g., an Embera shaman's making of a model of a gringo spirit ship — might have an influence on the writing practice of the ethnographer. His suggestion is that a mimesis practiced by the ethnographer will have an estranging effect on writing, distancing it from its traditions of representation to allow it to approach alterity rather than appropriating it.[101]

In addition to providing an approach to alterity, Taussig counts on mimesis to help him recognize the appropriating nature of his own representational practices. By paying attention to how alterity has mimed the West or "first world," he seeks a mimetic vertigo that will disrupt the Western narrative of encounter with the peoples of the non-West. To the extent that one can see the West as "mirrored in the eyes and handiwork of its others," it might undermine the ethnographic project of "intellectual mastery" that has characterized Western knowing.[102]

As Taussig notes, this ethnographic project of "intellectual mastery" has not been isolated in academic intellectual space; it has been articulated with projects of political domination, as for example in its construction of "good savages" and "bad savages," with the good as a "presentation of unsullied origin" and the bad a sign of "waste, degeneracy, and thwarted narrative."[103] These signs, which "fell on the Indian" have been part of a practice of both appropriation and erasure of "Indian-ness" in Western narratives of political evolution.

Taussig's struggle against such representations is an attempt to restage the encounter with the "Indian," to allow their stories and practices to migrate into ethnographic writing practices. This will, among other things, aim the Western stories back on themselves, allowing those who have lived by them to reassess their self-understandings, their stories of who they have been. For example, Taussig cites a mimetic practice of the women of the Cuna tribe of Panama: their use of the RCA Victor talking dog logo on the appliqued mola blouses they make.[104] From the point of view of the Western intellectual project, the recording device played a significant role in the discovery and recording of "primitive peoples."

In contrast, Taussig allows the mimetic practice of the Cuna women, who copy the talking dog as a magical emblem, to influence his rethink-ing of the power of the RCA logo in the Western commercial sphere. While RCA had thought the power of the logo lay in its symbolism of fidelity — making use of the old Western allegory that produces the dog as a symbol of faithfulness — Taussig, heeding the practice of the Cuna women, treats "the way it exploits the alleged primitivism of the mimetic faculty."[105] In this reading, the logo can be thought of as displaying a mimetic superpower in action, the mimetically capacious dog straining itself pleasurably to distinguish copy from original as it comes through the ear trumpet of the phonograph. Here Taussig allows a mimetic prac-tice to help him disclose a suppressed magical practice in a West that has attributed such practices wholly to the Other.

Perhaps most striking, however, is the way Taussig's writing mimes the disruptive effects of the mimetic practices that are his subject. In a section on the spiritual geography of Cuna cosmology, a series of non-Euclidean landscapes, Taussig treats the irony of Western ethnography as it attempts to contain conceptually a mimetic practice within a rep-resentational one; he allows Cuna mimetic geography, a play of visual translations between women's bodies and spirited landscapes, to create the mimetic vertigo in his own writing, which plays metaphorically with images of mimesis:

Thus the joker in the mimetic pack is smartly dealt. We are lost, yet perhaps not uncomfortably between so-called levels of reference, cross reference, and . . . all-of-a-sudden altering landscapes in which the Great Mother's house *is* another woman's body, more specifically, spirit copies of her womb genitalia.[106]

In the Western world of names, the myths of propagation, procreation, and rebirth (as well as constructions of female sexuality and male domination, which were undoubtedly deeply influential in the propri- etary impulses and practices with which landscapes are now controlled and invested) have been largely erased from a commercially and geopo- litically oriented cartography. Nevertheless, there is striking evidence of the imbrication of femininity, sexuality, and political/economic preda- tion in the West's fictional literature.

Anne McClintock has noted it in Henry Rider Haggard's *King Solo- mon's Mines*, a novel emerging out of the Western colonial mentality in the late nineteenth century, which is "far from innocent of the tensions of empire."[107] Haggard, who served in South Africa in British colonial administration, produced a best-seller in which a map, quite near the beginning, displays a radical entanglement between geopolitical domi- nation, the search for wealth, and a Western view of the sexuality of the black woman. Haggard's map, attributed in the story to a sixteenth- century Portuguese trader and used to guide English gentlemen treasure seekers, is organized in the form of a woman's body. Dominated by two mounds denoted as "Sheba's breasts," an inverted view of the map re- veals it as "the diagram of a female body." Moreover, "the body is spread eagled and truncated — only those parts are drawn which explicity de- note female sexuality."[108] As McClintock puts it, the map "assembles in miniature the three narrative themes which govern the most widely read and influential late victorian novels: cartography as a form of mil- itary appropriation, the transmission of white male power through control of the black female body, and the plundering of the land's riches."[109]

Two implications can be drawn from this mimetic dimension of Haggard's map. First, we are able to recognize that the mimetic prac- tice, now largely suppressed within contemporary cartography, has nevertheless been part of an otherness *within* Western practices of pro- ducing the Other. Second, while in Haggard's case, mimesis was complicit with a colonial imperialist project, producing a "conflation of the themes of colonial space and sexuality,"[110] in Taussig's it belongs to an ethics of writing. In contrast to Haggard's reinscription of a dominance structure of representation, a conceptual vertigo is manifested in Taussig's writing. *His* incorporation of a mimetic influence constitutes a moment of unmapping of contemporary, forgetful cartographic practices. Rather than resisting the mimetic practices of an-Other, Taussig allows himself to be affected by them, and to register the impact in his writing.

In *Slow Homecoming,* Peter Handke, writing in a different genre, the novel, practices a similar unmapping.[111] He also performs an ethical relation to alterity through a writing that is an unreading of the dominant discourse of place. Like Taussig's, Handke's writing struggles to free itself from a violent patrimony. While Taussig has seen himself as heir to an appropriating ethnographic practice of representation, Handke, an Austrian by birth, has seen himself as heir to a European vocabulary of space and identity that has bred violence. Concerned, like Levinas, with the Holocaust as a paradigmatic event (although descended from victimizers rather than being a survivor) Handke attempts to escape his patrimony in this literary performance. His protagonist, Sorger,[112] an alter ego who is an Austrian geoscientist, ultimately has his speech restored to him as he travels through various landscapes. He is freed from being "the faithful replica of death-cult masters."[113] Finding that he must "hate himself for having been possessed by dead monsters, as though they were kinsmen," he wants to say "I no longer have a father."[114]

To appreciate Sorger's struggle it is necessary to glimpse the narrative as a whole in which, like Levinas, Handke favors the saying over the said. Handke's writing is performative as Sorger enacts an ethical relationship with places and peoples. Sorger's "slow homecoming" begins in "the Far North," designated as such because Handke is avoiding the violence of names, pointing significantly at the outset to a contrast between conceptual and proximity practices respectively, as Sorger's abode is described as both a laboratory and a "dwelling."[115]

At work on an essay entitled "On Spatial Configurations,"[116] Sorger finds that he cannot rely on "the conventions of his science," seeing instead that landscapes become accessible to him only when "the mind has time to find ties with it."[117] Very much in keeping with the Derridean/Levinasian recognition of the violence of representation, Sorger "at times felt that his study of landscape was a science of peace."[118] It is soon evident that the peace or nonviolence can be achieved through Sorger's ability to contact or speak directly to alterity, rather than accepting the already inscribed designations of persons and places.

In a moment that evokes Taussig's use of mimesis to unmap representational practices, Sorger is sketching a tract of land that had been turned upside down by an earthquake. It was only "as he sketched" that he could "sense the overpowering force of the tremor."[119] His mimetic encounter with this piece of landscape affords him a hitherto prohibited appreciation of the mimetic practices of the Indians of the region (with whom he had only one intimate contact, a sexual relationship with someone referred to only as "the Indian woman").[120]

As he sketched, "he observed how the formless mound of clay transformed itself into a grimace, and then he knew he had seen that grimace before—at the Indian woman's house, on the dance mask that was supposed to represent an earthquake."[121] Sorger's epiphany is then generalized, for at that moment "he gained a sudden understanding of masks in general," and "this led to the idea of a series of dance steps, and in a single moment Sorger experienced the earthquake and the human earthquake dance."[122] In short, through a mimetic rather than a conceptual practice, Sorger/Handke moves toward an understanding and respect for both places and peoples who dwell in them. Able finally to dwell in this ethical sense, resisting the violence of inherited and distancing conceptualizations and naming practices, Sorger leaves "the Far North" and travels through what Handke calls "places of names." Having appreciated an ability to know a landscape and its people in a way unmediated by language, Sorger is struck with how his travels to "places of names" disorient his sense of space. He feels excluded and as if his voice has been lost or belongs to someone else.

This is what leads to Sorger's recognition that he must cast off dead monsters and develop his own mode of saying, his "science of peace." The "said"—the history of the inscription of place names—can be cast aside, for Sorger has learned "that history is not a mere sequence of evils, which someone like me can do nothing but despise—but has also, from time immemorial, been a peace-fostering *form* that can be perpetuated by anyone (including me)."[123]

Handke's story *about* Sorger's rejection of the violence of names— as he travels through such places as "Mile High City," "The Big City," and so on—is reflected not only in the narrative of Sorger's various experiences and thoughts, but also in his writing style. Throughout the early part of the narrative, the story is told in the third person. After Sorger's epiphany, his recognition that he can cast off the already said, "he" becomes an "I,"[124] and by the end of the narrative, Sorger addresses himself from the vantage point of an-other as "you."[125]

Through his grammatical play, narrating while shifting narration standpoints, Handke enacts an ethics of nonviolence as his Sorger changes to a mode of proximity with alterity through his rejection of preconceived scripts. Also, the ironic play with which Sorger discovers the violence of naming and the freedom to approach things himself performs an "ethical irony," a mode of linguistic practice that undermines fixities and coherences attached to named places and subjectivities.[126]

Thus, for example, when Handke's Sorger hears the expression "He's just an animal — an animal gone mad, and there's only one way to deal with mad animals, exterminate them," he is able to achieve an ironic distance by situating the remark in an unexpected way. In this case the remark turns out to be from a night clerk reading it to someone from a newspaper.

More generally, shedding the structure of past, violent inscriptions, Sorger is finally able to live in the present, to achieve a "presence of mind" in his reaching out to the world, to become "capable of penetrating to the depths of space and of participating in the peaceful beauty of his present."[127] This example can help produce an ethical regard more generally if we allow it, along with the foregoing ones, to migrate into our various political practices of space and identity. For those of us who write on global politics, the injunction amounts to a call for encounters, an unreading of the global histories and unmapping of the moral geographies that fix the violence of representations one simply reproduces when remaining unreflectively within the already said.

Notes

1. John Austin, *How to Do Things with Words* (Cambridge: Harvard University Press, 1962).

2. Austin did not make a sharp distinction between kinds of utterances. He argued that the descriptive (locutionary) and performative (illocutionary and perlocutionary) aspects of utterances are levels of force within a given speech act, not ways of characterizing different speech acts.

3. Jacques Derrida, *Limited Inc.* (Evanston, Ill.: Northwestern University Press, 1988), 14.

4. Ibid., 137.

5. Alasdair MacIntyre, *After Virtue*, 2nd ed. (Notre Dame, Ind.: University of Notre Dame Press, 1984), 73.

6. Ibid., 213.

7. Michel Foucault, "Friendship as a Way of Life," in Sylvere Lotringer, ed., *Foucault Live*, trans. John Johnson (New York: Semiotext(e), 1989), 209.

8. Edward Said, *Culture and Imperialism* (New York: Alfred A. Knopf, 1993), xiii.

9. For a significant challenge to the "ethics of international affairs" tradition, see David Campbell, *Politics without Principle: Sovereignty, Ethics, and Narratives of the Gulf War* (Boulder, Colo.: Lynne Rienner, 1993).

10. J. B. Harley, "Cartographic Ethics and Social Theory," *Cartographica* 27, 2 (summer 1990): 1–23. "Morality" as a problem has been too much absorbed into a temporal rather than a spatial model, one that privileges individual consciousness rather than discourse. For this reason, Foucault has suggested that a recognition of the ethico-political implications of discourse requires "the use of spatial, strategic metaphors."

11. See Homi Bhabha, "Anxious Nations, Nervous States," in Joan Copjec, ed., *Supposing the Subject* (London: Verso, 1994), 201–17, for a discussion of the construction of the "unchosen" in the narrative and spatial construction of the "nation-state."

12. Shaun Irlam, "Gerrymandered Geographies: Exoticism in Thomson and Chateaubriand," *MLN* 108, 5 (December 1993): 892–93.

13. The expression belongs to Paul Virilio, *The Vision Machine* (Bloomington: Indiana University Press, 1994), chapter 1.

14. This tradition in ethics is most clearly represented in the essays, written mostly by academics, found in the journal *Ethics and International Affairs*, published by the Carnegie Council on Ethics and International Affairs.

15. Jarat Chopra, Thomas G. Weiss, "Sovereignty Is No Longer Sacrosanct: Codifying Humanitarian Intervention," *Ethics and International Affairs* 6 (1992): 98.

16. Bernard Nietschmann, "The Third World War," *Cultural Survival Quarterly* 11 (1987): 1.

17. Ibid., 7.

18. G. W. F. Hegel, *Natural Law*, trans. T. M. Knox (Philadelphia: University of Pennsylvania Press, 1975), 60–61.

19. Ibid., 77.

20. Carlos Fuentes, "Writing in Time," *Democracy* 2 (January 1982): 61.

21. Ibid.

22. Ibid., 64.

23. Ibid., 69.

24. The relevant work is Adam Smith's *Theory of Moral Sentiments*. I treat the problems associated with constructing ethics around a moral psychology such as Smith's elsewhere: Michael J. Shapiro, *Reading "Adam Smith": Desire, History, Value* (Newberry Park, Calif.: Sage, 1993).

25. Emmanuel Levinas, *Time and the Other*, trans. Richard Cohen (Pittsburgh: Duquesne University Press, 1987), 75.

26. Emmanuel Levinas, *Totality and Infinity*, trans. Alphonso Lingus (Pittsburgh: Duquesne University Press, 1969), 251.

27. Sean Hand, ed., *The Levinas Reader* (London: Basil Blackwell, 1989), 82.

28. Levinas, *Totality and Infinity,* 39

29. Jacques Derrida, "Violence and Metaphysics," in *Writing and Difference,* trans. Alan Bass (Chicago: University of Chicago Press, 1978), 38.

30. Levinas, *Time and the Other,* 40.

31. Ibid., 41.

32. Levinas, *Totality and Infinity,* 80.

33. Emmanuel Levinas, *Difficult Freedom,* trans. Sean Hand (Baltimore: Johns Hopkins University Press, 1990), 7.

34. Ibid., 8.

35. Levinas, *Time and the Other,* 42.

36. Emmanuel Levinas, "The Trace of the Other," trans. Alphonso Lingus, in *Deconstruction in Context,* ed. Mark C. Taylor (Chicago: University of Chicago Press, 1986), 348.

37. Lars Gustafsson, *Funeral Music for Freemasons,* trans. Yvonne L. Sandstroem (New York: New Directions, 1983), 122.

38. Levinas, *Difficult Freedom,* 16.

39. Emmanuel Levinas, *Otherwise Than Being: or Beyond Essence,* trans. Alphonso Lingus (The Hague: Martinus Nijhoff, 1981), 37.

40. Emmanuel Levinas, "Meaning and Sense," in *Collected Philosophical Papers,* trans. Alphonso Lingus (Dordrecht: Martinus Nijhoff, 1987), 102ff.

41. Ibid., 103.

42. Derrida, *Violence and Metaphysics,* 141.

43. Ibid., 130.

44. Ibid., 95.

45. This subject is treated in many places, but for a succinct and focused account, see Valerie I. J. Flint, *The Imaginative Landscape of Christopher Columbus* (Princeton, N.J.: Princeton University Press, 1992), 3–41.

46. Hand, *The Levinas Reader,* 294.

47. Levinas, *Difficult Freedom,* 216.

48. Ibid., 217.

49. Emmanuel Levinas, *Outside the Subject,* trans. Michael B. Smith (Stanford, Calif.: Stanford University Press, 1994), 117.

50. Levinas, *Difficult Freedom,* 217.

51. Hand, *The Levinas Reader,* 82.

52. Levinas, *Outside the Subject,* 123.

53. Levinas, *Difficult Freedom,* 216.

54. Simon Critchley has an excellent discussion of Levinas's difficulties with "the feminine." Simon Critchley, " 'Bois': Derrida's Final Word on Levinas," in Robert Bernasconi and Simon Critchley, eds, *Re-Reading Levinas* (Bloomington: Indiana University Press, 1991).

55. Levinas, *Difficult Freedom,* 31.

56. Ibid.

57. Mieke Bal, *Death and Dissymmetry* (Chicago: University of Chicago Press, 1988), 170.

58. Ibid., 169.

59. Ibid.

60. For a reading of Levinas's treatment of Israel as an "ethical nation," which, it is argued, displaces his ethics, see George Salemohamed, "Levinas: From Ethics to Political Theology," *Economy and Society* 21, 2 (May 1992): 192–206.

61. Bal, *Death and Dissymmetry*, 14.

62. Ibid., 171.

63. Ibid., 169.

64. Emmanuel Levinas, *Nine Talmudic Readings*, trans. Annette Aronowicz (Bloomington: Indiana University Press, 1990), 37.

65. Ibid., 39.

66. My discussion of Levinas's reading of the Talmud has benefited from the excellent treatment by Jill Robbins, *Prodigal Son/Elder Brother* (Chicago: University of Chicago Press, 1991), 100–32.

67. Influenced in part by Levinas, John Caputo has a provocative treatment of responsibility as a fact with which to begin, rather than as a problem to be worked out. See John Caputo, *Against Ethics* (Bloomington: Indiana University Press, 1993).

68. Levinas, *Nine Talmudic Readings*, 34.

69. Edmund Leach, "The Legitimacy of Solomon," in Michael Lane, ed., *Structuralism: A Reader* (London: Jonathan Cape, 1970), 248–92.

70. Ibid., 248.

71. Ibid., 257.

72. Ibid., 258.

73. Ibid., 266.

74. Ibid., 271–74.

75. Analyses that emphasize the performative dimensions of identity include Victor Turner, *Dramas, Fields, and Metaphors* (Ithaca: Cornell University Press, 1974); Richard Schechner, *Between Theater and Anthropology* (Philadelphia: University of Pennsylvania Press, 1985), and Judith Butler, "Performative Acts and Gender Constitution: An Essay in Phenomenology and Feminist Theory," in Sue-Ellen Case, ed., *Performing Feminism: Feminist Critical Theory and Theater* (Baltimore: Johns Hopkins University Press, 1990).

76. Michael Walzer, *Exodus and Revolution* (New York: Basic Books, 1985).

77. Ibid., 29–30.

78. Ibid., x.

79. Ibid., 12.

80. Ibid.

81. Ibid., 102.

82. Michael Walzer, "An Exchange: *Exodus and Revolution*," *Grand Street* 5 (summer 1986): 247.

83. The idea of the violence of representation is elaborated in Derrida's "Violence and Metaphysics."

84. Edward Said, "Michael Walzer's *Exodus and Revolution*: A Canaanite Reading," *Grand Street* 5 (winter 1986): 86–106.

85. Ibid., 104–5.

86. Walzer, "An Exchange," 247.

87. There is also, of course, a heading or aim to Said's discourse. It is produced on behalf of Palestinian entitlements, seeking to head off the forward motion of Is-

raeli national consolidation. But in this particular exchange, the primary force of Said's writing is deconstructive, i.e., aimed at displacing closure with aporia.

88. Jacques Derrida, *The Other Heading: Reflections on Today's Europe,* trans. Pascale-Anne Brault and Michael B. Naas. (Bloomington: Indiana University Press, 1992), 15.

89. Ibid., 38–39.

90. Ibid., 41.

91. Ibid., 49.

92. This dilemma faced by Levinas is treated by Derrida in "Violence and Metaphysics," Robbins in *Prodigal Son/Elder Brother,* and Critchley in *The Ethics of Deconstruction.*

93. Critchley, *The Ethics of Deconstruction,* 43.

94. Derrida, "Violence and Metaphysics," 102.

95. Jürgen Habermas, *Justification and Application: Remarks on Discourse Ethics,* trans. Ciaran Cronin (Cambridge: Massachusetts Institute of Technology Press), 5.

96. Sylviane Agacinski has offered a similar critique, noting that Habermas's notion of communicative rationality contains a theory of the subject that posits an "initial atomism." See Agacinski, "Another Experience of the Question, or Experiencing the Question Other-Wise," in *Who Comes After the Subject?* ed, Eduardo Cadava, Peter Connor, and Jean-Luc Nancy (New York: Routledge, 1991), 13.

97. The Lacanian idea of the denial of debts to alterity is elaborated by Samuel Weber, *Institution and Interpretation* (Minneapolis: University of Minnesota Press, 1987).

98. Derrida, "Violence and Metaphysics," 80.

99. Michael Pomedli, *Ethnophilosophical and Ethnolinguistic Perspectives on the Huron Indian Soul* (Lewiston: Edwin Mellen, 1991).

100. Michael Taussig, *Mimesis and Alterity* (New York: Routledge, 1993), 2.

101. Ibid., 16.

102. Ibid., 236–37.

103. Ibid., 142.

104. Ibid., 212.

105. Ibid., 213.

106. Ibid., 122.

107. Anne McClintock, "Maidens, Maps, and Mines: The Reinvention of Patriarchy in Colonial South Africa," *South Atlantic Quarterly* 87 (winter 1988): 48.

108. Ibid., 150.

109. Ibid., 149–50.

110. Ibid., 152.

111. Peter Handke, *Slow Homecoming,* trans. Ralph Manheim (New York: Farrar, Strauss, Giroux, 1985).

112. Sorger, which translates as "one who cares," is contrasted with Lauffer, his scientific colleague in "The Far North."

113. Ibid., 60.

114. Ibid.

115. Ibid., 3.

116. Ibid., 71.

117. Ibid., 72.

118. Ibid., 73.

119. Ibid., 74.

120. Handke has Sorger and "the Indian woman" both avoid the violences in their respective patrimonies because they converse in English, which is not the "native language" of either.

121. Ibid., 75.

122. Ibid.

123. Ibid., 114.

124. Ibid., 129.

125. Ibid., 136.

126. The expression belongs to Gary Handwerk, *Irony and Ethics in Narrative* (New Haven: Yale University Press, 1985).

127. Handke, *Slow Homecoming*, 135.

CHAPTER FOUR

The Scandal of the Refugee:
Some Reflections on the "Inter" of International Relations and Continental Thought

Michael Dillon

> If you gaze long enough into an abyss, the abyss will gaze back into you.[1]

In seeking to advance an argument concerning the relevance of continental thought to international relations, and vice versa, this paper makes the following moves. The continental thought to which it refers is the return of the ontological begun with Nietzsche, developed by Heidegger, and exploited and contested in their different ways by Derrida and Levinas. Lacan, Foucault, Deleuze, Lyotard, Agamben, and Nancy remain important figures here as well. So do certain feminist thinkers, including Julia Kristeva and Judith Butler, who share a fundamental philosophical position deeply indebted to the breach in traditional thought originally made by the first group of thinkers (albeit Kristeva's debts are also to psychoanalysis).

What I take to be the defining feature of this continental thought is a comprehensive reappraisal of metaphysics that provided both a fundamental critique of epistemology and a new point of departure for political and philosophical reflection. Whether or not that point of departure is characterized as ontological, one defining feature continues to distinguish it—one that is also shared by all so-called poststructural thinkers. That feature is the insistence on the concurrent operation of a difference inhabiting existence whose coincidental recoil upon identity stops any identity or meaning from ever becoming fully stabilized. There is then an instability constitutively integral to all thought and practice.

Such a point of departure problematizes the very foundations of traditional philosophical and political thought. In other words, the *Fragestel-
lung* of politics is thoroughly re-posed. This opens up both positive and
critical possibilities for the study of politics and international relations,
as well as for continental thought.

The term *poststructural* has gained widespread currency, but unfortunately it has been used to obscure rather than clarify highly contested
philosophical positions, and the very significant differences that exist
between these thinkers respecting such disputes. The very difference
whose concurrent operational force is thought to be so disruptive varies
considerably among all these thinkers. Moreover, the different ways in
which they figure that difference determines the accounts they give of
the way it works and the effects it has. For example, Heidegger figures
it as the ontological difference between being and beings, Levinas figures it as the advent of Alterity, Derrida figures it as *differance,* and Lacan figures it as the barrier that distinguishes the symbolic from the
Real. For Heidegger *angst* at the nothingness of being serves to promote
the project of authenticity. For Levinas Alterity ramifies into an account
of our encounter with it as the advent of an ethical obligation that promotes the project of the ethical subject's substitution for the Other. Derrida's *differance* plays the motility of temporality much more extensively
into the operation of difference and promotes the project of deconstruction, which is its principal operational effect. Misfires of the symbolic
bring the intractability of the Real into play for Lacan, thus promoting
the project of Desire. The implications of the return of the ontological
were developed by Foucault in terms of a critical genealogy of political
problematizations consequent upon a fundamental reappraisal of the
basic categories of philosophical modernity, specifically the ways in
which its understanding of narrative, order, value, identity, and continuity, and of a rigorously methodological access to truth and totality
secured from the perspective of the *cogito,* without asking about the *sum,*
were disrupted by the ontological turn. It was precisely because the ontological turn did, of course, concentrate upon the *sum* that the puta-
tively secure ground of the *cogito* was radically unsecured.

An additional development made available by the return of the ontopolitical consequent upon the return of the ontological is, however, a
return of political thought to thinking about that which gives rise to it
in the first place, namely the question of the political. Here the political

is seen to arise out of the *plethos* insinuated into the very existence of human being by the concurrent operational force of a difference that can never be rendered the same. Such a difference, it has to be added, is more than oppositional difference and so the thinking of it is not dialectical. Neither does it offer the saving turn of an *aufhebung* or synthesis, which Hegelian negation and difference continuously promises. This makes available an account of difference that is intra rather than merely inter, and which is a positive process of differentiation, not simple negation. Human being, then, becomes that which is necessarily a stranger to itself because, always already both more and less than one, bearing difference within itself, it is never fully at home with itself.

The afoundationalism of such thinking is a denial only of some transcendental or final *arche* or ground. That there is no such ground does not, however, mean that there is no grounding. Out of this arises the possibility of another political thought: the "Law of the law"[2] for human being is the circumstance of an abyssal freedom in which, while necessarily having to decide how to take up its freedom — of determining what is just and what is unjust and, therefore, what to do — it has to find ways not simply of being hospitable to others, but of being hospitable, also, to the very Otherness or strangeness that inhabits it, and of which its own individual existence is, consequently, also always already composed. Created yet creative and, therefore, neither merely made nor given, the human is something *in-between*. Specifically, in between birth and death and always already, therefore, on the way into a future in which it becomes that which it has also never yet been, the human is always in the condition in which something is called for in the way of interpretation, decision, and action. Not simply occurring in history, then, the event of human existence within the event of existence itself is a radical hermeneutico-phenomenological experience — the continuous play of an interrogating presence and absence within the horizon of time — which first makes history possible. The political is intimately related as well, therefore, to this essentially active and futural character of the mobile temporality of human freedom.

One of the challenges with which continental thought confronts students of politics and international relations is that of finding some "concrete" site upon which this turn in thought can be shown to have direct purchase. This essay argues that the figure of the refugee provides precisely that. The refugee is successively presented and explored, therefore, as a figure of the "inter'—or the *in-between*—of the human way of being, as a figure of the "inter" of international relations and as a figure of the political abjection that is integral to the political subjectification of political modernity.

The advent of the stranger is, therefore, fundamentally deconstructive. It always brings to presence the strangeness, heterogeneity, and supplementarity of the human way of being as such, and thereby, also, the political challenge human being faces to address that strangeness in survivable and hospitable ways. Estrangement is consequently a condition of human existence as a how, a way of being, and not a what, an object whose essence may be captured in a concept. As a how, human being is always already a form of relating. Relating not only to other beings, the human is also always in the position of having to relate to its own existence. As a form of relating it is therefore always with other beings, both human and nonhuman. Even alone it is always with it-self, for it is a relation to its own existence that propels a relation with other beings. Human being is then a being-with, within a relation matrix that some call a world. Here, in this hyphenated—literally articulated—condition, human being is challenged to acknowledge a belonging together in the very absence of any predetermined designation of what it is to be human. The advent of the stranger in the form of the refugee emphasizes, by amplifying and intensifying, that human being is always in the position of articulating this "we" without the authorization of any God, Leader, Party, Nation, or State. Indeed, it is most often in the position of having to do so despite, or against, the authorizations of any God, Leader, Party, Nation, or State.

The refugee is then a scandal for philosophy, and specifically for epistemology, in that the refugee recalls the radical instability of meaning and the incalculability of the human. The refugee is a scandal for politics also, however, in that the advent of the refugee is always a reproach to the formation of the political order or subjectivity that necessarily gives rise to the refugee. The scandal is intensified for any politics of identity that presupposes that the goal of politics is the realization of sovereign identity, and for any politics that presupposes that the goal of politics requires epistemology's promise of secure political knowing.

This challenge extends the register of what it is to be democratic, and such an extension is integral to an international relations that takes the thought of the "inter" seriously as its point of departure for its reflection on human being and global politics. For the question, integral to democratic thought, of who belongs to the demos, always arises at the limit of the demos — quite literally, in a Levinasian sense, at the inter-face — wherein native, subject, citizen, or people receives its designation as such from the way the human encounter with the stranger and the strange is assumed. How a people is a people, not what the people is; how a people is a people — in recognition of the others and of the Otherness that are constitutive also of it — and not simply who or what represents a people; such issues not only extend the register of democratic thought, they do so through the "inter." They inevitably do so also, therefore, through the "inter" of international relations.

In short, it is the "inter" — the articulated and articulating *in-between* — that continental thought and international relations share. And it is through the "inter" that the one may usefully illuminate the other.

The Return of the Ontological

Perhaps the most important development in the history of philosophy in the last hundred years has been the return of the ontological in continental thought. By this I mean that since Nietzsche and Heidegger, in particular, and the crisis of historicism, in general, ontology has not only become the principal focus of thought, but the onto-theological underpinnings of Western thought as a whole — the ways in which it had previously posed and addressed the very question of Being as such, from Plato's *eidos* to Hegel's Absolute Spirit, and through the theism of Christian theology — has been subjected to a devastating reappraisal.[3] That ontologizing move — in itself not a single monolithic but a plural turn of thought that, in the early Heidegger aspired to the production of a fundamental ontology and in the later Heidegger flirted with the possibility of escaping metaphysics altogether — was what gave rise to all subsequent debates about foundationalism and antifoundationalism.

The question of ontology was not only reposed, however; the charge was also laid, to equally devastating effect, that the onto-theological yearnings that characterized Western thought were the source of its own understated but pervasive life-inimical violence. The return of the on-tological (which occurred in part, also, through the so-called "Language Turn" in philosophy) was, therefore, no mere turn of thought. It was prompted by and resonated with the historical changes and events of the late nineteenth and early twentieth centuries: bureaucratization and rationalization, global industrialization and technologization, and the advent of mass society, world war, and holocaust, which themselves challenged statesmen and women, as well as thinkers, to reconsider the character of the civilization they inhabited and the trajectory down which its own dynamics seemed to be propelling it.

World War I was pivotal in this regard. The subsequent advent of totalitarianism, together with the destruction of European Jewry, the advent of genocide as a regular tool of policy, and the invention, employment, and global deployment of weapons of mass destruction completed the turn. Philosophy and politics were intimately, if obscurely and confusedly, allied in these developments, in respect not only of science and technology, but also in terms of political movements, ideology, and the evolution of the thought of politics itself. Whereas the political and economic character of the age seemed to demand a fundamental reappraisal of the fundaments to which it held, the philosophical reappraisal of the fundaments called, in their turn, for a political reappraisal of the age. Modernity became the question, but the question was increasingly formulated in ways that were concerned less with its realization and more with whether or not it was capable of being outlived. Heirs to all this, we find ourselves in the turbulent and now globalized wake of its confluence.

As Heidegger — himself an especially revealing figure of the deep and mutual implication of the philosophical and the political[4] — never tired of pointing out, the relevance of ontology to all other kinds of thinking is fundamental and inescapable. For one cannot say anything about anything that *is*, without always already having made assumptions about the *is* as such. Any mode of thought, in short, always already carries an ontology sequestered within it. What this ontological turn does to other — regional — modes of thought is to challenge the ontology within which they operate. The implications of that review reverberate throughout the entire mode of thought, demanding a reappraisal as fundamental as the reappraisal ontology has demanded of philosophy.

With ontology at issue, the entire foundations or underpinnings of any mode of thought are rendered problematic. This applies as much to any modern discipline of thought as it does to the question of modernity as such, with the exception, it seems, of science, which, having long ago given up the ontological questioning of when it called itself natural philosophy, appears now, in its industrialized and corporatized form, to be invulnerable to ontological perturbation. With its foundations at issue, the very authority of a mode of thought and the ways in which it characterizes the critical issues of freedom and judgment (of what kind of universe human beings inhabit, how they inhabit it, and what counts as reliable knowledge for them in it) is also put in question. The very ways in which Nietzsche, Heidegger, and other continental philosophers challenged Western ontology, simultaneously, therefore reposed the fundamental and inescapable difficulty, or *aporia,* for human being of decision and judgment.

In other words, whatever ontology you subscribe to, knowingly or unknowingly, as a human being you still have to act. Whether or not you know or acknowledge it, the ontology you subscribe to will construe the problem of action for you in one way rather than another. You may think ontology is some arcane question of philosophy, but Nietzsche and Heidegger showed that it intimately shapes not only a way of thinking, but a way of being, a form of life. Decision, a fortiori political decision, in short, is no mere technique. It is instead a way of being that bears an understanding of Being, and of the fundaments of the human way of being within it. This applies, indeed applies most, to those mock-innocent political slaves who claim only to be technocrats of decision making.

While certain continental thinkers like Blumenberg and Lowith, for example, were prompted to interrogate or challenge the modern's claim to being distinctively "modern," and others such as Adorno questioned its enlightened credentials, philosophers like Derrida and Levinas pursued the metaphysical implications (or rather the implications for metaphysics) of the thinking initiated by Kierkegaard, as well as by Nietzsche and Heidegger. The violence of metaphysics, together with another way of thinking about the question of the ethical, emerged as the defining theme of their work.[5] Others, notably Foucault, Deleuze, Lyotard, Baudrillard, and Bataille turned the thinking of Nietzsche and Heidegger into a novel kind of social and political critique of both the regimes and the effects of power that have come to distinguish late modern times; they concentrated, in detail, upon how the violence identified by these other thinkers manifested itself not only in the mundane practices of modern life, but also in those areas that claimed to be most free of it, especially the freedom and security of the subject as well as its allied will to truth and knowledge. Questioning the appeal to the secure self-grounding common to both its epistemic structures and its political imagination, and in the course of reinterrogating both the political character of the modern and the modern character of the political, this problematization of modernity has begun to prompt an ontopolitically driven reappraisal of modern political thought. This means that the ontological constitution of politics itself— its legislating categories of time, space, understanding, and action, and of what it is to be— prompted by the politics of the specific (ontological) constitutional order of political modernity, has begun to come under sustained scrutiny.

Taken up first (outside philosophy) in the study of literature, psychoanalysis, and sociology, the reception of this movement of thought was necessarily colored by the historical predispositions and disciplinary preoccupations into which it was first received, in North America especially and later in Britain. Without being diverted into an interdisciplinary excursus and without diminishing the continuing significance of the following issues or their relevance to the political, this accounts, at least in part, for the early preoccupations with textuality (poststructuralism), subjectivity (individual and collective), and epochality (identification of a new epoch, the postmodern).

The political implications of the return of the ontological have always been evident, but they were hardly the principal concerns of literature, psychoanalysis or even sociology. This meant that (with the exception of the critical members of the Frankfurt school and thinkers such as Carl Schmitt in Germany) they did not engage with the tradition of political thought until somewhat later. The work of Butler, Connolly, Dallmayr, Dumm, Flynn, Honig, Kateb, Shapiro, Strong, Villa, Warren, and White in the United States, and of Agamben, Haar, Kristeva, Lacoue-Labarthe, Lefort, Laclau, Mouffe, Nancy, and Zizek in Europe is evidence of a plural body of thought that now does just that.

Hannah Arendt stands out here, not just for the individuality, extent, and quality of her political thought, but because she was there before all the rest. Her adherents, however, did not appreciate the extent to which her political thinking was enabled by Heidegger's early search for a fundamental ontology and his allied destruction of metaphysics, simply because until recently, the tradition of political thought has been largely ignorant or dismissive of these developments.[6] Much of that has now begun to change in a widespread and positive revival of interest, for example, in Arendt herself.[7] It is, perhaps, ignorance of its own ontological indebtedness that (among other reasons) accounts for the continuing lack of interest in Arendt's thinking displayed by international relations, despite the ways in which it has been opened up to related currents of thought in recent years.[8]

Thinking the political in the way we do because of the way we think, this turn in thought has profound implications for the thought of politics as well. The return of the ontological, in other words, necessarily prompted a return of what Connolly has aptly called "the ontopolitical," something I want to turn to later.[9] One of the most important features of this development has been to concentrate the attention of political thought on the question of the political as such.[10] Part of the argument I make here is that international relations, once the citadel of metaphysical understandings of the political, may instead become a prime site for that very ontopolitical reappraisal of the political — in which political thought rethinks itself by turning back to that which it is given to think, namely the political — called for by the ontological turn.[11]

Inasmuch as we also think international relations in the way we do because of the way we think, and that international relations — even when it most claims to be something else, something apolitical — is also a mode of political thought, the return of the ontopolitical has profound implications for international relations as well, not only for what is thought through international relations, but also for the very way in which international relations as a mode of thought is itself construed and may be further reconstrued.

What is ordinarily most difficult here, however, is finding how the wider philosophical issues raised by the ontopolitical turn can be shown to have direct critical purchase not only on the construal of that discipline as a domain of thought, but also on the international politics of decision and judgment, comprehension of which international relations claims as its definitive distinctive competence. What is required therefore is some "concretization," some location in readily appreciated international political circumstances or events, of these more philosophically derived issues, so that both the political implications of the philosophy and the character of political decision itself can be simultaneously illuminated.

My other principal argument, then, is that what I call the scandal of the refugee presents such a conjunction. It illuminates both the fundamental ontological determinations of international politics and the character of political action because the refugee is a function of the intentional political destruction of the ontological horizons of people's always already heterogeneous worlds, and effects an equally fundamental deconstruction of the ontological horizons that constitute the equally heterogeneous worlds into which, as refugees, these people are precipitated. It is precisely on this concrete and corporeal site that both the ontological horizons and the allied political decision making of modern politics are thrown into stark relief and profoundly called into question. For it is precisely here that the very actions of modern politics — decisions and judgments together with how those decisions and judgments are framed and determined by their own ontopolitical assumptions — both create and address the incidence of its own massive and self-generated political abjection. If that is one of the principal ends of international relations, one is forced to ask, what does it take as its beginning? If, in other words, the vernacular political architecture of modern international power commonly produces forcibly displaced people globally, one is inclined to ask about the foundations upon which that architecture is itself based.

The "Inter" of International Relations

Neither a co-national nor another national, the refugee is, instead, distinguished precisely because s/he is located in the strange territory of estrangement that is located between the two; denaturalized, as a recent study of migration notes, means having "no means of identification."[12] Neither in nor out — while nonetheless actually bearing the name of some previous identification and existing in a carefully defined nowhere place within the boundaries of some other nation or state, so clearly also undeniably present — s/he brings the very "inter" of international relations to the foreground in a disturbing and unusual way, insisting that it become the concentrated focus of attention that it deserves to be.

In search of a home because forcibly deprived by violent and sustained political intent of their previous home, the refugee brings to presence the very question of the home as such and of its relation to politics. The refugee is a suppliant in search of a home, with painfully indelible memories of a home that once was, and often with an abiding, seducing nostalgia for a home that never was. For the violent event of displacement, of dislocation and subsequent diaspora, generates a necessary re-presentation of home that inevitably calls into question what home was really like. No one knows what home was really like, however, because the home recalled is not the home that was; and yet, also, the home that was could not have been the securely domesticated home one thought it was because it proved so susceptible to radical dispersal and dissolution. The question of the home is therefore radically problematized by the unsettled, and is never resettled even when the unsettled regains a home.[13]

How, then, in all the senses of this term, is one to address the refugee? And how does that problem of address illuminate what the refugee illuminates about the human condition as such? For while intentionally displaced, the refugee is not purposefully sent. Equally, while in desperate need of sustainable and survivable means of habitation, the refugee is not destined for some previously inscribed forwarding address. This experience — literally, of no known address — discloses something that is itself fundamental to the human: its very own lack of address, its own unsettledness. Their names erased, or Babelized, the places from which they fled changed beyond original recognition by the violence of expulsion itself, the refugee is one who, no longer safely responding to their previous name, cannot be hailed securely by that original ethnic, religious, social, or political designation. An administrative category for that which is no longer reliably fixed, locatable, or designatable, one waiting in a sometimes interminable line, camp or holding tank for some other assignment, the refugee is human or s/he is nothing, or at least nothing but raw stuff. Here, then, is the inescapable and irresolvable, yet also practical and immediate — indeed, in our times massively posed — ontopolitical question that the refugee brings to presence: What is it to be human, when the human is precisely that which is in-between — neither simply one thing, nor the other, precisely "inter" — without a secure term or dwelling place? And how are not only politics but the thought of the political related to this question? The very advent of the being who is precisely without secure and unambiguous home, identity, or name, the refugee raises our need while challenging our capacity to articulate or acknowledge the "we." That, I suggest, is not only the territory of the political in an age that has to be outlived if the human is to have a future; it is also, and quite precisely, the territory of the inter of an international relations that is capable of outthinking its own traditional designation, as a *techne* skilled in calculating the intersubjective political arithmetic of modernity's given political subjectivities. For it is precisely that arithmetic obsession — the *techne* of modern political subjectification and governance itself — which now produces its own massive political abjection in the form of the refugee.

The Refugee as Constitutive Outsider

> Exactly because s/he destroys the old trinity of state-nation-territory, the refugee, an apparently marginal figure, deserves on the contrary to be considered the central figure of our own political history.[14]

What historical politicality (the quality or project of being political, circumscribing the very domain of political intelligibility) is raised here by the advent of the refugee? What are we to make of what is going on when the political discourse of state-nation-territory does not merely enact that which it names, materializing the state, the nation, and the territory, but the very "outside" upon which it draws for the articulation of its most traditional legitimatory functions, representation of the people, and the monopoly not only of the legitimate use of force for the purposes of security, but also the prior monopolistic determination of the definition of threat? What conclusions are we to draw from the following observations? That the harder a politics is conditioned to secure the material production of the coherent identity to which its discourses refer, the more it seems to produce "the unspeakable, the unviable, the non-narrativizable . . . the traumatic,"[15] upon which it relies. Yet, also, the more it produces that which it cannot abide, the more the impossibility of its project is confirmed, such that what remains outside the political subject, set there by the very acts that found the subject, persists as an integrally defining negativity.[16] In what ways might this seemingly paradoxical political condition have become not only the condition, but also the very occasion of some further, of some other, political thought and action?

This essay on the theme of the refugee is not, therefore, an essay in the largely policy-analytic tradition of refugee studies. Neither is it simply an essay in identity politics, whereby the fear of the other, enemy, or stranger is exploited in the contestation over the constitution of certain kinds of political subjectivity. The scandal to which it refers is a quite different register of scandal also from that in which we are usually invited to share when we are gathered by political and media representations of it to witness the spectacle of the refugee's abjection.

Moving beyond that register of scandal, the essay offers a different one, and seeks as well to indicate the measure of its political implications. This register of scandal is plural. It refers to the scandal of the human as such. It addresses also the scandal of the inhospitability of the *techne* of modern politics: politics understood as *techne*, politics technologized by *techne*, politics whose end has become the application and operation of *techne*. Finally, and relatedly, it provokes the scandalous thought that the political project to which modern politics itself now gives rise is precisely not that of its self-realization, not that of the instantiation of sovereignty, not that of the securing of a home, not that of the resolution of alienation, not that, even, of the representation of the people. It is the challenge to outlive the global politics of modernity itself. Outlive, that is, in all of the senses of that phrase: to survive, to exceed, to transcend, to live more fully than the totality that the modern in modern politics both promises and threatens, though it is, ordinarily, bound to renege on the promise and fail fully to realize it as a threat.

Different identity politics, of course, determine different things to be alien to them. How the alien appears, and the experience of the alien as alien, also waxes and wanes, however, according to different times and different philosophical systems. How the alien is alien similarly determines how the self-same, in both philosophy and politics, is itself not simply constituted, but continuously reinaugurated in the process of trying to make the alien proper. There brews, therefore, beneath all identity politics and beneath all allied philosophical systems a secret *horror alieni* that insidiously seeks to dispel all aliens—alienness itself—to divest things of everything enigmatic and strange. If they cannot do that, they seek instead to drive out the stranger, making that estrangement the bearer of all that such systems find fearsome and threatening, evil, sinful, and barbarous.

The constitution of any social group or political community is a matter of the exercise of inclusions and exclusions. The semantic field of the alien is, therefore, manifold and its political register is determinative of political community. All this is, by now, well appreciated.

Mass expulsion and forceful displacement of peoples are not, of course, modern phenomena. Equally, exile and diaspora are not exclusively modern experiences. But if all philosophical systems, and all social and political groupings, are constituted on the basis of complex practices of inclusion and exclusion, then the nature of modern inclusions and exclusions is peculiar to and discloses something fundamental about the particular character of political modernity. The sheer scale of the mass forced displacement of peoples globally in our times, for example, seems to be distinctive, and it has given rise to analytical crises in the areas of migration and refugee studies, as well as political crises in those areas of national and international policy making concerned with immigration, emigration, refugee protection, humanitarian intervention, asylum seeking, and regulation.[17] Crises serve here, however, as a pretext that, in addition, possesses a powerful rhetorical appeal for broaching a discussion that would apply even if there were only one displaced, one nonassignable, human being in the world.

The violent character of modern global estrangement also seems to be extraordinarily diverse. Consider, for example, the list of outcasts that distinguishes modern forced displacement of peoples: refugee, political refugee, development refugee, internal refugee, asylum seeker, oustee, deportee, relocatee, involuntary displaced person, involuntarily resettled person, forced migrant, involuntary migrant, and so on. Consider, too, the portfolio of policies that have given rise to them: war, internal security actions, low-intensity operations, pacification, ethnocide, genocide, pogroms, political repression, racial and religious discrimination, conquest, colonization, territorial appropriation, state building, nation building, self-determination, famine, urbanization, industrialization, and development. In 1993, out of a world population of about five billion, the United Nations High Council for Refugees (UNHCR) estimated that around one in every 130 people had been forced into flight across state borders.[18] Given the complexity and confusion surrounding the production and movements of refugees, together with the shifting legal politics of classification that characterizes the categorization of people as refugees, the precision of these figures is questionable and said to significantly underestimate the scale of the phenomenon. Later reports, which include people forced into flight within their own state territories, thus classifying refugees as part of an extraordinarily large and variegated global phenomenon of coerced displacement, record that approximately one in 115 people find themselves in this condition.[19]

While "there are as many reasons for moving as there are migrants,"[20] globally (and it is now increasingly difficult for migration analysts and legislators to distinguish between voluntary migration, involuntary migration, forced migration, and expulsion) the production of the modern refugee is distinctive and differs from earlier, particularly nineteenth-century refugees, in the way in which it is defined in terms of the whole-sale devastation of the very ontological horizons of their worlds and their reduction to worldless beings unwelcome among the worldliness of others. Attributed to a complex combination of war; violent mass political repression; geopolitical instability; regional and global economic transformation in the form of the redivision and redistribution of capital, labor, and industry; man-made environmental disaster; and civil conflict, the most overwhelmingly important reason now is violent internecine conflict. The vast majority of refugees are precipitated by generic violence against civilian populations. "Virtually all of the refugee producing conflicts taking place in the world during the early part of 1993," according to the UNHCR study, "were within states rather than between them."[21] Development studies have, however, documented how development itself generates at least equal numbers of refugees. In short, the modern refugee is an (inter)national political production of its age and cannot but disclose the fundaments of it.

It is not my intention, however, to refine the taxonomies of these modern outcasts or the policies that have given rise to them. Taxonomies are generally concerned with advancing knowledgeable control of the objects of study by refining their categorization. I want instead to probe into what the refugee as such discloses about modern politics. I am concerned with precisely that which, while categorizable, nonetheless exceeds categorization, like the refugee. For the refugee, like the human itself, is always both more and less than human. Thus, while the manifold ways in which expulsion and revulsion are experienced can be taxonomized, and taxonomic precision has its advantages in other forms of argument, expulsion and revulsion (the effect of being strange or estranged) always bring to presence the uncanniness of strangeness as such. That is to say, the uncanniness of being within a category categorized as being without a category — that of the refugee — discloses the very uncanniness of the human itself, its improbable condition of always already containing both more and less than it seems it ought naturally to contain.

Because the constitution of any social group or political community is a matter of the exercise of inclusions and exclusions does not mean that one set of inclusions and exclusions is the same as any other. Nor is it true that because there have always been people who have been outcasts we can legitimately concentrate on the native and the home, and thus forget about the stranger and the outside. On the contrary the "we" is integrally related to, because formed by, this relationship with the alien. Given the horrors inflicted on the alien, it is understandable, indeed almost orthodox, to deny difference and urgently champion an all-encompassing inclusion so as to mitigate or eradicate the terrors of exclusion.

Here, too, however, arises a further reverberation of the scandal of the refugee in the form of another scandalous thought. Being more fully "we" might precisely *not* entail being a more inclusive "we." The politicality of such a way of being would necessarily also comprise other, precisely deconstructive, political entailments, practices, dispositions, and sensibilities extending, and differing quite significantly from, those of any politics or project of inclusivity. It might, instead, entail different ways of thinking about, and different ways of seeking to entertain, that very relationship of alienness—what Nancy calls the "we" of being-with—which literally articulates us the human; expresses and joins, joins by expressing, links through the medium of language itself.

All order, in short, encounters the alien or the strange, which is defined not in relation to itself at all. Such alienness is beyond the trial of propriety to which strangeness is continuously submitted, including especially those codified in immigration and asylum-seeking procedures, an instance of which follows:

Are you or have you at any time been an anarchist, or a member of or affiliated with a Communist or other totalitarian party?

Have you advocated or taught, by personal utterance, by written or printed matter, or through affiliation with an organization (a) opposition to organized government; (b) the overthrow of government by force; (c) the assaulting or killing of government officials because of their official character; (d) the unlawful destruction of property; (e) sabotage; (f) the doctrines of world communism, or the establishment of a totalitarian dictatorship in the United States?

Have you engaged in or do you intend to engage in prejudicial activities or unlawful activities of a subversive nature?

Are you afflicted with psychopathic personality, sexual deviation, mental defect, narcotic drug addiction, chronic alcoholism, or any dangerous contagious disease?

Are you a pauper, professional beggar or vagrant?

Are you a polygamist or do you advocate polygamy?

Have you committed or have you been convicted of a crime of moral turpitude?[22]

These are among the questions you would have to answer should you be seeking to join, and be accepted as a proper member of, the United States. Other trials of propriety, however, are more Kafkaesque than farcical.

The alienness I refer to now concerns an alienness that is not the property of any person, people, place, or thing. It does not belong to entities, albeit that it comes to presence in the appearance of persons or things. Propriety does not attach to it all. Hence it is not a property of the world but an indelible, if fugitive, aspect of the world within whose horizon it is continuously and variously encountered. The semantic field, and thus also the political register of the alien, here through the figure of the refugee, in always disclosing this alienness consequently also simultaneously betrays the philosophical register of the *horror alieni* as well. Buried in the political register of that *horror alieni* therefore is something more fundamental about the fundaments of being that philosophy, and thus political Modernity, is inclined to express.

The refugee alerts us to, by bringing to presence our awareness of, a different ontological condition definitive in many ways of the ontological turn — that of the ontological difference between beings and Being as such. Recognition of the ontological difference is recognition of the mutually disclosive belonging together of Being and beings, of the excess that always already inhabits the being of human being, whose absent presence does not come to presence as such, which gives rise to the deconstruction that is always already at work in the coming to presence of human being and language, the mode in which it comes to presence. Thus deconstruction is less a technique than the irresistible consequence of the ontological difference whose play makes of human being a free and incomplete *plethos*.

Alert to this ontological dimension of identity politics, we can be alerted also to that other register of scandal I referred to in my opening. It is that strangeness, the strangeness that comes to presence with the advent of the stranger or the alien, that takes this essay not only through but also beyond identity politics — where the alien or the stranger is regarded as virulent because the idea of order is premised on the oper-

ation or realization of a unity, even of an ensemble of many beings —
to scandalize its philosophical underpinnings: traditional understandings of the idea, the *eidos,* of unity as such. For the advent of any stranger
is the limit at which the integral and indelible strangeness of the human condition makes its appearance.

Accepting that other times and other forms of life have treated
strangers badly, or manufactured strangers of themselves, does not,
then, deny that modern estrangement happens in its own modern way
and for its own modern reasons. We can therefore note that our age is
one in which political order is not simply premised on the realization
of a unitary identity, but on a certain kind of technological, utile uniformity of, identity; in pursuit of which the very activities of their own
states, together with the global capitalism of states and the environmental degradation of many populous regions of the planet, have made
many millions radically endangered strangers in their own homes, as
well as criminalized or anathematized strangers in the places to which
they have been forced to flee. Although we have some sense of why it
was, it is, nonetheless, still utterly astonishing that while millions upon
millions of people were engaged in massive transoceanic Euro-American
and intra-European migration, itself accompanied by the forcible transfer of at least equal numbers of people through the globally commer-
cialized slave trade and, later, the so-called "coolie migration," it was
insisted that politics be understood as grounded upon a secure trian-
gulation of territory, nation, and state; when the facts so massively spoke
of the mobility of people, the mutability of boundaries, the mongrel-
arity of nations and the specular artificiality of the state.

The scale of the politically instrumental — deliberate, legal, and policy-
initiated — manufacture of estrangement in world politics necessarily
calls into question, therefore, the very moral and political foundations
and accomplishments of the modern age, particularly those of the state
and the international system of states.

In such circumstances — and given the vaunted political and moral
claims made on behalf of states and of the international state system,
as well as of so-called international society — we seem increasingly left
not knowing to what symbolic space, to what understanding of the human way of being, we can entrust what we variously call freedom and
humanity.[23] Modern politics, the politics of modernity, continuously undermines, however, its own most violent, most intense, most totalizing

attempts to securely free humanity. And this is not because of some technical deficiency on its part — the global politics of modernity is the expression of politics as *techne*. It is because it is not realizable. In the process the modern expression of identity politics, while thus disclosing something also about the modern world's response to strangeness as such, provides a powerful intimation that the reception that the modern we accords the strangeness of the human way of being is what the very (dis)order of political modernity itself calls into question.

Specifically, modern political subjectification creates its own peculiar form of political abjection. Originally applied to French Huguenots who fled to England after the revocation of the Edict of Nantes in 1685 — and therefore a direct function of early modern absolutist understandings of the entailments of stable, legitimate, and authoritative political order, and their consequences — the refugee is precisely the figure that identifies the political abjection of the modern age.

Abject means cast out; abjection means also the act of expelling. It marks the failure of the political subject to be a pure political subject even in the act of trying to realize that ideal. Marking the porosity of the limits of that which seeks to be the self-same, it is the waste that continuously disturbs identity, system, and order because as the outside produced by the inside, it continuously irrupts in a way that erodes the very parameters by which the inside seeks to be defined. That which the effort to subjectify creates, its production marks the impossibility, the abject failure, of what modern political subjectification idealizes and aims to realize. For the political practices of burning, chasing, raping, expelling, degrading, murdering, humiliating, terrorizing, excoriating, removing, burying, hiding, suppressing, and devastating invent and reinvent the very waste they name and exorcise in the process of continuously reinaugurating, as politics, a certain imperative of political unity and malleable uniformity. Waste, as Ricoeur noted, is not waste without its wasting processes: its protocols of purgative production.[24] Neither is it undifferentiated since its processes of production are themselves plural. Abjection — the system's own self-produced and self-producing perturbation — is neither inside nor outside but the in-between, the boundary or limit that enacts the differentiation. Abjection is (inter)national politics, and as (inter)national politics, it insists on a preoccupation with the inter anterior to the national.

Since the seventeenth century, of course, while the international definition of the refugee specifies the crossing of state borders, the incidence of "refugeeism" (to coin an awful neologism for an awful condition) has been extended in many intensive ways to the massive forced relocation of peoples within their existing territorial boundaries and for the purposes of "development" and "resettlement" rather than from traditionally religious or political persecution. Social scientific research on involuntary resettlement mushroomed between 1984 and 1994 in response to the discovery that World Bank-funded development projects—notably those concerned with the building of large-scale dams—manufactured massive impoverishment instead.[25] Complexly complicit in the violent appropriative and exploitative politics of the political and economic elites of the recipient states, politically mandated mass relocations of people did not merely enrich some and pauperize most, in ways systematically related to the mutations of global capitalism, but effectively and radically de-worlded those who were resettled. That in turn provoked reformations of identity borne out of resistance to the experience itself. Here, then, is a further mutation of the processes and protocols of the production of abjection which discloses something else about the governmental imperatives of politics in late modern times. In consequence: "Development-caused displacements, that seemed to be piecemeal occurrences and were estimated as totalling far less than the number of refugees world-wide, have turned out to be a *much larger process than all the world's new refugee flows.* Refugees and development displacees, of course, are not 'numbers' that compete with each other, but are global parallel dramas sometimes intertwined."[26]

The principal difficulty with the overwhelming volume of this research is, however, the propensity to depoliticize the issue by translating it into precisely that technical policy-analytic enframing that contributed to the production of the problem in the first place. Technology thus translates the question of the political into certain kinds of problematizations requiring rigorous calculability, utility, and governmentality. It then feeds itself on the history and further elaboration of the very problematizations it introduces.[27]

Albeit, then, that the theme of abjection also arises here, this essay is not a treatment of the refugee as victim. Refugees have always offered, and been, more than mere objects of pity and suffering, something the

Huguenots themselves, of course, also demonstrated.[28] As abjection, refugees consequently also call into question the foundational under-pinnings both of the community from which they have been expelled and the community into which they seek to be received. What is at issue, in short, is the very question of human dwelling and belonging in a world. That in turn raises the point, well made by Judith Butler in an-other discussion, of how "such socially saturated domains of exclusion" can be recast from their status as constitutive-outsiders "to beings that matter."[29] I take the refugee to be a being that matters in respect of the world (dis)order of political modernity, the requirement to outlive it, and the possibility of the possibility of doing so. The essay is thus, in-stead, a contribution to what political theorist William Connolly has called "ontopolitical interpretation."

By the ontopolitical, Connolly refers to the way in which every polit-ical interpretation invokes a set of fundaments about the necessities and possibilities of human being; about, for instance, "the forms into which human beings may be composed and the possible relations which humans may establish with nature."[30] For the *on*, or the *onta*, of ontol-ogy refers to the reality of really existing things. In making his point about the way in which all political interpretation is simultaneously also ontopolitical because it cannot but disclose the ontology sequestered within it (to repeat, making any statement about what *is* is always al-ready to find oneself within an understanding of the *is* as such) Connolly demurs at the logos of ontology because he finds the idea of the logic of reality apart from appearance too determinative and restrictive. It suggests a principle or design of being, when it can and has, of course, been argued that the fundamental thing about being is that it exhibits no such overriding logic or principle.

Surveying the various means by which modern political thought has elided the ontopolitical — modern secularism (Lowith or Blumen-berg), pragmatism, and epistemological realism, for example — Connolly concludes that this elision also obscures a convergence of ontological views. Asking rhetorically, "What if some common presumptions of our times...contain dangerous demands and expectations within them? What...if the points of ontopolitical convergence in the late-modern nation-state turn out to be exactly the domain in need of reassessment today?"[31] Connolly notes that this is precisely what that strain of think-ing from Nietzsche onward, to which I referred earlier as the ontologi-

cal turn, contends: "that every detailed interpretation presupposes answers to fundamental questions of being, and that this is indeed one of
the territories of modern discourse that requires critical reflection."[32]

My contention is that the advent of the refugee brings that very territory of modern discourse directly into question because the refugee
is a function of the dangerous ontopolitical convergences that Connolly
notes. Specifically, that ontological narcissism, to which he refers in his
essay on "Freedom and Contingency," in which freedom has become associated with the security of being in command, the corollary of which
appears to mean being subjected to intensifying control.[33] Among other
things, therefore, outliving the modern is critically associated also with
outliving these dangers. The advent of the refugee — one whose very
own ontological horizons have been devastated, one removed from a
world — thereby dramatically exposes and radically disrupts the ontopolitical horizons not only of the hosts in which they arise, but also
of political Modernity as such. Finally, the essay seeks to draw out a
significantly different set of ontopolitical suppositions that the advent
of the refugee also helps to disclose.

If this provides some early, if all too brief, indication of what I mean
by outliving the modern, I cannot give some comparable and positive
indication of what I mean by the scandal of the refugee without also
elaborating on the very different ontopolitical fundaments that the advent of the refugee brings to presence. Just as Connolly draws on a certain range of philosophical resources to make his point about the eli-
sions and dangers of the ontopolitics of late Modernity, I draw on the
same resources to offer this alternative ontopolitical account of the human, in which its estrangement from itself is the very scandal that the
refugee brings so forcefully and politically to presence in the (dis)or-
dering of world politics. It is that estrangement, itself an ontopolitical
point of departure, that is both the condition and the occasion of another politics.

The Ontopolitical Condition of Worldly Estrangement

> What becomes of being-with when the *with* no longer appears as
> composition, but rather as dis-position?[34]

In excess of the humanitarian scandal of the refugee, and in excess of
the policy analytic and policy-making crisis induced by the astonishing

growth of refugees in the past ten years. In excess, also, of the political crises that the advent of large numbers of refugees excite in the countries to which they flee, or in countries like the United Kingdom, in which the narcissistic politics of identity seems designed to go phobic at the least provocation of alienness, the scandal of the refugee is not only the scandalous thought that political Modernity has to find a way of outliving rather than of realizing itself. In excess of, but also in alliance with, these other registers of scandal, the advent of the refugee always brings to presence this: the scandal of the human as such. That scandal is the scandal of human freedom that makes both politics and law possible without making either politics or law certain. It is a scandal from which the telic understanding of politics, as a form of making that results in a technologizing of politics, seeks to save us; and in the process subjects us to novel, possibly terminal, globalized terrors and dangers.

Human being is a mobile way of being on its way from birth to death that lives life without owning whatever gives life. It is, then, in the condition of an originary dispossession because it enjoys no security of tenure over the freehold of its existence. That leaves it in the curious position of having to own itself without possessing original title to itself. It simply does not, and cannot, possess a secure property right in itself, of itself. In consequence, it makes up wonderfully implausible stories to account for this predicament and binds itself to and with them in the hope that they may make such a peculiar way of being somewhat easier to bear. Technological mastery of ourselves and "nature" through submission to the spectacular power and productivity of representative calculative thought projected on and through, rather than grounded in, the idea of a sovereign reasoning subject, is the specular mythological achievement that distinguishes and determines our own politically modern times.

Philosophers (some philosophers) call this difference — the difference between beings that exist and existence as such — the ontological difference. Insinuated into the very being of human being, it is what makes human being plural; more than one. That plurality is not, it should be noted, the plurality of many human subjects, however those subjects are specified: people, nation, class, race, religion, or even citizen (by virtue of subscription to the constitution of a republic and its civic culture). An even more disturbing phenomenon, that plurality is what might be called an onto-plurality. Installed within the being of every human be-

ing, the plurality of such a difference is not a Hegelian relational concept of difference either, in which difference (some would call it Otherness) is only difference in relation to me and, therefore, not truly different or Other at all.[35] Rather, it is an irreducible and irremissible
Otherness or difference that, constitutive of human being, is nonetheless beyond its mastery. What identifies human being—its freedom, in
raising and answering the question of its own existence, also to recognize this Otherness or difference that is integrally constitutive of it—is
simultaneously what disrupts its identity with itself as well.

Enjoying an existence that is plural as such—itself a *plethos* rather
than merely composed of a plurality of beings—the human inhabits a
strangeness that also inhabits it. A being that is itself radically transitive,
occurring through time and so originally historical rather than merely
mobile, the worldly estrangement of human being is an interrogatory
way of being that, in having only itself hermeneutically to answer to, is
nonetheless in the position of having to answer to a mystery.[36] To be
worldly here is to have a certain modality of alienation "inscribed at
the heart of one's existence, and to give this alienation an extremely positive validation."[37] On its way from birth to death, and consequently always
already on the move into a future in which it becomes that which it has
never yet been, human being necessarily also remains fundamentally a
stranger to itself. The scandal of the refugee is that the human is itself
not simply natural, not—to play on the scan of scandal—reliably met-
rical. Calculative, it nonetheless simply does not add up. The scandal, in
short, is that the human is itself alien; in that, while of necessity it dwells
in a world, it is not, and cannot be, fully at home there because it never
received vacant possession, does not own the freehold, and has no security of tenure in it. The hope that therefore arises with the refugee
exceeds the hope that the alien might find a "home" and entertains the
possibility that the onto-alienness of human being might ultimately also
find ways of being hospitable to itself. Finding such ways and articulating such a hope are, I believe, also ways of newly understanding the project of democratic politics, provoked by the advent of the refugee and
dramatized by the dangers of world (dis)order in late modern times.

Such a condition—freedom to give the law that is a freedom before
the law of that which is, in Nancy's paradoxical phrase, "legitimately without law (*de droit sans droit*)"[38]—is not just a scandal to reason, it is also
ethically scandalous as well, which is to say, a "snare," "trap," or "cause

of moral stumbling . . . a stumbling-block" [OED].[39] Continuously having to find its feet, the human way of being is thus simultaneously, also, the occasion of its downfall as well. Nothing bears it up in its disposure other than its composure. That composure, however contrived, even under modern forms of representative democratic government, which ground their legitimacy in the representation of "the people," is a fallible act made possible by virtue of that ontological freedom. Such composure is not, however, the telos or end of a politics of making, of politics understood to be a process of fabrication. Rather, it is the endless work of assuming the burden of being free, of laying down the law, to be interpreting the law in consequence of the exception to the law that the law itself necessarily brings to presence. To have an end is only possible in the condition of not having any end as such. Political — I would add, democratic — composure is the deferral of the end that would end all purposefulness. It is a tricky act to pull off because, continuously disrupted, human being nonetheless has to continuously come to terms with its original disposure: its thrownness into a world in which it knows not from whence it came, nor where it is headed.

To note and consider the ontologizing effect of the refugee, however, does not mean abandoning the economic, political, or personal dimension of the refugee, any more than it means abandoning the terrain of judgment. The ontologizing effect does not remove us to some abstract or speculative region at all. It is a question of entering these other so-called empirical (but in Arendtian and Heideggerian language simply worldly) regions differently. For the word means the thought of existence, and the status of it today means thinking our, especially political, existence on the level of the challenge that the refugee brings to our capacity, less to secure a home and more to create and live in habitable worlds. Hence, we are ontopolitically indebted to the refugee. That debt cannot be repaid, but it can be explored and acknowledged through a political thought other than that which has helped to make the refugee one of the principal bearers of the cost of the political (dis)order of the modern world, where the technological understanding of politics as fabrication — state-building, nation-building, nation-state-building, hegemonizing, counterhegemonizing — is paramount. To bring the derelicted into thought in this way is neither to patronize, nor to avoid the devastation of their dereliction. It is an exercise of neither good nor bad conscience. It is to respond positively, instead, to the refugee's profound provocation of political thought, by which I mean the provocation both to think politically and, in thus thinking politically, to think against the ontopolitical convergences that distinguish modern political thought.

For the refugee raises the question of association beyond, outside, in the margins, or in excess of, established political sociation, because the refugee is by definition asocial, apolitical. Being political, or as one might say the being of politics, is profoundly at issue here, in and through the presence of the refugee. The figuration of the abjection at the heart of modern political subjection, of the associational poverty at the center of so much political sociation, and of the impoverishment of being-with in today's global togetherness, the refugee exposes how belonging together politically has become belonging together at the production of the spectacle of politics, including that of the abjection integral to it. The advent of the refugee nonetheless still ruptures the horizons—spoils the show—of societies that desire to be left only to themselves, seeking to affirm their social and political being by reference to no horizon but themselves. What emerges from taking the refugee even more seriously, therefore, than refugee studies might perhaps unfairly be said to do, is not the idea of some sovereign individual or communal, rights-based, understanding of human being, which requires extension to the being that has been expelled from its world.

The problem with rights in this argument concerning the politically dislocating ontologizing effects of the advent of the refugee—that is to say, aside from any tactical questions concerning the provision of some means of protection to the outcast—is that it appeals to one of two grounds, each of which is equally unsustainable in the face of the alienness that the refugee brings to presence. On the one hand rights are the fruit of the enforceable law of a community. On the other, rights are said to be the natural endowment of what it is to be human. The refugee is, of course, refugee in virtue of its expulsion from, and very often by, the enforceable law of a community. There is no enforceable communal law to which the refugee has recourse; UN conventions on refugees are just that, conventions that the existing legal communities of states interpret for themselves, and may or may not apply to themselves.[40] That is the point to being a refugee. Conversely, the appeal to what is said to be the natural endowment of the human raises the ontological question of the natural. Here the advent of the refugee is radically disruptive because the event of the refugee's alienness calls to mind the alienness of the human as such: the very non-naturalness of the onto-plurality, the thrownness and responsibility of its abyssal freedom. For if the human were simply natural it would not have this freedom — with all its attendant burdens of decision — to be.

The question of taking the refugee even more seriously is not, however, simply a question of some sociality or alterity that problematizes the authority of the subject understood as a *solus ipse:* "It is more than this and something else entirely."[41] It is a matter of the *ipse* itself, of its very belonging together in and through its inherent plurality. That with which we are associated, and that which associates us, in short our capacity to say "we" the human, is what is at issue: mundanely, corporeally, and increasingly, in our world, massively. The advent of the refugee, therefore, poses both the ontological question politically and the political question ontologically. Hence the dramatic, and dramatically disruptive, ontopolitical valence of the refugee. Neither a neighbor nor a friend, not linked by a politically fraternal, communal, or national bond, the advent of the refugee poses the question of the "we" of the human as such and discloses its co-ipseity beyond, or other than, our current understandings of the belonging together of the human way of being. That co-ipseity is obscure, enigmatic, and opaque. Readily deniable, it is nonetheless also impossible to escape. Inescapably ethical,[42] its inescapability has also gone global, and sets up aporetic perturbations in all settled systems of political order and understanding, including those of communitarian and liberal thought.[43]

Michael Walzer, for example, admits as much. At the extreme, he notes in *Spheres of Justice,* "the claim of asylum is virtually undeniable. I assume that there are in fact limits to our collective liability, but I don't know how to specify them." But if that is true, he went on, "[W]hy stop with asylum? Why be concerned with men and women on our territory who ask to remain and not with men and women oppressed in their own countries who ask to come in? Why mark-off the lucky or aggressive, who have somehow managed to make their own way across our borders, from all others? Once again I don't have an adequate answer to these questions."[44]

Raising the question, the capacity, and our necessity to be able to say "we," the refugee does so in circumstances that are not authorized, therefore, by God, the Leader, the Nation, the State, or the People. Rather, the refugee not only raises that need in the circumstances in which none of these ontopolitical figures says it for us, but does so also, and crucially, in precisely those circumstances when these figurations of the ontopolitical convergences of modern times — those very ontopolitical signifiers that operate as rallying points for mobilization and politicization fated nonetheless to dishonor their promise "both to unify the ideological field and to constitute the constituencies they claim to represent"[45] — tell us, instead, exclusively to say "I." Not being able to say "we" in the circumstances in which it is most called for — that is to say, when we are not authorized to do so, and when it is the strange and different that we are entertaining (consider Oskar Schindler, the Nazi Party member and war profiteer, in his enigmatic relationship with his Jewish slave-labor force) — is precisely, however, what allows each "I" the dementia that ultimately results in individuals not being able to say "I" any more either.[46] That is what makes the refugee a touchstone for the very democratic politicality of any community — its capacity, in making way for other beings, to make way for other ways of political being to be in its very own way of being.[47]

The "we" is in question as a question, then, when faced with the refugee because the refugee poses the very questionability of the "we" at us directly and politically, but in a way in which the answers we have currently settled upon — and in — no longer answer. That "we" obliges us to find other ways of saying "we" again, and through that inescapable insistence binds us in a peculiarly ethical form of "commonality." Once more our ontopolitical indebtedness to the refugee surfaces, for the refugee attests to the very aporeticness of the "we" and reopens it for us. In the process — precisely because the "we," however enigmatically, is — we, however we are, are continuously reconfigured. Herein, then, lies the intimation of the possibility of a different ontology of the species of political being: of one always already strange to itself, one more equipped to address the plurality always already insinuated into being. Here the "with" of association is what the political takes as its question, not its ground, precisely because it is human being's very own questionability. And it assumes as the commission of that very omission, precise lack of any secure answer to what the human is, the commitment to keep the with of that indefinable "we" open.

I want to conclude, then, in a kind of amplified and intensified Arendtian way, that it is this *plethos* that allows for the very possibility of politics, because it constitutes an ontological freedom that, in distinguishing human being as the way of being that is obliged to raise and respond to the question of its existence, without ever being in a position to answer it, devolves upon it the responsibility to lay down the law, and thus order its own affairs. It is not simply, then, the question of the "inter," but of its very irresolvable questionability, that gives rise to politics at all.

I would call that politics democratic that did not merely claim to represent "the people," did not begin with a subject individual or collective, but was committed instead to continuously forestalling the foreclosure of freedom entailed in having to give an answer to the question of the self and of the community. Indeed, that had no understanding of the self that was not also and simultaneously always already a being — within the Otherness of the ontological difference. I would also call that politics democratic if it was one that was thus committed to the project of keeping open the question of who "the people" (the demos) is; that is, of continuously disclosing, rather than foreclosing, the "inter" or "we" in the human way of being. Democracy to come would thus be — always already is — the forestalling of the foreclosing of this questionability, even in its own foreclosing.[48] Is it not this that constantly takes place in the "inter" of international relations, despite what international relations once thought itself to endorse, as knowledge and as politics, and so to be as a discipline?

Notes

1. Friedrich Nietzsche, *Beyond Good and Evil,* trans. R. J. Hollingdale (Harmondsworth: Penguin Books, 1990), 102.

2. To use an expression that Derrida coined in his essay, "Force of Law," in *Deconstruction and the Possibility of Justice,* ed. Drucilla Cornell et. al., (New York: Routledge, 1992).

3. See, for example, Nietzsche, *Beyond Good and Evil,* and *The Birth of Tragedy and The Genealogy of Morals* (New York: Doubleday, 1956). For Heidegger, see especially, *Being and Time* (Oxford: Blackwell, 1988), *The Fundamental Concepts of Metaphysics* (Bloomington: Indiana University Press, 1995), *Basic Questions of Philosophy* (Bloomington: Indiana University Press, 1994), *The Basic Problems of Phenomenology* (Bloomington: Indiana University Press, 1988), *Hegel's Phenomenology of Spirit* (Bloomington: Indiana University Press, 1988), *Kant and the Problem of Metaphysics* (Bloomington: Indiana University Press, 1990), and also the two-volume

study *Nietzsche* (San Francisco: Harper Collins, 1987). Kierkegaard's work was also an important influence in this movement of thought; see, in particular, *Fear and Trembling* (Princeton: Princeton University Press, 1974), *The Sickness Unto Death* (Princeton: Princeton University Press, 1974), *Philosophical Fragments* (Princeton: Princeton University Press, 1974), and *Journals and Papers* (Bloomington: Indiana University Press, 1970).

4. There is a very large literature on Heidegger and politics, much of it polemical and some of it bad. To my mind, the issue is neither the man nor simply the thought, much less being able to indict the one so as to forget about the other. The issue is the fundamental relationship between politics and philosophy; for that reason, some acquaintance with both is necessary. That specifically means understanding is also needed about the crisis of German historicism, which was, in effect, the crisis of German philosophy at the end of the nineteenth and the beginning of the twentieth centuries. See in particular Charles R. Bambach, *Heidegger, Dilthey, and the Crisis of Historicism* (Ithaca: Cornell University Press, 1995), and, less philosophically, Hans Sluga, *Heidegger's Crisis: Philosophy and Politics in Nazi Germany* (Cambridge: Harvard University Press, 1993).

5. The ethical is of course the preoccupation of all of Levinas's work. See, for example, the two major treatises *Totality and Infinity* (Dordrecht: Kluwer, 1991) and *Otherwise Than Being: Or Beyond Essence* (Dordrecht: Kluwer, 1991). The most ethico-politically intriguing of Derrida's recent work includes: *The Other Heading* (Bloomington: Indiana University Press, 1992), *Given Time. I, Counterfeit Money* (Chicago: Chicago University Press, 1991), *Aporias* (Stanford: Stanford University Press, 1993), *On the Name* (Stanford: Stanford University Press, 1993), *The Gift of Death* (Chicago: Chicago University Press, 1992), and *Specters of Marx* (London: Routledge, 1994).

6. One can track this evolution through the shift that occurs in Margaret Canovan's second major study of Arendt. See Canovan, *Hannah Arendt: A Reinterpretation of Her Political Thought* (Cambridge: Cambridge University Press, 1992). Bernard Flynn's work, however, is exceptional in this regard. See, especially, his essay on Arendt in the outstanding collection *Political Philosophy at the Closure of Metaphysics* (Atlantic Highlands, N.J.: Humanities Press, 1992). See also the excellent study by Dana Villa, *Arendt and Heidegger: The Fate of the Political* (Princeton: Princeton University Press, 1996).

7. In addition to the works already cited, see Seyla Benhabib's *Hannah Arendt* (London: Sage, 1996).

8. See, among others, Richard Ashley, "Untying the Modern State: A Double Reading of the Anarchy Problematique," *Millennium* 17 (1988); Jens Bartelson, *A Genealogy of Sovereignty* (Cambridge: Cambridge University Press, 1995); David Campbell, *Writing Security* (Minneapolis: University of Minnesota Press, 1998); William E. Connolly, *Identity\Difference* (Ithaca: Cornell University Press, 1991); James Der Derian and Michael Shapiro, eds., *International/Intertextual Relations* (Lexington, Mass.: Lexington Books, 1989); David Campbell/Michael Dillon, eds., *The Political Subject of Violence* (Manchester: Manchester University Press, 1993); Michael Dillon, *Politics of Security: Towards a Political Philosophy of Continental Thought* (London: Routledge, 1996); R. B. J. Walker, *Inside/Outside: International Relations as Political Theory* (Cambridge: Cambridge University Press, 1993).

9. William E. Connolly, "Nothing Is Fundamental," *The Ethos of Pluralization* (Minneapolis: University of Minnesota Press, 1995), 1–40.

10. See especially Fred Dallmayr, *The Other Heidegger* (Ithaca: Cornell University Press, 1993), and Simon Critchley, *The Ethics of Deconstruction: Derrida and Levinas* (Oxford: Blackwell, 1992).

11. See Dillon, *Politics of Security.*

12. Sarah Collinson, *Europe and International Migration* (London: Pinter for RIIA, 1994), 37.

13. See, for example, Daniel Warner, "The Community of the Refugee," *International Journal of Refugee Law* 3, 4 (1991): 731–34. More philosophically, see Robert Bernasconi, "On Deconstructing Nostalgia for Community in the West: The Debate between Nancy and Blanchot," *Research in Phenomenology* 23 (1993): 3–21.

14. Giorgio Agamben, "Beyond Human Rights," *Liberation,* 9 June 1993, 8 (my translation).

15. Judith Butler, *Bodies That Matter: On The Discursive Limits of "Sex"* (London: Routledge, 1993), 188.

16. See also Slavoj Zizek, *The Sublime Object of Ideology* (London: Verso, 1989).

17. See Aristide Zolberg, "The Next Waves: Migration Theory for a Changing World," *International Migration Review* 23, 3 (1988): 403–30; Christopher Mitchell, "International Migration, International Relations, and Foreign Policy," *International Migration Review* 23, 3 (1989): 681–708; and, classically, the recent report from the UNHCR, *The State of the World's Refugees: The Challenge of Protection* (Oxford: Oxford University Press, 1995).

18. UNHCR, *The State of the World's Refugees.*

19. Hans Thoolen, Regional Representative for the Nordic and Baltic Countries of the UNHCR, Report, 10 October 1994.

20. UNHCR, *The State of the World's Refugees,* 13–14.

21. Ibid, 14–15.

22. I am indebted to David Campbell's provocative study *Writing Security,* 41, for this list.

23. Jean-Luc Nancy, "War, Law, Sovereignty— *Techne,*" in Verena Andermatt Conley, ed., *Rethinking Technologies* (Minneapolis: University of Minnesota Press, 1993), 28.

24. Paul Ricoeur, *The Symbolisation of Evil* (Boston: Beacon Press, 1969).

25. See Michael M. Cernea, *Involuntary Resettlement in Development Projects. Policy Guidelines in World Bank Financed Projects* (Washington, D.C.: World Bank Technical Paper 80, 1988); *Tribal Peoples and Economic Development. Human Ecological Guidelines* (Washington, D.C.: World Bank, May 1982); *Development in Practice. Governance. The World Bank Experience* (Washington, D.C.: World Bank, May 1994); Leila C. Frischtak, *Governance Capacity and Economic Reform in Developing Countries* (Washington, D.C.: World Bank Technical Paper 254, 1994); *Resettlement and Development: The Bankwide Review of Projects Involving Involuntary Resettlement, 1986–1993* (Washington, D.C.: World Bank Environment Department, 8 April 1994).

26. Michael M. Cernea, "Understanding and Preventing Impoverishment from Displacement. Reflections on the State of Knowledge," in C. McDowell, ed., *Resisting Impoverishment: Tackling the Consequences of Development-Induced Population Displacement and Resettlement* (Oxford: Berghahn Books, 1995).

27. See Graham Burchall et al., eds., *The Foucault Effect* (London: Harvester Wheatsheaf, 1991).

28. This point could and has been argued in book-length studies. See, for example, Collinson, *Europe and International Migration*. It is an important corrective to the ways in which economic, racial, and other fears of the outsider are habitually exploited in domestic politics. In consequence, it is ironic to note that at the height of the most recent employment of the fear of the outsider in British politics, and a further restricting of asylum in the United Kingdom, that a research study by the British Home Office should have provided further evidence for the point. See Jenny Carey et al., *The Settlement of Refugees in Britain* (London: Home Office Research Study 141, HMSO, 1995).

29. Butler, *Bodies That Matter*, 189.

30. Connolly, "Nothing Is Fundamental," *The Ethos of Pluralization*.

31. Ibid., 4.

32. Ibid.

33. William E. Connolly, "Freedom and Contingency," in S. K. White, ed., *Life-World and Politics: Between Modernity and Postmodernity* (South Bend, Ind.: Notre Dame University Press, 1989).

34. Jean-Luc Nancy, *Being-With* (Colchester, England: University of Essex Centre for Theoretical Studies, Working Paper No. 11, 1996), 5.

35. See Rodolphe Gasché, *Inventions of Difference: On Jacques Derrida* (Cambridge: Harvard University Press, 1994).

36. This is, of course, the radical hermeneutical approach to the human condition, derived from Heidegger's radical phenomenological and hermeneutical moves. See the following for an account of its development and character: John Caputo, *Radical Hermeneutics* (Bloomington: Indiana University Press, 1987); Gerald Bruns, *Heidegger's Estrangements: Language, Truth, and Poetry in the Later Writings* (New Haven: Yale University Press, 1992), and *Hermeneutics Ancient and Modern* (New Haven: Yale University Press, 1992).

37. Villa, *Arendt and Heidegger*, 203.

38. Nancy, *Being-With*, 6.

39. Oxford English Dictionary, s.v. "scandal."

40. See Michael Dillon, "Sovereignty and Governmentality: From the Problematics of the New World Order to the Ethical Problematic of World Order," *Alternatives* 20 (1995).

41. Nancy, *Being-With*, 5.

42. See how David Campbell works this point in relation to territory in "The Deterritorialization of Responsibility," this volume.

43. See, for example, how Thomas Dumm explores this point in relation to Charles Taylor in "Strangers and Liberals," *Political Theory* 22, 1 (February 1994): 167–75.

44. Michael Walzer, *Spheres of Justice: A Defence of Pluralism and Equality* (Oxford: Basil Blackwell, 1983), 51. The difficulties lie, of course, in pluralism and equality—a phenomenological symmetry and asymmetry (to use Derrida's Levinasian gloss on Heidegger)—which radically disrupts Walzer's project. It is precisely that phenomenological symmetry and asymmetry that the refugee brings so forcefully and corporeally to presence.

45. Butler's gloss on Zizek, in *Bodies That Matter*, 191.

46. I work this point out of Nancy's *Being-With*. I am generally indebted to the thought of "freedom" and "being-with" that he has developed in the following: *The Experience of Freedom* (Stanford: Stanford University Press, 1993), *The Birth to Presence* (Stanford: Stanford University Press, 1993), and *The Inoperative Community* (Minneapolis: University of Minnesota Press, 1991).

47. Connolly, *The Ethos of Pluralization*.

48. In respect of the idea of "democracy to come," see Critchley, *The Ethics of Deconstruction*.

CHAPTER FIVE

Suffering, Justice, and the Politics of Becoming

William E. Connolly

Suffering and Ethics

People suffer. We suffer from illness, disease, unemployment, dead-end jobs, bad marriages, the loss of loved ones, social relocation, tyranny, police brutality, street violence, existential anxiety, guilt, envy, resentment, depression, stigmatization, rapid social change, sexual harassment, child abuse, poverty, medical malpractice, alienation, political defeat, tooth-aches, the loss of self-esteem, identity-panic, torture, and fuzzy categories. We organize suffering into categories to help cope with it, but often these categories themselves conceal some forms of suffering, even contribute to them. This latter experience leads some to suspect that suffering is never entirely reducible to any determinate set of categories. To suffer is to bear, endure, or undergo, to submit to something injurious, to become dis-*organized*. Suffering subsists on the underside of agency, mastery, wholeness, joy, and comfort. It is, therefore, ubiquitous.

Severe suffering exceeds every interpretation of it while persistently demanding interpretation. Without suffering, it is unlikely we would have much depth in our philosophies and religions. But with it, life is tough ..., and miserable for many. Does the polycultural character of suffering reveal something about the human condition? And how contestable and culturally specific are the medical, psychological, religious, ethical, therapeutic, sociostructural, economic, and political categories through which suffering is acknowledged and administered today? Is "suffering" a porous universal, whose persistence as a cultural term reveals how conceptually discrete injuries, wounds, and agonies are experientially fungible, crossing and confounding the fragile boundaries we construct between them? Or is it a barren generality, seducing theorists into metaphysical explorations far removed from specific injuries in need of medical or moral or religious or political or therapeutic or military attention? Any response to this question draws upon one or more of the theoretical paradigms already noted. A political theorist might focus on power struggles between disparate professionals over the legitimate definition and treatment of suffering. An evangelist might minister to instances that fit the Christian model. And a physician might medicate theorists and spiritualists burned out by the projects these faiths commend. Is the bottom line, then, that today people go to the doctor when they really need help? Perhaps. But they might pray after getting the treatment. Or file a malpractice suit. Or join a political movement to redesign the health-care system. Sufferers are full of surprises.

Among field contenders for primacy in the domain of suffering, ethical theory has pretty much dropped out of the running. The reason is clear, even if astonishing. Contemporary professional paradigms of ethics, represented fairly well by John Rawls and Jürgen Habermas, have drifted far from the putative object of ethical concern.

Even though professional ethicists have relinquished authority over suffering, *morality*—as a set of cultural interpretations of goodness, obligation, and evil—continues to play a major role in its delineation and treatment. But morality, as played out in this culture, is divided against itself over the interpretation of suffering. Some modes of suffering, say child abuse, are said (by some) to be caused by immoral behavior by others; others, say alcoholism, to be caused by the immorality of the sufferer herself; others, say racism, to be caused by the cultural hegemony of vindictive moral codes; and others yet, say terminal patients who seek to end their own lives because they roll in agony, to be rendered otiose by traditional moral codes. And we disagree within and between ourselves about which instances fall under which categories.

John Caputo, in a fascinating study entitled *Against Ethics,* seeks to cut through the abstractions of contemporary ethical theory. He elevates suffering itself to the center of moral attention. Drop punitive gods. Forget Rawls. Bypass Nietzsche's coldness toward suffering. Avoid entanglement in the coils of Derrida. Pour salt on Foucault's critique of normalization. Be wary of the spiritualism of Immanuel Levinas. Step outside the conflictual world of political partisanship. Concentrate, instead on suffering of the flesh, and on the obligation of those in the vicinity of suffering to respond to it. Let's make obligation, Caputo says, palpable, specific, situational, and guttural. Let's rescue it from theology and philosophy. Let's respond to suffering without mediation by a god, a Greek ideal of beauty, a teleological principle, a veil of ignorance, an overlapping consensus, or a (non)metaphysics of *differance* to govern the response.

Obligation is not commanded on high, nor is it grounded in reason, nor does it filter into life through mystical experience. Caputo, a theologian and philosopher, has gone practical. He still loves the old texts. But obligation, he says, simply happens: "Obligation means the obligation to the other, to one who has been laid low, to victims and outcasts. Obligation means the obligation to reduce and alleviate suffering."[1]

Moral codes grounded in a law of laws, such as the commands of a god or the dictates of a categorical imperative, are too blunt, crude, and closed to respond to suffering equitably. Those grounded in a fictional contract are not much better. Besides, both types purport to ground morality in certitudes that are highly questionable and debatable. People spend so much time debating the certitudes they never get around to suffering. Even moralities built around appreciation of the human as an essentially embodied being tend to slide over suffering. Though they come closer. The thing to do is to move through gods, transcendental commands, principles, contracts, and bodies to the experience of human flesh. "Flesh is soft and vulnerable. It tears, bleeds, swells, bends, burns, starves, grows old, exhausted, numb, ulcerous. . . . Flesh smells."[2] Flesh is the soft, perishable medium in which suffering occurs. "What is suffering if not this very vulnerability of the flesh, this unremitting unbecoming. This liability to suffer every breakdown, reversal and consumption?"[3] If you bind suffering to flesh and flesh to obligation, you both cut through systems that try to ground obligation in some solid finality and render obligation more sensitive to the palpable hunger, sickness, desperation, and helplessness humans often face. Flesh moves you from us to them, without complex argumentation. We are all made of it.

Caputo knows things are not quite that simple. He knows that to reach the flesh it has been necessary to write an entire book entangled in a host of controversial arguments. But, still, he hopes he has built a cantilever upon which a certain amount of moral weight can be placed. He hopes to pull us away from metaphysics and systematic doctrines toward the suffering and obligation that both inspire the constructions of metaphysics and engender its obfuscation. "Flesh fills metaphysics with anxiety."[4] Flesh, first, challenges the systematicity that governs metaphysics. For flesh is vulnerable. It absorbs burdens, blows, injuries, and shocks. It compromises agency. Flesh suffers. But the very vulnerabilities of flesh, second, often prod humans to construct metaphysical systems to elevate them above its softness, smell, and bloodiness. (Caputo does not evince old worries about temptations of the flesh.) Or it prods them to embrace systems that show why limits of the flesh are deserved. But you never escape the flesh, and Caputo counsels you to stay close to it when you let obligation happen.

Can such a recipe be followed? Caputo concedes formally that he reinscribes himself in the world of metaphysics even as he struggles to write himself out of it. For he uses an inherited language.[5] Caputo has read his Derrida. Indeed, he has written books on language. Nonetheless, we can stay close to the experience of suffering, Caputo thinks, if we strive for "metaphysical minimalism." "Minimalism is a metaphysics without a meta-event, a kind of decapitated metaphysics. . . . Minimalism lets events happen, lets them be, lets them go, without imposing grand and overarching schemata upon them, without simplifying them. It has decided to come to terms with intractable plurivocity."[6]

Caputo, I should tell you, professes to love many of the prophets he criticizes. He loves Abraham, Kierkegaard, Nietzsche, Deleuze, and Levinas for starters, partly because he is so indebted to them while diverging from them. Well, I love Caputo. I love his critique of monotheistic and secular moralities alike. I respect his quest to bring suffering back to the center of ethics. I appreciate his sense of the fragility of obligation combined with the insight that attempts to write fragility out by constructing automatic foundations for ethics themselves foster new cruelties. I love much in his sensibility. But, still, Caputo, to focus our attention on suffering and to make obligation simple, has submerged some dilemmas in the ethics of responsiveness.

Caputo's "metaphysical minimalism" is a nonstarter. It contains some admirable ingredients, but it does not succeed in its objective. Rather, Caputo replaces a familiar set of metaphysical doctrines with an alternative that is just as fundamental. And Caputo does not identify anything within his perspective (within the perspective I share up to a point) that might *inspire* the spirit of obligation he pursues. You are either moved or unmoved by the stories Caputo tells. Obligation either "happens" or it does not. And Caputo's "minimalism" compels him to reduce his injunctions to the "I" far too often: "I feel," "I avoid," "I love," "I must." Minimalism reduces Caputo to a Christ figure without transcendental portfolio. Either *he* moves you to read suffering as he does, or nothing happens.

Most significantly, Caputo's metaphysical minimalism impels him to treat devastated groups and helpless individuals as *paradigm* objects of obligation. Sick, homeless, helpless individuals. Peoples laid low by floods, conquest, famine, holocaust. Caputo issues a charity model of obligation, in which virtuous helpers are pulled by the helplessness of the needy: "the power of obligation varies directly with the powerlessness of the one who calls for help, which is the power of powerlessness."[7]

Such situations often occur, and their moral importance is undeniable. But they may not pose the most difficult cases in ethics. Some of the most difficult cases arise when people suffer from injuries imposed by institutionalized identities, principles, and cultural understandings, when those who suffer are not entirely helpless but are defined as threatening, contagious, or dangerous to the self-assurance of these identities, and when the sufferers honor *sources* of ethics inconsonant or disturbing to these constituencies. And this suffering, too, invades the flesh. It engenders fatigue; it makes people perish; it drives them over the edge. To simplify obligation in an era of political pessimism, Caputo has quietly emptied ethics of its political dimension.

The most difficult cases require not an ethics of help for the helpless but a political *ethos of critical engagement* between interdependent, contending constituencies implicated in asymmetrical structures of power. Indeed, some ways of acting upon obligations to the deserving poor or victims of natural disaster provide moral cover for the refusal to cultivate an ethics of engagement with constituencies in more ambiguous, disturbing, *competitive* positions. The most complex ethical issues arise in those ambiguous contexts where suffering is intense and the injuries suffered by some contribute to the sense of self-confidence, wholeness, transcendence, or cultural desert of others. That is, the most pressing, difficult cases of ethics are political in character. They often revolve around what I will call the politics of becoming.

The politics of becoming occurs when a culturally marked constituency, suffering under its current social constitution, strives to reconfigure itself by moving the cultural constellation of identity\difference then in place. In such situations either the condition of the subjugated constituency or the response required to open up a new line of flight is not acknowledged by some of the parties involved. And sometimes by none. Under these circumstances it takes a militant, experimental, and persistent political movement to open up a line of flight from culturally induced suffering. Such a movement, to succeed, must extend *from* those who initiate cultural experiments *to* others who respond sensitively to those experiments even while they disturb their own sense of identity.

I honor, then, the politics of *becoming,* not the politics of realization of an essence or universal condition already known in its basic structure by reasonable people. Indians, slaves, feminists, Jews, homosexuals, and secularists, among others, have participated in the politics of becoming in the last couple of centuries in Euro-American societies. But many citizens who now acknowledge the fruits of these movements, who repudiate the negative marks inscribed upon such constituencies in the past, also forget how the politics of becoming proceeds when it is in motion. They treat retrospective interpretations of the politics of becoming as if these definitions and standards were actually or "implicitly" available to participants when things were in motion. They act as if the initiating constituency either exposed *hypocrisy* in the profession of universal rights by dominant groups or prompted a cultural *dialectic* that fills out the implicit logic of the universal. They reduce the politics of becoming to a social logic.

Caputo is wary of both the model of hypocrisy and the model of dialectical progress. I am with him here. But his minimalist response to these two metaphysics flattens out the modes of suffering he can recognize. Caputo's perspective does appear "minimal" by comparison to the models of a commanding (Christian) god and/or a teleological principle. Measured by these two perspectives, it *lacks* a god and *lacks* reference to a fundamental purpose of being. Lacking these supports Caputo is pressed to give (apparently) simple examples of suffering and to make obligation just "happen."

The two interdependent traditions Caputo resists only appear to exhaust metaphysics if *meta* is (mis)translated as "beyond."[8] For then metaphysics would inform you of what precedes the physical world. Perhaps a god or an intrinsic purpose. But if you construe metaphysics to be any reading of the fundamental character of things, it becomes clear that every positive cultural interpretation is inhabited by a metaphysical dimension. The call to metaphysical minimalism now becomes either a command to conceal the perspective that moves you or a doomed attempt to live, act, judge, and respond without engaging in positive interpretation.[9]

Caputo takes a step in the direction I endorse when he speaks of an "intractable plurivocity" coursing through things. But his drive to minimalism stops him from pursuing this thought. Does he lament the *loss* of a god who could communicate clear commands or draw us closer to the fundamental design of things? His critical reading of Nietzsche suggests this possibility, anyway; for Caputo reduces the thinker who pursued the theme of fundamental plurivocity more fully than anyone preceding him in the West to a visionary of a cold, cruel, world who is indifferent to suffering. Often Caputo simply bypasses the element of joyfulness, abundance, and possibility that Nietzsche locates in the multiplicity of being; and the Nietzschean generosity he does acknowledge is never pure enough to fit the disinterested model of obligation Caputo demands.

My Nietzsche offers a positive metaphysic that breaks with the familiar options of theism, secularism, and metaphysical minimalism. He does so to fend off the "passive nihilism" that so readily accompanies the liquid diet of metaphysical minimalism, to fend off, that is, the cultural enervation that readily accompanies the doomed attempt to live without interpreting life actively. Nietzsche affirms that action is impossible without interpretation, that every particular interpretation invokes a fundamental conception of the world, and that every interpretive perspective remains questionable and contestable. He affirms, that is, life, in its ambiguous conditions of possibility. So Nietzsche interprets actively from within a distinctive reading of the fundaments of things. Here is one formulation of those fundaments, offered by his sidekick Zarathustra, while preaching about "Old and New Tablets":

> When the water is spanned by planks, when bridges and railings leap over the river, verily those are believed who say, "Everything is in flux...."
> But when the winter comes...,then verily, not only the blockheads say, "Does not everything stand still?"
> "At bottom everything stands still" — that is truly a winter doctrine...O my brothers is everything not in flux now? Have not all

railings and bridges fallen into the water? Who could still cling to "good" and "evil"? . . . The thawing wind blows — thus preach in every street my brothers.[10]

Several thoughts mingle in Zarathustra's saying. First, things are mobile at bottom, rather than still or fixed. This experience of the mobility of things has profound, corrosive effects upon winter conceptions of nature, divinity, identity, truth, and ethics that have prevailed in the West.

Second, winter thoughts keep reinstating themselves in ways that treat the cultural ice as if it were frozen all the way down. This drive to find a solid bottom is particularly powerful when suffering is intense or profound. For sufferers often seek relief from the riddle of suffering, and they often find solace when things appear still at the bottom. Suffering readily fosters winter doctrines. But, sometimes, as in the case of Nietzsche, individuals struggle against these pressures to come to terms critically with the existential needs impelling them in this direction. They then struggle to gauge the cruelties and exclusions that regularly accompany the hegemony of winter doctrines.

Third, Zarathustra's perspective is paradoxical and contestable. He can point to multiple disturbances and surprises that disrupt each new winter doctrine; he can provide *pointers* to a mobility of things that exceeds the reach of cognition. But he cannot freeze this contestable experience of flux in truth. Truth cannot be a relation of correspondence for Nietzsche. Truth changes its *place* as well as its meaning in his thought. "Truth," in one of its valences, is those indispensable cultural productions that freeze things (representations of nature, identities, moral codes) temporarily and incompletely. Truth, as solidification, occurs in a "regime of truth," as Foucault would say. On another register — for Nietzsche plays with "truth" — the Nietzschean true *is* the flux out of which solidifications occur in society and nature (for nature is not finished), the surplus and noise that circulate through every solid formation and create possibilities for new becomings. Truth, so rendered, casts off the dimension of final *solidity* so crucial to the correspondence model while retaining the dimension of *fundamentality* also invoked by that model. The true becomes unsusceptible to correspondence. By disaggregating two elements the correspondence model binds together, Nietzsche recovers an alternative orientation to truth. Along *this* dimension, Nietzsche is closer to a-theologies of god(s) as absence, excess, or "nothing" than to secular conceptions of truth as correspondence, coherence, rational consensus, or pragmatic success.

Fourth, Nietzsche and Zarathustra tap into this fugitive and cognitively indirect experience of the protean diversity of life, cultivating *gratitude* for the rich abundance of life. They cultivate gratitude toward the abundance of being that endows life with mobility. They cultivate gratitude both to life and to the excess that provides one of its conditions of possibility. Such a gratitude is "religious" without necessarily being theistic. It finds more intense expression at some times than others. "What is astonishing about the religiosity of the ancient Greeks is the lavish abundance of gratitude that radiates from it. Only a very distinguished type of human being stands in *that* relation to nature and to life. Later, when the rabble came to rule in Greece, *fear* choked out religion and prepared the way for Christianity."[11]

Gratitude for the abundance of life, then, carries acceptance of a contestable conception of being into ethics and politics. But this temperament is not located beyond the play of identities, understandings, and principles. Rather, it is inserted into these media, rendering them more responsive to that which exceeds them, more generous and refined in their engagements with difference. Without the infusion of such gratitude, high-sounding principles will be applied in stingy, punitive ways. A theistic or secular perspective that exudes it can foster ethical generosity while trimming some cognitive fat from its theological or secular diet.

This contestable faith in the abundance of being, this impious, nontheistic reverence for life, can render a postsecular ethic both alert to the fragility of ethics and open to the play of difference in cultural life.[12] These two dispositions support one another. Those inspired by an ethos of generosity participate in the politics of becoming without having to ground their ethic in something solid, fixed, or frozen. Because we can act ethically without being commanded by a god or transcendental imperative to do so, we can also deploy genealogy, deconstruction, and political disturbance to cultivate responsiveness to movements of difference. Our commitment to these activities does not dissolve ethics: it only does so for those who cannot be ethical without solid foundations. We do not have to pretend that obligation just happens either. Acceptance of obligation grows out of a protean care for the world that precedes it. Indeed, the demand for purity in obligation strips it of implication inside those human identities and interests that might mobilize it as an active force. For to retreat to the view that "obligation happens" is to retain the Christian form of obligation as obedience while stripping off the transcendental command that authorizes it.

A postsecular ethic thus situates itself within the discordant experience of the *indispensability and constitutive fragility of ethics*. It renounces the assurance of solid grounds to enable it to explore unnecessary and injurious limits to life supported by the very provision of such assurances. Those who participate in such an ethos cultivate critical generosity to those differences upon which the specification of their own identities depend, in part by responding to those differences outside that are regulated in themselves to enable them to be what they are and in part by recalling that they inhabit a world where the admirable possibilities of being outstrip the time and corporeal capacity of any particular individual or culture to embody them all.

Fifth, the first four themes do not make Nietzsche indifferent toward suffering. They drive him to make a crucial division *within* suffering. He resists pity for those who demand a winter doctrine that redeems the suffering that comes with life or proves how human beings deserve to be punished. For such doctrines express ressentiment. They express persistent resentment against the flesh, pain, limited capacity to know, vulnerability to disorganization, and susceptibility to death that mark the human condition. They thereby resent conditions of possibility for human life itself. This existential resentment infiltrates into stingy moral ideals, conceptions of truth, practices of identity, judgments of normality, and systems of punishment. Every individual and culture struggles with ressentiment, according to Nietzsche. And every generous disposition issues in resentment, anger, or fear on occasion. Indeed, such responses are sometimes appropriate to specific circumstances. But moral dispositions governed by ressentiment regularize war against the diversity of life in the quest to transcendentalize what they already are or pretend to be. Or so my Nietzsche thinks.

Nietzsche resists pity for those who demand a transcendental reason for suffering. Secularists, on this reading, too often join too many theists in placing such demands on being. (There is no doctrinal imperative, recall, that either party *must* do so.) This demand finds expression in the conceptions of truth, reason, justice, and nature they insist upon without being able to prove. Pity for existential suffering too often squashes individuality, distinctiveness, nobility, and difference under the stars of universality, metaphysical necessity, and civilizational regularity. The problem is that the first sort of pity seldom articulates itself exactly as Nietzsche defines it. It often takes cover under rubrics of love, universal principle, desert, freedom, and civilizational necessity. It must be sniffed out before it can be combated.

Moreover, some forms of suffering provide conditions of possibility for admirable achievements. The refinement and maintenance of a mode of individuality, for example, requires considerable work by the self on the self. And its very particularity carries losses with it. "How is freedom measured, in individuals as in nations? By the resistance which has to be overcome, by the effort it costs to stay *aloft*."[13] Every way of being involves considerable work to maintain itself — to stay aloft — and too many individuals and groups both resent this condition of life and take revenge against others who seem not to require *the same combination of regulations and restraints to be what they are*. The key is to work to stop the suffering tied to staying aloft from fueling resentment against external expressions of differences regulated in you that allow you to be what you are.

That being said, it must be emphasized that Nietzsche is not against pity or compassion per se, despite what Caputo and several other commentators suggest. He resists compassion for selective modes of suffering to express it actively for others. As he puts the point: it is "compassion, in other words, against compassion," one type of compassion against another.[14] Nietzsche pits compassion for that suffocated by the normalizing politics of "good and evil" against compassion for existential suffering. The latter compassion must be redirected, and the demand to which it responds must be overcome, if an ethic of generosity in relations of identity\difference is to be cultivated. Nietzsche might have striven to develop more respectful distance from the mode of suffering he finds most offensive and dangerous. But he, like everyone else in *this* respect, is *compelled* to be selective with respect to suffering. His open selectivity challenges concealed principles of selection in other moral perspectives. Is it because his selectivity pits him against powerful currents flowing through sacred and secular moralities in Western societies that representatives of these traditions so often read him to be against compassion and benevolence per se?

There are plenty of ways I dissent from Nietzsche: his cultural aristocraticism, which prizes becoming and plurality among a "noble" (though

often unmonied) few while condemning "the herd" to a cultural dogmatism it is said to be predisposed toward; his (sometimes appealing)
fantasy of residing on the margin of society beyond the reach of organized politics; his tendency (following from the first two themes) to neglect the *politics* of becoming in favor of cultivating individual distinctiveness; his profound ambivalence toward the basis and effects of gender
duality; his periodic delight in petty cruelty against carriers of ressentiment (though I feel some ambivalence here). I do not, then, endorse
numerous themes represented today under the name "Nietzsche," but I
do subscribe to the five stated above. Call them if you wish, *my* "democ-
ratization of Nietzsche." I doubt whether I could enunciate them without drawing considerable sustenance from the work of Nietzsche.[15] And
I suspect that some who *reduce* their Nietzsche to some ugly mixture of
coldness, indifference, and cruelty do so to suppress these themes themselves from ethical discourse, sinking them in filth so as to return ethical
authority to the narrow, formal, stingy options with which they began.

The Politics of Becoming

By the politics of becoming I mean that paradoxical politics by which
new cultural identities are formed out of old energies, injuries, and differences. The politics of becoming emerges out of the energies, suffering, and lines of flight available to culturally defined differences in a particular historical constellation. To the extent it succeeds in placing a
new identity on the cultural field, the politics of becoming changes the
shape and contour of established identities as well. The politics of becoming thus sows disturbance and distress in the souls of those disrupted
by its movement. In a (modern?) world where people are marked and
known through their identities, difference and becoming are ubiquitous.
If each positive identity is organized through the differences it demar-
cates, if difference circulates through it as well as around it, if movement by some of these differences compromises its quest to present itself as natural, transcendent, complete, or self-sufficient, then the politics
of becoming imperils the stability of being through which dominant constituencies are coddled and comforted.[16] The question of ethics emerges
within this complex set of relations. If becoming is as fundamental to
life as being, the question becomes: which sort of suffering is most worthy of responsiveness in which contexts? That which the politics of becoming imposes on the stability of being? Or that which established iden-

tities impose upon the movement of differences to protect their stability? In contemporary American culture the operational answer often precedes the question. Here, frozen codes of morality and normality weigh in heavily on the side of being, stasis, and stability without acknowledging how the moral scales are tipped. And this is probably true more generally as well. To attend to the politics of becoming is to shift the cultural balance between being and becoming without attempting the impossible, self-defeating goal of dissolving solid formations altogether.

The politics of becoming is paradoxical. A new cultural identity emerges out of old injuries and differences. But because there is not an eternal model, it copies as it moves toward new definition, and because it meets resistance from identities counting upon its neediness or marginality to secure themselves, the end result of the politics of becoming is seldom clear at its inception. Indeed, becoming proceeds from inchoate injuries and hopes that may not be crisply defined until a new identity has been forged through which to measure those injuries *retrospectively.*

If and as a stigmatized identity attains a more positive standing, it may be an exaggeration to say that it has arrived at what it truly is at bottom or in essence. No positive identity can be judged final in a world where things are mobile at bottom. Of course, it is also hard *not* to pretend such a final state has been approximated. The presumptions of (at least) European languages press in this direction. So do persistent human interests in regularity of expectation and stability of judgment. But a successful movement of becoming stirs up this cultural field of identities, standards, and procedures; *it thereby alters to some degree the measure by which its previous suffering and the responsibility of others to it are culturally defined.* Moreover, the new movement, if it is not squashed, sets up new intrasubjective and intersubjective differences. It might thereby enable some new positive possibilities by engendering new modes of intrasubjective and intersubjective suffering not yet crystallized as injuries. Perhaps it is wise to assume that admirable modes of being tend to crowd each other out in a world not predesigned to house all together. Perhaps, too, suffering of the flesh is somewhat less variable within and across cultures than the formation of positive identities. These two premonitions inform those who seek to come to terms ethically with the constitutive tension between the powers of being and the energies of becoming.

The politics of becoming is purposive without being teleological. It engages actors who, as they pursue a line of flight, do not remain sufficiently fixed across time to be marked as consistent and masterful agents. Those who initiate the politics of becoming make a difference without knowing quite what they are doing. In this respect they amplify under-appreciated dimensions within human agency in general.

The politics of becoming requires specific conditions of possibility. It flourishes in a culture that incorporates most of its members into the good life it enables, that is already *pluralistic* to a considerable degree, and that has cultivated an ethos of critical responsiveness to new drives to *pluralization*. Here many constituencies appreciate a little more actively the uncertain element of contingency in their own constitution, and this discernment informs their responses to movements by alter-identities to reconstitute the terms of their cultural identification. The responding constituencies recognize that to create space for the politics of becoming they must render themselves available to modification in one way or another. They convert cultural disturbance of what they are into energy to respond reflectively to new lines of flight. If they are pluralists, they appraise each new drive to identity first according to the likelihood that it will support a culture of pluralism in the future.

An ethos of responsiveness to becoming is never entirely reducible to obedience to a preexisting code of morality. Some elements in the existing code itself must be modified if space is to be created for something new to emerge. In a pluralizing culture two interdependent dimensions of ethics are perpetually poised in tension: the *obligation* to abide by the existing moral code and the *cultivation* of an ethos of critical responsiveness to the movement of difference. Without a code, the regularity of judgment deserved and expected by existing constituencies would be lost. But a congealed code also poses dumb, arbitrary barriers to the politics of becoming. This is what Nietzsche means by the "immorality of morality." While a moral code is indispensable to social regulation, judgment, and coordination, it is also too crude, blunt, and blind an authority to carry out these functions sensitively and automatically. An ethos of critical responsiveness, when active, navigates between these interdependent and discordant dimensions of ethical life.

In American life, historical examples of the politics of becoming can be found in antislave movements, feminism, gay/lesbian rights movements, the introduction of secularism, the effort to place "Judeo" in front of the "Christian tradition," the right to die, and so on. But few participants in such movements interpret themselves entirely through the politics of becoming. Many claim to pursue an essence that has been culturally occluded or to fill out a universal set of rights that contain hypocritical exclusions. Yet, some difficulties speak against these essentialist self-interpretations: they often create implacable conflicts between contenders for the title of *the* natural, true, or intrinsic identity; they underplay the work required to cultivate generosity in social relations by pretending the end they pursue is already *implicit* in the culture; they discourage winners of one round from coming to terms actively with the contingency of their own identity, thereby setting the stage for a new round of resistances to the politics of becoming by newly dogmatized identities; and they discourage cultivation of gratitude toward the rich ambiguity of life, a gratitude that sustains responsiveness to the politics of becoming.

There is always a new round in the politics of becoming. For in a world where things are mobile at bottom, Being, as stable essence, never arrives. Let us set these general formulations in the context of a couple of contemporary examples, examples still poised in the uncertain space between obscure suffering and the possible consolidation of something new.

Jan Clausen is a beneficiary of, and participant in, gay and lesbian movements in America. Because of them it became more feasible to establish sensual relations with women without self-hate and without encountering quite as much social stigmatization as heretofore. She knows these collective achievements are partial and precarious. But through them she has developed a critique of "essentialist thinking" and has come to terms more actively with the constructed, conflicted, and sometimes mobile character of sexual identity. While "socially powerful groups have a stake in promoting the illusion of unconflicted identity because maintenance of their power depends on keeping in place a constellation of apparently fixed, 'natural,' immutable social relationships," Clausen joins others in engaging the "resistance to identity which lies at the very heart of psychic life."[17] The community she belonged to until recently believes, for example, that both "heterosexuality" and "homosexuality" are complex organizations of sensual energy rather than cultural fixtures to be graded according to a natural scale of normality and abnormality.

Clausen, though, recently found that this collective knowledge did her little good when her affections shifted from a woman to a man. She faced charges of betrayal and responses of rejection strangely reminiscent of those she had encountered in disturbing the code of heterosexual normality. These responses were understandable, given the beleaguered condition of gay and lesbian communities. Still, they may point to powerful tendencies in most cultural groupings to naturalize what they are; they may suggest how the naturalization of identity functions simultaneously to protect collective bonds, to provide security for certain individuals, and to create hardships for those whose contingent condensation of life and desire does not fit into defined cultural slots.

Clausen's "interesting condition" shows how the politics of becoming at one historical junction readily solidifies into a mode of being at another. For Clausen, alert to a fluidity of desire that may settle for a time and then start moving again, needs a new social movement to modify one she still identifies with to a considerable degree. Clausen's interesting condition enables her to amplify a common, though rather subterranean, experience of ambiguity and resistance within identity. It encourages her, therefore, to become more responsive to alternative sensualities struggling to form themselves within the social matrix. Out of such a series of intersections between old and new participants in the politics of becoming, she can hope for a new cultural coalition to bestow greater ethical attention upon becoming itself. As she puts it, experience "in a particular community of women convinces me that all human connections are risky, fragmentary, and non-ideal"; but participation in coalitions between disparate social constituencies connected by multiple knots of affinity and sympathy also convinces Clausen of the possibility of people combining together "from incredibly different places" from time to time to vindicate the politics of becoming.[18]

Mrs. Lin, a daughter of Chinese intellectuals who died while being abused during the Cultural Revolution in China, is in a more abject situation. Her "symptoms" include headaches, difficulty sleeping, poor appetite, low energy, anxiety, and fantasies of death. They lead to the diagnosis of neurasthenia by Chinese psychiatrists, while they might issue in the diagnosis of depression in the United States.

> For a North American psychiatrist, Mrs. Lin meets the . . . criteria for a major depressive disorder. The Chinese psychiatrists . . . did not deny she was depressed, but they regarded the depression as a manifestation of neurasthenia. . . . Neurasthenia — a syndrome of exhaustion, weakness, and diffuse bodily complaints, believed to be caused by inadequate physical energy in the central nervous system — is an official diagnosis

in China; but it is not a diagnosis in the American Psychiatric Association's latest nosology.[19]

Arthur Kleinman, a medical anthropologist with degrees in medicine and psychiatry as well, doubts that either diagnosis fits the case perfectly.[20] While the first focuses on bodily symptoms and the second on psychological states, neither pays much attention to the complex intersections between social stress, corporeal experience, and professional diagnoses of the symptoms that issue from this combination. And Kleinman's extensive interviews with Mrs. Lin convince him that her situation cannot be "diagnosed" until the stresses, punishments, and dislocations imposed upon her as a cultural dissident are drawn into the diagnosis. If they are included, the prescribed responses to Mrs. Lin's condition will include changes in the system of social stress and surveillance in which her suffering occurs. Psychiatry will become more explicitly engaged in the political context in which it is always already set.

In the United States, too, there is considerable resistance to a cultural broadening of psychiatric perspective. It would require psychiatrists to explore complex relations between social stress and bodily experience, to study how corporealization of cultural experience occurs, to explore general limits to the human body's tolerance of stress, disruption, fixed routine, and so on, and to reflect upon the connections between contemporary practices of medical diagnosis and the professional identities psychiatrists themselves seek to maintain. It would implicate psychiatrists in wider political debates from which the *medicalization* of suffering and illness may now insulate them. Mrs. Lin, and her equivalents in the United States, need a political movement to reconfigure the psychiatric approach to mental disorder. Such a politics of becoming would profit from recent movements in the United States that sharpened awareness of complex interconnections between social stress, human suffering, medical diagnosis, and medical treatment in the domains of race, gender, and sexuality.

Any such movement would be filled with uncertainty and risk, of course. Even Arthur Kleinman shies away from it. His last chapter is not entitled "Social Movements and the Psychiatric Sensibility," but "What Relationship Should Psychiatry Have to Social Science?" The latter is doubtless an important topic. But it stretches the experience of psychiatry while remaining within the bounds of academic interdisciplinarity. Kleinman, I suspect, would be responsive to a new political movement to connect psychiatry, social stress, and corporeal experience, a movement that opened up new investigations in psychiatry by altering the cultural pressures in which it occurs. His subject position, however, makes it difficult to *initiate* such a politics of becoming.

Justice and the Politics of Becoming

The element of paradox in the politics of becoming is that before success, a new movement is typically judged by the terms through which it is currently depreciated, and after success a new identity emerges that exceeds the energies and identifications that called it into being. We are morally primed to expect a new identity to precede our recognition of it; but, given the paradox of becoming, the way in which this moral expectation closes off lines of flight from suffering often turns out retrospectively to be immoral. An ethos of critical responsiveness negotiates these discordant imperatives: it ushers new identities through the barriers that normality and morality pose to becoming. Participants in such an ethos appreciate how something admirable might become out of obscurity or difference. Critical responsiveness is anticipatory, critical, and self-revisionary in character.

Critical responsiveness is *anticipatory,* in that it responds to pressures to become even before they have condensed into a firm, definite identity. It also subjects the politics of becoming to *critical* appraisal, alert to the possibility a new movement might congeal into a fundamentalism that forecloses the future becoming or might force certain constituencies into an abject position. Finally, and most crucially, critical respondents engage in practices of *self-revision* as they respond to the politics of becoming. For example, when heterosexuals endorse diverse sensualities they also acknowledge that heterosexuality is neither firmly grounded in the universality of nature, nor the automatic outcome of normal sensual development. And for whites to challenge established assumptions of racial difference is to come to terms with how "whiteness" has been culturally constructed by aligning diverse skin shades and tones with a set of social privileges, a gender-graded code of parenthood, and middle-class expectations.[21] Critical responsiveness to the claims of difference calls forth a partial and comparative denaturalization of the respondents themselves; it also opens up possible lines of mobility in what you already are. These effects are possible because every effective movement of difference moves the identities through which it has been differentiated. It is thus not surprising that the time in which politics on behalf of the pluralization of identities intensifies is also the time in which counter drives to the fundamentalization of disturbed identities also becomes tempting.

Consider, then, the ambiguous relation the practice of justice bears to the politics of becoming. The politics of becoming repositions selected modes of suffering so that they move from an obscure subsistence or marked identity *below* the register of justice to a visible, unmarked place on it. In a modern world of justice as fairness between *persons,* this means that modes of being consciously or unconsciously shuffled below normal personhood become modified and *translated into the dense operational rubric of personhood itself.* A mode of suffering is thereby moved from below the reach of justice to a place within its purview, and now the language of injury, discrimination, injustice, and oppression can apply more cleanly to it. It is *after* a movement crosses this critical threshold that a mode of suffering becomes unjust.

Thus, the coarse practice of justice regularly poses barriers to the politics of becoming before providing support for it. Failure by some liberal theorists to acknowledge the fundamental ambiguity in the center of justice disables them from registering the importance of an ethos of responsiveness to justice itself. This does not mean that the politics of being (justice, common standards, shared understandings, and so forth) is irrelevant to ethico-political action. It does mean that the "we's" who act together are more pluralized than some traditions recognize and are susceptible to periodic movement through the politics of becoming.

Take John Rawls. Rawls promises to adjudicate between just and unjust claims. He encounters several difficulties in fulfilling this promise, including the inability to decide whether his exclusion of animals, nature, and mentally retarded humans from the scales of justice exposes limits to his theory or the relative unimportance of these issues to the public life of a just society. I will concentrate here, though, on two ways in which the Rawlsian rendering of "persons" engaged in "fair cooperation" poses ill-considered barriers to the politics of becoming.

Rawls now concurs that justice as fairness cannot be derived from the calculations of rational agents. The outcome of rational calculation depends on the premises adopted. Self-interest, for instance, does not serve as a sufficient basis for justice. "What rational agents lack is the particular form of moral *sensibility* (my emphasis) that underlies the desire to engage in fair cooperation as such."[22] What else is needed, then? Well, agents of justice are "reasonable" people. They are willing to accept reciprocal limits. The word "reasonable" may suggest that this sensibility is a sibling of rationality, while it is actually a kissing cousin of traditional theories of virtue.[23] For by what procedure or mode of argument is reasonableness attained? On what logic is it grounded? Rawls says the disposition comes from a fortunate cultural tradition that already embodies it. It is nested, that is, within cultural practices never entirely reducible to a logic or rationality.

Note that Rawlsians are now unable to find the sufficient basis for justice they habitually accuse post-Nietzscheans of lacking. Reasonableness finds its grounds in itself if and when it is already widely shared in a culture. But what does a Rawlsian moralist appeal to when such a tradition is deeply conflictual, or weak, or active in some domains and absent in others? What do Rawlsians appeal to, that is, when the appeal is most needed? Rawls has nothing compelling to say in such cases. This is because, in a way reminiscent of Caputo, Richard Rorty, and Jürgen Habermas, he rules "comprehensive doctrines" out of public discourse to protect the impartiality of justice. But the Rawlsian imperative to silence at such junctures has become a dangerous eccentricity. Since every other contemporary constituency articulates some of its most fundamental presumptions in its public presentations, the eccentric liberalism of John Rawls marginalizes liberals on the most hotly contested issues of the day. Sure, they still claim that unreasonable people explicitly refuse what their conduct in other domains "implicitly" presumes. But, given the slack, uncertainty, and slipperiness within the operational terms of public discourse, there is always room to slip out of such a putative logic of social implication when people are motivated to do so.[24] The moral power of the logic of cultural implication itself grows out of the sensibility it purports to sustain. Rawls himself occasionally recognizes this point, though he does not apply it to this domain. The reasonableness Rawlsian justice requires rests upon movable conventions disconnected from any "comprehensive doctrine" of the human condition.

Post-Nietzschean gratitude for life and its ambiguous conditions of possibility, while not widely thematized today, does speak at exactly the juncture where Rawlsians lapse into silence. Moreover, it challenges all the way down the presumptions of the theistic and secular fundamentalisms Rawls himself resists.[25] For this fundamental perspective anticipates noise, surplus, and inchoate energy coursing over and through every winter doctrine. It draws an ethos of generosity from the cloudy atmosphere in which established conventions and identities are set, rather than resting it on a fictive ground or binding it *entirely* to the existing shape of those conventions themselves. It therefore has resources to draw upon in fighting cultural forces disposed to the moral negation, punishment, or marginalization of differences that disrupt their sense of naturalness or self-assurance. Nor is it pressed to hide ugly forces within contemporary life behind a veil of ignorance to protect the fiction that existing conventions sufficiently sustain the cultural background (the "reasonableness") justice requires. And, of course, the very presumption of irreducible surplus alerts post-Nietzscheans to the insufficiency of justice to itself and, therefore, to the need to cultivate critical responsiveness to the politics of becoming.

The second, most direct way in which Rawls forecloses the politics of becoming follows from his conception of the person. The loss of traditional grounds for "the good" means, Rawls says, that justice must be insulated as much as possible from irresolveable debates over the good. So Rawls seeks a fixed conception of persons appropriate to justice as an internal practice, dependent only on the (supposedly modest) externality of cultural reasonableness. Sure, Rawlsians say a thin conception of the person allows concrete persons to develop rich, individual selves. But the very formality of this permission obscures how dense cultural differentiations and hierarchical rankings of *types* of self (identities) precede and shape the practice of justice. It deflects ethical attention from thick cultural determinations of what is already inside, marginal to, and excluded from personhood *before* justice as fairness appears on the scene. A veil of ignorance thus screens the ethical importance of becoming from the practice of justice.

This way of putting the point exaggerates slightly. Rawls now emphasizes how the fortunate becoming of liberalism out of a historically specific modus vivendi forms an indispensable background to justice as fairness. And this thought about the ethicization of a modus vivendi contains valuable possibilities. *But this is the last historical moment in the politics of becoming his categories allow him to acknowledge.* Rawls wants to freeze the liberal conception of the person today while everything else in and around it undergoes change. The result is to surround justice with a stingier sensibility than Rawls intends. Persons just are,

for Rawls, at least after the modus vivendi of liberalism. "No construc-
tivist view, including Scanlon's, says that the facts that are relevant in
practical reasoning and judgment are constructed, any more than they
say that the conceptions of person and society are constructed."[26] Then
he states the implications of this theme for the injustice of slavery: "In
claiming that slavery is unjust the relevant fact about it is not when it
arose historically, or even whether it is economically efficient, but that
it allows some persons to own others as their property. *That is a fact
about slavery, already there, so to speak* [my emphasis], and independent of the principles of justice. The idea of constructing facts seems
incoherent."[27]

Rawls levels persons to make social facts simple, and he pursues these
two agendas to secure an unequivocal conception of justice. But the most
relevant moral/cultural fact about slavery, to slaveholders and defenders, was that slaves did not count as full persons. They could, therefore,
endorse the Rawlsian formula of fairness to persons while contesting
its application to slaves. If they did so, Rawls would say that they were
simply wrong in this respect: his judgment fits the facts while slaveholders misrepresented them. There is something to this point. But the
way in which Rawls treats this specific, retrospective judgment as if it
revealed a timeless and sufficient paradigm of personhood again obscures
two crucial dimensions in the politics of becoming: 1) the contemporary importance of dense, institutionally embedded discriminations between conditions that cross the threshold of personhood and numerous culturally defined afflictions, inferiorities, liabilities, disorders, and
defects that fall, in one way or another, *below* this threshold, and 2) the
contemporary importance of political performances and enactments in
moving and modifying those dense codes of cultural presumption that
always surround and inhabit us. Thus: Slaves were said by many to be
inhabited by natural inferiorities pushing them below the threshold of
personhood; John Brown, the abolitionist, was widely declared to be a
"monomaniac" (a type, I believe, no longer recognized in the official
nosology of psychiatry) who also fell below that standard in another way;
women were widely held to be equipped for the immediate ethics of
family life but not for the abstract deliberations essential to public life;
atheists were (and still are) said (e.g., by Tocqueville and the America he
registered) to be too materialistic, narcissistic, and selfish to hold public office, though they were persons enough to participate in employ-

ment, commerce, and military liability; "homosexuals" were (are) said to deserve justice as persons *and* to be marked by an objective disorder and/or sin shuffling their sensualities below the reach of justice; "postmodernists" (who now occupy the subject position once reserved for atheists) are sometimes said to be cool, amoral, and antihumanist, lacking the prerequisites to be taken seriously as moral agents; doctors who assist terminally ill patients die were (and often are) defined as murderers because of the generic Christian injunction against taking one's own life; and Rawls himself now treats the mentally retarded as something less than full persons because they cannot participate fully in the practice of "fair cooperation" upon which his scheme of justice rests.

Rawls is superb at acknowledging the justice of newly defined claims and constituencies once the politics of becoming has carried their voices within range of his hearing. And within a period of thirty years or so Rawlsians have acknowledged the claims of Indians, women, and gays *after* a series of social movements began to reshape the complex cultural identifications in which they are set. But Rawls pretends (and his categories presume) that he is *now* in the same position with respect to a large variety of unpoliticized injuries today that he is with respect to constituencies whose cultural identification and institutional standing have been changed through the politics of becoming. And he also acts as if his own identity (as "a person") can remain untouched and unchanged as he responds to new movements of difference.

The point is not to criticize previous "oversights" of Rawlsians, as if *we* have a god's eye view above the fray that they lack. *Such a model of moral criticism would merely reiterate Rawlsian insensitivity to the politics of becoming.* The point, rather, is to press Rawlsians (and others they stand in for) to *cultivate a bivalent ethical sensibility responsive to both the indispensability of justice and the radical insufficiency of justice to itself.* For it is extremely probable that all of us today are unattuned to some modes of suffering and exclusion that will have become ethically important tomorrow after a political movement carries them across the threshold of cultural attentiveness and redefinition. This is so because each effective movement of difference toward a new, legitimate identity breaks a constituent in its previous composition that located it beyond the operational reach of justice by rendering it immoral, inferior, hysterical, unnatural, abnormal, irresponsible, monomaniacal, narcissistic, or sick.

Often enough, of course, such a movement does not succeed; and sometimes it should not. Many conclude that they have good reason to refuse some of its claims, even after the movement opens up previously concealed issues. But this constitutive uncertainty at the center of becoming does not defeat the central point.[28] Rather, it reminds us how ethical uncertainty haunts the politics of being and becoming and how important it is to cultivate an ethos of critical responsiveness never entirely reducible to a fixed moral code. For often enough, obscure pains, objective disorders, low levels of energy, perverse sexualities, basic inferiorities, uncivilized habits, hysterical symptoms, inherent abnormalities, and unreliable moral dispositions become reconfigured through a politics of becoming and critical responsiveness that first exceeds the official reach of justice and then places new dimensions of life on its register. And these effects show justice to be an essentially ambiguous practice, insufficient unto itself. No general concept of the person can resolve that constitutive ambiguity into a sufficient code or set of criteria: it will either (like the Rawlsian model) be too formal to reach deeply enough into the density of culturally constituted identities or (like the communitarian model) too specific to respond to diverse possibilities of being that may turn out to be acceptable or admirable after the politics of becoming brings them into being. It is better to respond to this constitutive ambiguity by cultivating critical responsiveness to the politics of becoming, acknowledging that the practice of justice depends on an ethical reserve it is incapable of subjecting to definitive regulation.

Rawls is pulled by the demand that things be still at bottom. He wants — after the historical becoming of liberalism — persons and the generic facts about them to remain stationary so that liberal justice can be (nearly) sufficient onto itself. One should offer a moment of tribute to those who cling to such a winter doctrine during difficult times. They do honor one important dimension of ethical life in the face of forces that press relentlessly against it. But it is even more important to emphasize how things don't stay still. Any doctrine of liberalism that pretends they do poses barriers to modes of becoming to which it might otherwise be responsive. This drive to stillness is the crucial, secular, Rawlsian sensibility to contest by those who think the politics of becoming never ends. Because Rawls hides his comprehensive doctrine inside a closet in the private realm, the contestation has to proceed through symptomatic readings of the effects the underlying doctrine has on publicly articulated conceptions.

Dialectical Progress and the Politics of Becoming

But isn't it time for a postsecularist, too, to become reasonable? Doesn't the trajectory of change in the shape of western universals reveal a historical dialectic filling the universal out progressively? Doesn't it show, retrospectively, how historically tolerable suffering imposed upon slaves, women, Indians, atheists, and homosexuals was actually unjust, and hence, how an enriched cultural universal draws us ever closer to the universal? If we can't be Rawlsians, can we not at least become neo-Hegelians?

We *can*. It is indeed very difficult not to from time to time — whenever we honor the politics of becoming retrospectively. Rawls, for instance, is a neo-Hegelian with respect to the historical becoming of liberalism. And there *is* an ethical compulsion to treat the latest filling out of persons as the highest standard of personhood. It is just that this viable ethical compulsion soon bumps into a discordant ethical imperative: to pursue practices of genealogy, deconstruction, political disturbance, and the politics of becoming through which contemporary self-satisfied unities are rendered more problematical and more responsive to new movements of difference. Attunement to the politics of becoming, then, engenders a bivalent ethical sensibility in which critical tension is maintained between these two interdependent and dissonant ethical imperatives.

I resist, therefore, the winter satisfaction of dialectical progress without being able either to forgo its imperatives and comforts at some moments or to disprove it definitively.[29] Perhaps every new constellation of cultural identities, even as it relieves palpable modes of suffering, introduces new *artifacts* of identity and difference onto the social register. Perhaps these historically contingent forms carry a series of surprises with them, including modes of suffering exceeding the capacities of this cultural constellation to recognize and respond to it. The publication of these obscure injuries will be entangled in a new round in the politics of becoming. What if a) the energy and suffering of embodied human beings provides a starting point from which becoming and critical responsiveness proceed, *and* b) no intrinsic pattern of identity\

difference on the other side of suffering consolidates being as such? Would it not then be wise to maintain *ethical* tension between being and becoming, even to sanctify becoming so as to counter powerful tendencies normally in place to tilt moral energies in the other direction?[30]

When a dialectical rendering of the politics of becoming suggests that the most recent identities are the most true, natural, or advanced, it discourages proponents from cultivating now that partial, comparative sense of contingency in their own identities out of which responsiveness to new claims of difference might proceed. A dialectician must be poised in front of a final act always about to commence *or a dialectical reading of things cannot be vindicated.* For how could a dialectical reading of things be sustained unless the standard that redeems it is now discernible in vague outline just over the horizon? Contemporary dialecticians, therefore, always proceed as if they were on the cutting edge of the last historical moment. Most have learned just enough from the record of Hegel, Marx, and Fukuyama to refrain from shouting this presumption out, but not enough to fight against obscure injuries it legitimizes today.

If a politician of the dialectic thinks that things have been developing up to *this* penultimate moment on the edge of stasis, the politician of becoming thinks it is critical at this same moment to initiate the politics of becoming in some domain and/or to cultivate critical responsiveness to some forces pressing against existing stabilizations. Moreover, the politician of becoming thinks a generous ethos emerges when a number of constituencies engage actively and comparatively those differences in themselves and others the regulation of which enables them to be what they are. This end, then, forms a regulative *ideal* for the politician of becoming, a complex, final act never entirely susceptible to completion because some of its components are never entirely synchronized with the others at any particular time. It places two politicians of difference fairly close to one another, along one dimension for a moment. If these two types were to converge upon an ambidextrous characterization of the regulative ideal, other differences between them would fade, though they would still debate which *vocabulary* best expressed that convergence and what *balance* between being and becoming must be sought at any particular moment. Such debates remain crucial to the ethics of engagement, as long as the tension between being and becoming persists, enough people care about the constitutive tension between

suffering and the play of cultural possibility, and public discourse remains relatively open.

Notes

1. John Caputo, *Against Ethics* (Bloomington: Indiana University Press, 1993),
145.

2. Ibid., 158.

3. Ibid., 203.

4. Ibid., 200.

5. "We cannot just avoid or simply step outside metaphysics, which would mean
to step outside the logic and ontologic of our grammar and our intellectual habits."
Ibid., 221.

6. Ibid., 222.

7. Ibid., 4.

8. The prefix *meta* "is joined chiefly to verbs and verbal derivatives; the principal notions which it expresses are: sharing; action in common; pursuit or quest;
and, especially, change of place, order, condition, or Nature." (OED)

9. The issues are still more complicated, of course. It is very difficult, some say
impossible, to write and speak a European language without invoking implicitly a
fundamental order or logic that governs everything. Caputo acknowledges this. He
has read his Derrida. But I concur with Nietzsche, Michel Foucault, and Gilles
Deleuze that we do possess some resources within these languages to press a positive alternative forward that is not completely captured by the old doctrines. This
is a debate I will not pursue here.

10. F. Nietzsche, *Thus Spoke Zarathustra*, trans. Walter Kaufmann (New York: Penguin Books, 1978), 200–201.

11. F. Nietzsche, *Beyond Good and Evil*, trans. Marianne Cowan (South Bend,
Ind.: Gateway Editions, 1955), 58.

12. Is "gratitude" the right word here? If so, it has to be reworked so that it is not
governed by the idea that you are always grateful to some agent(s). But every word
Nietzsche tries in this domain has to be reworked to play the role he asks it to play.
Wonder, (nontheistic) reverence, awe, affirmation are other possibilities, equally in
need of reworking. Is it Nietzsche's fault that the language of the Christian/secular
West is often inadequate to his thought? Reworking familiar terms is part of the
ethical project.

13. F. Nietzsche, *Twilight of the Idols*, trans. R. J. Hollingdale (New York: Penguin
Books, 1968), 151–52. I am grateful to comments by Jill Frank, Mort Schoolman,
and George Shulman that have helped me to crystallize this point.

14. Nietzsche, *Beyond Good and Evil*, 151–52.

15. Some themes in the relation of ethics to the politics of becoming cannot be
pursued here. For example, "gratitude" is certainly not a sufficient basis of ethics
on my reading; it is, rather, an element that must flow through established codes,
contracts, identities, interests, and habits of responsiveness if they are to be generous, if care for difference is to find operational expression in them. This essay is a
companion to another that sets forth other elements in this perspective. See Con-

nolly, "Beyond Good and Evil: The Ethical Sensibility of Michel Foucault," *Political Theory* 21, no. 3 (1993): 365–89.

16. William E. Connolly, *Identity\Difference: Democratic Negotiations of Political Paradox* (Ithaca: Cornell University Press, 1991).

17. Jan Clausen, "My Interesting Condition," *Outlook: National Lesbian and Gay Quarterly* (1990), 19.

18. Ibid., 20–21.

19. Arthur Kleinman, *Rethinking Psychiatry: From Cultural Category to Personal Experience* (New York: The Free Press, 1991), 7.

20. The following statement by I. Rosenfield, quoted by Kleinman, makes contact with the Nietzschean conception of nature as unfinished: "There are good biological reasons to question the idea of fixed universal categories. In a broad sense they run counter to the principles of Darwinian theory of evolution. Darwin stressed that populations are collections of unique individuals. In the biological world there is no typical plant.... Qualities we associate with human beings and other animals are abstractions invented by us that miss the nature of biological variation." Ibid., 19.

21. For example, a child of a "colored" mother was automatically defined as black, regardless of skin tone, during the period of slavery in America. This protected the sexual rights of white fathers over slave mothers and exempted them from embarrassment or responsibility for the consequences. This, in turn, supported a double imperative against white women having sex with black men, an injunction still operative to a significant degree; for that combination would visibly compromise the "purity" of the white race. Sons and daughters of mixed parenthood today still bear effects from these two legacies. They are presumed "black," unless a whole set of other social factors override this presumption. "Whiteness" is the absence of that which makes you "black."

22. John Rawls, *Political Liberalism* (New York: Columbia University Press, 1993), 51.

23. For a very thoughtful effort to locate Rawls in the tradition of "virtue theories," see Bonnie Honig, *Political Theory and the Displacement of Politics* (Ithaca: Cornell University Press, 1993).

24. "All this presupposes the fundamental ideas of justice as fairness are present in the public culture, or at least implicit in the history of its main institutions and the traditions of their interpretation." Rawls, *Political Liberalism*, 78. Here is a set of Rawlsian considerations that could be brought to bear against this implicit/explicit logic, but are not: "a) the evidence... bearing on the case is conflicting and complex.... b) Even when we agree fully about the kinds of considerations we may disagree about their weight.... c) To some extent all our concepts... are vague and subject to hard cases.... d) To some extent... the way we assess evidence... is shaped by our total experience, our whole course of life up to now.... e) Often there are different kinds of normative considerations... on both sides of an issue.... f) Finally..., any system of social institutions is limited in the values it can admit so that some selections must be made from the full range of moral and political values that might be realized." Ibid., 56–57. Rawls seems to think these factors enter into general reflections of reasonable persons about fundamental doctrines, but not necessarily or so actively into the practice of justice that they can share while holding a variety of reasonable doctrines. That is what makes the first quote above congruent with the second.

25. I discuss "Fundamentalism in America" from this perspective in William E. Connolly, *The Ethos of Pluralization* (Minneapolis: University of Minnesota Press, 1995). That book, more generally, explores the constitutive tension between pluralism and pluralization in ways that converge with the argument in this essay.

26. Rawls, *Political Liberalism*, 118.

27. Ibid., 122.

28. It actually reinforces the central point. For if you could devise a sufficient *code* in advance to adjudicate between acceptable and unacceptable movements of difference, critical responsiveness would not be required as an ethical counter and supplement to justice. An additional point: in this essay I focus on the relation of "critical responsiveness" to the politics of becoming. I do so because this dimension has been underplayed by both theorists of sufficient justice and defenders of the politics of becoming. But of course agents of *initiation* are extremely crucial to the politics of becoming. You might be on one side of that line in some instances (for example, a woman involved in feminist initiatives) and on the other side on others (for example a white, Christian, heterosexual woman responding to the politics of becoming by blacks, gays/lesbians, and atheists). Often, you will be on both sides to different degrees on the same issue. And so on. The politics of becoming probably has a better chance in a culture where most "subject positions" are multiple, and where most people find themselves on the initiating side in some domains and the responsive side in others. But these are elaborations.

29. I criticize Seyla Benhabib's dialectical interpretation of the politics of becoming in *The Ethos of Pluralization*. It now seems to me that I deemphasized too much there my own ambivalent implication in the model of progression she develops. I like this rendering better than that one.

30. A Heideggerian might resist this distinction between being and becoming on the grounds that difference inhabits Being as such and that the "oblivion of Being" in western history is bound up with the demand to make Being into a solid ground. I concur in this reading, but an important point is underlined by juxtaposing being and becoming in the way this paper does. It focuses attention on the ethical importance of the *politics* of becoming out of the oblivion of Being, an issue which Heidegger, particularly in his late work, shied away from. See Martin Heidegger, *Identity and Difference*, trans. Joan Stambaugh (New York: Harper and Row, 1969).

CHAPTER SIX

Critical Humanism:
Postcolonialism and Postmodern Ethics

Kate Manzo

Savage Scholarship, Moral Fictions

This paper addresses three questions about ethics, postmodern scholarship, and postcolonial political thought. First, do ethical politics require the universalization of moral judgments and codes of conduct? Second, do African critiques of colonialism and nationalism appeal, in Kantian fashion, to an ethically universal humanism? And third, does the "human impulse" displayed in such works render them "not an ally for Western postmodernism but an agonist," as Kwame Anthony Appiah has claimed?[1]

"Philosophical reflections on the ethical" (to borrow a phrase from David Theo Goldberg) have been part of wider relations of power and global modes of oppression. Goldberg has pointed out that "moral discourse has both reflected and refined social relations, centrally defining changed images of social subjectivity across time and space."[2] Of particular importance to this paper is Goldberg's connection of racial hierarchies to "the historically prevailing conception of moral subjectivity." He argues that in the philosophy of Immanuel Kant and others, the colonized "Savage Man" was deemed lacking in moral understanding and incapable of ethical behavior. Kant assumed that "Orientals" were more evolved than "Negroes." This reflected the racial theories of the time and was not an idea original to Kant. But racial theory did condition Kant's philosophical reflections. The "lower" races were not held to the standards of behavior expected of the "higher" ones because of their supposed absence of moral reasoning. At the same time, the ethical principle that all men are created equal did not extend to them. Kant's universal principles of correct conduct applied only to those considered fully human. Kant was for Goldberg "a moral rationalist" who "turned Hume's empiricist endorsement of racial subordination into an *a priori* principle."[3]

It is thus necessary to beware of what Goldberg calls "moral fictions," namely philosophies that "purport to furnish us with an objective and impersonal criterion of morality but in practice do not." He applauds "postmodernist accounts of ethics" that emphasize the "inherently social character" of a prevailing moral order.[4] This begs the question, though, of how a postmodernist account of ethics is different from those not identified as such by their authors. John Hodge, for example, has argued that "an ancient moral concept — the dualism of good and evil" has helped "maintain oppression by making social relationships that are objectively oppressive appear subjectively reasonable both to the oppressors and to the beneficiaries of oppression."[5] For Hodge, "a modern society based on equality without dualism" is preferable to one still permeated (albeit often unconsciously) with ancient political thought.[6] The analysis and conclusion are notably sensitive to the inherently social character of an established good/evil dichotomy. Yet Hodge does not identify himself as postmodernist.

Arguably, a postmodern analysis of ethics is distinguishable from accounts such as Hodge's on one of two principal counts. On the one hand, there is political deconstruction of modern morality. Moral concepts and ethical values are connected not only to dominant power relations but also to modern conceptions of human identity and difference. For example, there is ethical value now in human rights. The founding charter of the United Nations commands universal respect "for human rights and fundamental freedoms for all without distinction as to race, sex, language, or religion." The rights concept "has served as a rallying point for the oppressed and has given pause to oppressors."[7] Yet the 1944 commitment to racial nondiscrimination that underpinned the UN charter guaranteed only "just treatment" for colonized peoples within an International Trusteeship System administered by colonial powers. Liberation from colonial rule did not qualify as a universal human right or fundamental freedom, even though Japan in 1919 and China in 1944 argued for liberation in the moral terms of racial equality and a human right of all races to self-determination.[8]

Goldberg's claim that the global authority enjoyed by rights depends on moral worth attaching to equal and autonomous individuals makes his account postmodern in a way that Hodge's is not. Virtue is described as a classical moral principle, and evil or sin as definitive of medieval Christianity. Autonomy and obligation, Goldberg argues, marked the Enlightenment shift from Christian to secular ethics: "Self-commanding reason, autonomous and egalitarian, but also legislative and rule-making, defines in large part modernity's conception of the self."[9]

The modern self is still to some extent traditional. As Hodge has demonstrated, an "ancient" dualism has persisted into the modern present. What the modern reworking of ethics means, for Goldberg, is not that the self is fully modern, but that struggles over rights are integral to modern politics:

> Rights are in their very formulation relative to their social recognition and institution. In this sense, they are never absolute or universal: rights exist and empower, if at all and even where they claim universality, only on the basis of some socially constructed and civil system already established by a specific process of politics and law... The reformulation of moral space in the twentieth century, in terms of radically atomized and isolated individuals vested with rights on the basis only of their contractual relations, has made conflicts of rights and dispute resolution central to moral and legal (self-) conception.[10]

Colonial power relations have been integral to modern politics as well. Global conflicts over moral concepts and ethical values did not disappear with the formal demise of colonialism or the founding of the United Nations. The UN became an arena where clashing conceptions of morality and ethics are contested. Is there, for example, a universal human right to language? Does there exist, more generally, a human right to cultural identity? Such questions are routinely debated within branches of the UN, where Rodolfo Stavenhagen has noted that "certain traditions and customs in indigenous cultures are considered by outside (mainly Western) observers to be in violation of universal individual human rights."[11]

Human rights are thus open to interpretation and redefinition. But so too is modernity's conception of the human in whom rights are vested. The political "goal of the oppressed" is not necessarily "to create equality of power and rights," as Hodge, for one, has assumed.[12] Citing Frantz Fanon as inspiration, Barney Pityana once said that the Black Consciousness movement in South Africa had "values and standards which are bound to be different from those of the whites . . . I am not aspiring to be equal to a white man but I am determined to establish my worth as a God-created being. I have to assert my *being* as a person." Pityana's friend in Black Consciousness, Steve Biko, once "surprised" Donald Woods by saying that individual liberty was admirable but it was not his main priority. To this Woods replied: "That's a real Third World argument. Surely all other benefits flow from individual liberty."[13]

"The oppressed" have been known to embrace a universal, individual human right to liberty and equality. But they are not a homogeneous mass, and political theorists within those ranks have sometimes shared with postmodern analyses of ethics their second (as well as first) principal feature. That is philosophical reconstruction. A postmodern ethics attempts to reconstitute social relations based in concepts such as justice and freedom by rethinking the moral status of autonomous man.

Like "Savage Man" in the colonial age, those who do not treat certain principles as self-evident are judged lacking in moral understanding and incapable of ethical behavior. Only a "third-world" politics would fail to ground social freedom in individual liberty, for example. But Biko's "quest for a true humanity" called for a reexamination of all accepted concepts, values, and systems. His political philosophy tied liberation from *all* racialized categories (and not just the liberation of black people) to consciousness of colonial power relations in South Africa and elsewhere.[14]

To conceive (with Biko) of identity as an effect of power relations is to invite a redefinition of dominant conceptions of justice and community. David Campbell has suggested that the philosophies of Emmanuel Levinas and Jacques Derrida are both ethical in that sense.[15] Levinas treated his own being as inseparable from "the usurpation of spaces belonging to the other man whom I have already oppressed or starved, or driven out into a third world."[16] That echoes Pityana's insistence that "one has to take account of the years of indoctrination starting from the first encounter of the white colonists with black tribesmen, when whites were set up as a standard."[17] In both cases, identity and difference are interdependent. That is, identity is founded in relationships with others and is not the private property of autonomous human beings.

The *critical humanism* of the title is an umbrella term for reflections on the nature of humanity that theorize what it means, and how it is possible, for interdependent beings to attain dignity, worth, and freedom. Finding that humanism in both Levinas (the "postmodern") and Pityana (the "postcolonial") does not mean that the latter was either a disciple of the former or self-consciously postmodern in attitude. If Pityana was indebted to Western philosophy at all it was indirectly, through a reading of Fanon's engagement with Hegel. As Paul Gilroy has pointed out, "a significant number of intellectuals formed by the black Atlantic have engaged in critical dialogues with [Hegel's] writings."[18]

My response to the opening questions is that common bonds unite seemingly "agonistic" bodies of scholarship, and that a critical humanist attitude is no less ethical than universal principles and codes of conduct. The remainder of the essay attempts to support that position. Part one engages with different meanings of the terms *postcolonial* and *postmodern*, for identifying common bonds depends to some extent on how such concepts are understood.

Identifying of affinities where others have found none depends as well on interpretation of particular texts. The second part of the paper engages with selected works of four "postcolonial" African theorists to show the critical humanism manifest in their writings. For reasons made clearer in part one, the four chosen are two novelists, Bessie Head and Ben Okri, and two writers of nonfiction, Frantz Fanon and Albert Memmi.

The Postcolonial and the Postmodern

> Far from being a celebration of the nation, then, the novels of the second stage — the postcolonial stage — are novels of delegitimation: rejecting the Western imperium, it is true, but also rejecting the nationalist project of the postcolonial national bourgeoisie. And, so it seems to me, the basis for that project of delegitimation is very much not the postmodernist one: rather, it is grounded in an appeal to an ethical universal . . . in an appeal to a certain simple respect for human suffering, a fundamental revolt against the endless misery of the last thirty years.[19]

Appiah's *In My Father's House* is a reflection on "Africa in the philosophy of culture" by a sympathetic critic of postmodern scholarship. His argument for a recovery of humanism within postmodernism depends on a double separation. As the above quote indicates, Appiah separates novels critical of nationalism from an earlier political fiction. The "first generation of modern African novels" is classified as nativist and nationalist. Its distinguishing feature is "the imaginative recreation of a com-

mon cultural past that is crafted into a shared tradition by the writer."
Liberation from colonialism is sought in political sovereignty and (after formal independence) in the cultural restoration of native man and
precolonial society. This fiction is likened more to the literary nationalism of early modern Europe than to the projects of delegitimation undertaken by Yambo Ouologuem and others.[20] In Appiah's terms, Bessie
Head and Ben Okri qualify as postcolonial writers.

The more contestable separation is of postcolonial literature from
postmodern theory. Here the contrast is not between nationalism and
its discontents, but between universalism and relativism. After mention-
ing "the Kantian injunction to universalize our moral judgements," Appiah suggests that "we do not need the full apparatus of Kantian ethics
to require that morality be constrained by reason."[21] Yet the valued *humanism* is supposedly a synonym for "the ethical universal." The ethics
of the postcolonial novel are opposed to a postmodernism defined as
"irreducibly plural, with every perspective essentially contestable from
other perspectives." According to Appiah, "Ouologuem is hardly likely
to make common cause with a relativism that might allow that the
horrifying new-old Africa of exploitation is to be understood — legitimated — in its own local terms."[22]

Appiah's postcolonial/postmodern dichotomy depends on the particular meanings attached to two key terms, namely humanism and postmodernism. There is no need to "recover within postmodernism the
postcolonial writers' humanism" if the two genres of scholarship already
share the critical humanism mentioned previously.[23] What Appiah's association of postmodernism with relativism implies is that "postmodern ethics" is a contradiction in terms. Only Kantian ethics accommo-
dates "concern for human suffering," and a critical humanism that is
relativist by default does not qualify as humanism at all.

Appiah's understanding of postmodernism may be common but it is
not universal. Postmodernism as an intellectual movement has also been
linked, not to relativism but to a critical attitude and cultural consciousness. In analyzing "the cultural logic of late capitalism," for example,
Fredric Jameson writes that "it is safest to grasp the concept of the postmodern as an attempt to think the present historically in an age that has
forgotten how to think historically in the first place."[24] For Robert Young,
"postmodernism can best be defined as European culture's awareness that
it is no longer the unquestioned and dominant centre of the world."[25]

Given different definitions of the same concept (and to defend the notion of a postmodern ethics), it is important to explain what is meant here by "postmodern." In a reflection on Kant entitled "What Is Enlightenment?" Michel Foucault wonders "whether we may not envisage modernity rather as an attitude than as a period of history." If modernity is an attitude, one that "ever since its formation, has found itself struggling with attitudes of 'countermodernity,'" then so too is postmodernity.[26] The postmodern is a countermodernist attitude, or "white" consciousness, emergent with the globalization of capital and the decolonization of European empire.

A postmodern attitude is composed of three complementary components. The first is exemplified by Foucault's histories of sexuality, madness, and discipline and punishment.[27] Postmodernism posits that no element of humanity — even seemingly natural phenomena like sexual orientations and desires — can be unaffected by power or incapable of change. Identity is an effect of power, which is a social relationship and not a commodity. To study relations of domination and resistance is to analyze their production of the identities of all concerned.[28]

Second, while "modernity is often characterized in terms of consciousness of the discontinuity of time: a break with tradition, a feeling of novelty, of vertigo in the face of the passing moment," postmodernity is not willing to "'heroize' the present."[29] A postmodern attitude to time is summed up by Derrida when he says that "we must thus be suspicious of *both* repetitive memory *and* the completely other of the absolutely new."[30] The past and the future are always within the present, not behind or ahead of it.

Derrida noted in a reflection on contemporary Europe that the most egregious abuses of human beings have been conducted in the name of a revolutionary new man (for example, modern man or postcolonial man) who promises complete transcendence of tradition. He also noted that when the present form of something is treated as natural and its historical production forgotten, "one can be sure that one is beginning to be deceived, indeed beginning to deceive the other."[31] Promises of a revolutionary time and place beyond history are not to be believed, for such promises are destined to be broken.[32]

Derrida's discussion of what he calls *logocentrism* displays the third postmodern attitude: toward the binary oppositions indicative of modern attitudes about identity and difference.[33] Logocentrism is a predisposition for dichotomies such as white/black, colonizer/colonized, or human/animal. Logocentrism treats the familiar as natural and difference as self-evident, often saturating both categories of a dichotomy with moral judgments about good and evil. Biko's insistence that the black South African man "rejects himself precisely because he attaches the meaning white to all that is good, in other words he equates good with white," was a critique of the modern attitude that treats black as an inferior aberration from an accepted white norm.[34]

Simply inverting the conventional distinction, for example by insisting that truth and meaning reside with good black people instead of bad whites, was *not* Biko's response to the political problem he identified. Logocentrism is not challenged by treating each category as autonomous, and looking in one of them for an original source of goodness, humanity, and knowledge. A critical attitude attempts, as Jameson said, to "think the present historically" by asking, for example (as Biko did), how the white/black dichotomy came to be produced in the first place.

One pitfall of the term *postcolonialism* is the possible suggestion that colonialism has been transcended completely with formal political independence.[35] But Homi Bhabha has suggested that "if the jargon of our times — postmodernity, postcoloniality, postfeminism — has any meaning at all, it does not lie in the popular use of the 'post' to indicate sequentiality." For Bhabha, "the postcolonial condition" is one of desire: "The voyeuristic desire for the fixity of sexual difference and the fetishistic desire for racist stereotypes."[36] This recalls Appiah, for whom the postcolonial is a condition as well as a stage: "Postcoloniality has, also, I think, become a condition of pessimism."[37]

For Bhabha, though, postcolonialism is more than just a condition. "Postcoloniality" is a perspective on continuity: a "salutary reminder of the persistent 'neo-colonial' relations within the 'new' world order and the multinational division of labour." Beyond that is "postcolonial critique," a mode of inquiry that bears witness to those hybrid "cultures of a postcolonial *contra-modernity*" that challenge nationalist conceptions of history and community.[38] This recalls Edward Said on "the role of the postcolonial intellectual," which is "to clarify and expand upon experiences of colonialism which continue into the present."[39] Just as important, Bhabha's definitions of postcolonialism recall the treatments of change, continuity, colonialism, and nationalism in the African writings reviewed in the following section.

With the above understandings of postmodernism and postcolonialism in mind, the paper turns now to an effort to connect international relations to postcolonial theory.[40] Like Appiah's reading of African literature, Phillip Darby and A. J. Paolini do not find in "postcolonial discourse" a single voice or approach fully compatible with postmodernism. What they call an "overtly deconstructionist stance" indebted to Derrida is associated only with a recent movement led by Said, Bhabha, and Gayatri Spivak (the name of Henry Louis Gates Jr. could be added as well).[41] A movement critical of binary oppositions such as colonizer/colonized highlights heterogeneity, marginality, and hybridity. Postmodernism apparently "pervades this third movement of postcolonialism."[42]

Nationalist efforts to recover an authentic native identity or voice (Appiah's first-generation novels) are supposedly more typical of the second movement within postcolonialism. This is said to be a psychoanalytic perspective featuring a "Manichean, self-versus-other frame of reference, which characterizes the colonizer-colonized relationship very much in terms of polar opposites." Its exemplars are identified as Albert Memmi, Octavio Mannoni, and Frantz Fanon.[43]

The following section challenges the boundaries erected by Appiah, Darby, and Paolini. To that end it analyzes key themes in works by Frantz Fanon and Albert Memmi (Darby and Paolini's nationalist movement of postcolonialism) and in novels by Bessie Head and Ben Okri (Appiah's postcolonial fiction). Fanon and Memmi do not cite Foucault or Derrida, while Head and Okri certainly revolt against human suffering and misery. As challengers to existing divisions, therefore, these four are by no means as obvious as someone like V. Y. Mudimbe, an African philosopher, novelist, and Foucault admirer who revolts against human suffering while exploring questions of subjectivity.[44] Appiah, indeed, recognizes Mudimbe's work for its potential (if not actual) capacity to bridge the postcolonial and the postmodern.[45]

The African writers analyzed were chosen because they are *not* as obvious as Mudimbe. They illustrate that the direct influence of Derrida and Foucault on "third movement" postcolonial intellectuals is but one point of connection between the postcolonial and the postmodern. Also important is a shared attitude toward critical analysis, and a common endeavor that Young describes as a "widespread attempt to decolonize the forms of European thought."[46]

As I understand not only postmodernism but also Fanon and Memmi, the second movement of postcolonialism has more affinities with postmodernism (including the postmodernism of its own successor) than Darby and Paolini have suggested. The influence of Fanon as well as Derrida on some leaders of the third movement needs to be remembered, and not only because it complicates distinctions between movements two and three.[47] It is important not to fall into the trap of what Mudimbe has called "epistemological ethnocentrism; namely, the belief that scientifically there is nothing to be learned from 'them' unless it is already 'ours' or comes from 'us.' "[48]

Fanon called the triple dichotomies of good/evil, beauty/ugliness, and white/black a "manicheism delirium," so it is difficult to see how the label *Manichean* (my preferred term would be *logocentric*) applies to him.[49] Memmi's analysis is not Manichean either, because the colonizer-colonized relationship is analyzed for its creation of multiple identities (including hybrid ones like Memmi's own) and is not about the interaction of autonomous human beings. As for Head and Okri, they are not merely humanists in Appiah's (Kantian) terms because they do more than call for respect of Africans suffering under colonialism and nationalism both. Okri's text displays a markedly postmodern attitude toward time, and Head's reflects a "third movement" concern for heterogeneity, marginality, and hybridity.

There are differences among the four writers chosen, but all four offer important illustrations of a critical humanist ethics not dependent on universalized moral judgments or commands. That is, each shows how human identities and forms of suffering have been manufactured in relations of power, and all seek liberation (albeit in dissimilar ways) from closed communities defined by race.

The Effects of Power

Madness and Sexuality

> We have a full docket on you. Your mother was insane. If you're not careful you'll get insane just like your mother. Your mother was a white woman. They had to lock her up, as she was having a child by the stable boy, who was a native.[50]

The question of what constitutes madness is woven throughout Bessie Head's autobiographical novel, *A Question of Power*. Both Elizabeth (the heroine) and her mother are confined at times to mental hospitals. Both experiences are connected to race relations in South Africa. The mother was supposedly insane to have an affair with a black man, while racial hatred in South Africa was for Elizabeth "like living with permanent nervous tension."[51]

The action of the novel takes place in newly independent Botswana, Head's country of exile from South Africa.[52] Apparently, "a lot of refugees have nervous breakdowns."[53] An expatriate schoolteacher named Eugene claims that "South Africans usually suffered from some form of mental aberration."[54] But South Africa is not the only site of madness in the text. The old "world of the Pharaohs," supposedly analogous, in some ways, to contemporary Africa, is described as "insane."[55] A Danish development worker named Camilla — a representative of Western development efforts more generally — is described as "half-mad."[56] As for the African continent, the "social defect" of "witchcraft practices" is said to render its victims "stark, raving mad."[57]

Head's linkage of individual neuroses to relations of power is reminiscent of Fanon, particularly of *Black Skin, White Masks*. There Fanon describes black inferiority as a form of alienation, and as a mental ailment or neurosis. He speaks the language of psychoanalysis and psychopathology. But Fanon takes issue (for example in chapter four) with those who treat an inferiority complex produced in colonial relations of power as an autonomous "syndrome." Even the unconscious world of dreams, Fanon argues, must be situated in its "proper time" and "proper place."[58]

Mental suffering by colonized peoples is said to take the form of a desire to "turn white or disappear," to change racial identity through "lactification."[59] The association of whiteness with complete humanity is for Fanon socially produced, through comics and other stories that use Negroes and Indians to represent evil.[60] Of his typical psychoanalytic patient, Fanon argues: "If he is overwhelmed to such a degree by the wish to be white, it is because he lives in a society that makes his inferiority complex possible, in a society that derives its stability from the perpetuation of this complex, in a society that proclaims the superiority of one race; to the identical degree to which that society creates difficulties for him, he will find himself thrust into a neurotic situation."[61]

Neurosis is reflected in daily practices such as language use, in the desire to speak authentic French and not a hybrid dialect. The "Antilles

Negro who goes home from France" often "returns radically changed" and speaking a different language.[62] By listening for a moment or two, family and friends will know whether "a European has got off the ship."[63]

Another indication of how colonialism creates identity is the racial distinctions that colonized peoples draw among themselves:

> Some ten years ago I was astonished to learn that the North Africans despised men of color... The Frenchman does not like the Jew, who does not like the Arab, who does not like the Negro... The Arab is told: "If you are poor, it is because the Jew has bled you and taken everything from you." The Jew is told: "You are not of the same class as the Arab because you are really white and because you have Einstein and Bergson." The Negro is told: "You are the best soldiers in the French Empire; the Arabs think they are better than you, but they are wrong."[64]

Like Jean-Paul Sartre, Fanon insists that anti-Semitism creates the Jew and Negrophobia the Negro; neither category is naturally given or morally neutral.[65] He states that "the Negro symbolizes the biological danger; the Jew, the intellectual danger."[66] Yet despite being "separated by the sexual question," the Jew and the Negro are said to "have one point in common. Both of us stand for evil."[67]

If Jew and Negro are an effect of power relations that include conceptions of moral worth rooted in a good/evil dichotomy, so too are black and white. For Fanon, racial mythology is reproduced in colonial situations but it is not founded there. He traces it instead to a "collective unconscious" socially produced in Europe; "the sum of prejudices, myths, collective attitudes of a given group."[68]

Whatever his purpose in the colonies, "in Europe the Negro has one function: that of symbolizing the lower emotions, the baser inclinations, the dark side of the soul."[69] Through the projection of unconscious impulses and desires onto an encountered black world, "the European had tried to repudiate this uncivilized self" and absolve "every civilized and civilizing country of sin."[70] Fanon writes that "the Negro is not. Any more than the white man."[71] The constructed image of the Negro works to produce a mythical white man without sin, and reflects the alienation of European man from his physical self. Fanon describes the European as also a victim, "the victim of his unconscious."[72]

Fanon demonstrates in Black Skin, White Masks how racial identities condition sexuality. He argues that "if one wants to understand the racial situation psycho-analytically, not from a universal viewpoint but as it is experienced by individual consciousnesses, considerable importance must be given to sexual phenomena."[73] Of particular concern is what happens when the colonized African is "turned into a penis" and transformed into a racialized object called Negro.[74]

Fanon suggests that the objectification of black African men affects the sexual fantasies and desires of four groups of people. First, the African man, who treats sexual intercourse with European women as "a ritual of initiation into 'authentic' manhood."[75] There is also the woman of color, for whom "it is always essential to avoid falling into the pit of niggerhood."[76] While black women seek whiteness in relations with white men, white women (the third group) "invariably view the Negro as the keeper of the impalpable gate that opens into the realm of orgies, of bacchanals, of delirious sexual sensations." Sexual intercourse apparently "destroys all these beliefs."[77] But the sexual fantasies or rape nightmares of white women are experienced by the last group as well: white men. "The Negrophobic man," according to Fanon, "is a repressed homosexual."[78]

Sexuality is another key theme of *A Question of Power*. As a South African exile in Botswana, Elizabeth is dehumanized twice. First in apartheid South Africa, "a country where people were not people at all" and where she "lived the back-breaking life of all black people."[79] Dehumanization is a function of racial classification, for "in South Africa she had been rigidly classified Colored . . . they were races, not people.[80]

Elizabeth is dehumanized again under African nationalism, a mode of political exclusion compared in the novel to apartheid, Black Power, and Hitler's national socialism.[81] While in Botswana, "mentally, the normal and the abnormal blended completely in Elizabeth's mind."[82] Madness and sanity combine in Elizabeth's dreams, where she is subjected to the psychosexual tortures of a character named Dan. There is a real person called Dan, just as there is a living equivalent of Sello, another man who figures prominently in Elizabeth's nightmares. They are African nationalists who wear dark glasses and Western suits as markers of their identities.[83]

The sexual debauchery of the dreamed Dan is a reflection of two African social defects. These are "the African man's loose, carefree sexuality" and "a form of cruelty, really spite, that seems to have its origins in witchcraft practices."[84] In the context of post-independence Botswana, debauchery and torture symbolize African nationalism and its cults of personality. The mythical Sello is a dual figure, both good (when he appears as a monk) and evil (when he wears a brown suit). He seems to represent an Africa struggling for liberation from the twin forces of black nationalism and witchcraft.[85]

The power-maniac is one who "never saw people, humanity, compassion, tenderness . . . what did they gain, the power people, while they lived off other people's souls like vultures?"[86] Those who aspire to be God bring death to the souls of others, like Elizabeth,[87] but they kill their own souls as well.[88] Absolute or corrupted power thrives on narrowness and exclusion — "power people need small, narrow, shut-in worlds" — and on cults of personality.[89] Described early in the novel as Elizabeth's "own hell" and as one who "understood the mechanics of power,"[90] Dan is the principal symbol of power in the novel. He operates at times in concert with a "wild-eyed Medusa." She is the "surface reality" of Africa who wants to expel those, like Elizabeth, who have been constructed as different.[91]

The phantom Dan uses his sexuality to denigrate Elizabeth even as he claims to love her. A broken record turns in Elizabeth's head: "Dog, filth, the Africans will eat you to death."[92] Dan constructs Elizabeth as alien, a nationalist exclusion productive of her mental suffering and breakdown.[93] Consistent with Darby and Paolini's "third movement" of postcolonialism, power is exercised through racial classification and disavowal of hybridity, as when Elizabeth is denigrated as a "half-breed."[94] Racial hierarchy is described as a "nightmare" and racial oppression as "agony."[95]

For all her torture and suffering, Elizabeth admits to being attracted to Dan's "extreme masculinity."[96] His manhood is contrasted to an effeminate homosexuality characteristic (in the novel) of Colored men in South Africa. But reminiscent of Fanon, neither sexual orientation nor behavior is rendered independent of relations of power. An unnamed African in the novel gives "the most reasonable explanation" for Colored transvestism when he says: "How can a man be a man when he is called boy? I can barely retain my own manhood."[97]

Time and Memory

Famine (rather than malnutrition) and war (especially civil war or "tribal" conflict) are among the most tenacious images of decolonized Africa in media coverage of the continent. The "starvation" motif stems from the 1967 Biafra revolt from Nigeria, when swollen-bellied children were brought to the attention of the world. The "warfare" theme dates from 1960, when political violence and unrest followed the decolonization of the Belgian Congo (later Zaire, and now the Democratic Republic of Congo).

To accept that "too much of the reporting of Africa has been conditioned by a view of its people as an eternally miserable smudge of blackness stretching across the decades, from the Congo in the Sixties to Rwanda in the Nineties," is not to deny that suffering and misery have been perpetrated by nationalist rulers.[98] A revolt against man-made starvation and warfare is what Appiah expects from an ethical, postcolonial novel.

Ben Okri's *The Famished Road* is certainly a novel of postcolonial delegitimation, but its critique of broken promises and nationalist betrayals does more than appeal to an ethical universal. Through the allegorical use of its characters (in particular of Azaro, the "spirit-child" narrator), the novel tells of the birth of a decolonized nation-state. Like the biblical time of Genesis, this was "the earliest days of creation."[99] Azaro "realized that new forces were being born to match the demands of the age."[100] Not only birth, but *rebirth* of the nation through blood and sacrifice is a major theme: "Ours too was an abiku nation, a spirit-child nation, one that keeps being reborn and after each birth comes blood and betrayals, and the child of our will refuses to stay till we have made propitious sacrifice and displayed our serious intent to bear the weight of a unique destiny."[101]

Written by a Nigerian expatriate, the novel is somewhat reminiscent of Kwame Nkrumah of Ghana's "Motion of Destiny." In a bid for independence in 1953, Nkrumah recalled the birth and rebirth of his own nation, over time and in different guises.[102] The incorporation by Okri of figures from the spirit world into human life also recalls Nkrumah's claim that "ghosts" are "a very real part of tribal society."[103] But unlike Nkrumah, Okri does not equate political sovereignty with the end of history, or treat independence as a revolutionary time when native people fully "regain their ancient heritage."[104]

This is not a new beginning but the "second wave of our transformation;" not the end of time but the start of another historical cycle.[105] The novel at the outset speaks of "great cycles of time."[106] Such causes of suffering as violence, oppression, madness, inhumanity, patriarchy, and poverty are said to keep recurring, in part because of "the great curse

of forgetfulness."[107] Petty warlords are "the madmen of our history" rein-
carnated.[108] Events are restaged, seemingly without recollection. Azaro's
father throws two parties, he launches a boxing career twice, and there
are two political rallies.

Politicians are associated only with false promises and extortion. Con-
temptuous of the poor, they resort to thuggery, violence, and intimida-
tion to win votes. When the Party of the Rich holds the first political
rally, impoverished hecklers are silenced with a combination of "abun-
dant promises... future visions of extravagant prosperity" and an immediate offer of free milk. "The crowd poured after the [Party] van as
if in a holy crusade," whereupon henchmen threw "pennies and silver
pieces in the air" to divert attention and enable a getaway. A local photographer captured all on film.[109] The milk, it transpires, was poisoned.

At the onset of the second rally, Azaro comments on his neighbors'
amnesia: "The political season started up anew... I thought people would
remember how the very same party had poisoned them with bad milk
and had unleashed their rage upon our nights. But people had forgotten, and those who hadn't merely shrugged and said that it was all such
a long time ago, that things were too complicated for such memories,
and besides the party had new leaders."[110]

Azaro is an allegory for the decolonized nation-state. An early homecoming party (after Azaro has been held against his will) represents the
hoped-for establishment of an independent homeland: "I had brought
with me a new hope. They too [the women] became reasons for staying on this earth, to sometimes taste the joys of homecoming."[111] Initially at least the return is joyful: "In that room, in our new home, I was
happy because I could smell the warm presences and the tender energies of my parents everywhere."[112] Waiting for the party are the poor of
the community, whose "faces were bright with aroused appetites. There
wasn't a single throat that didn't betray the best hopes for a feast of abun-
dant cooking in which all anticipation would be fully rewarded."[113]

The idea that this is a time of revolutionary expectations, a "new era
that promised Independence," is captured through references to time
stood-still.[114] Azaro says that "we were in the divide between past and
future"; that "time did not move at all"; and that "time moved slower
than the hot air."[115] But in a rapidly disappearing forest that foretells of
capitalist development, Azaro glimpses "another reality, a strange world,
a path which had completed its transition into a road."[116] Azaro's pres-

ent is not a modern one, for it contains within it the old and the new and the past and the future.

Azaro's impoverished neighbors understand that "the world is turning upside down."[117] And like him, they soon realize that nationalism will not deliver on its promises. Even before elections to decide between the Party of the Rich and the Party of the Poor, it is evident that the promised "ecstasies of a secret homeland" will not be realized.[118] An herbalist's lament that "they are destroying Africa!" seems aimed at the new rulers of African states.[119] The late appearance of a family of mutilated beggars — described by Azaro's father as "once a great people" — seems to foretell of Africa's nationalist destiny.[120]

Both Parties make false promises, so betrayal is not the monopoly of the Party of the Rich. The foreignness of politicians and thus a neocolonial subtheme is suggested by their "talking in strange languages" and in "alien tongues."[121] Power is exercised by those who dispense money and patronage; who demand sacrifice; who poison the people; and who create myths and illusions. These, apparently, are the postcolonial national bourgeoisie. But oppression is also associated with militarism and patriarchy: "The thugs whipped themselves into future eras. They whipped themselves into future military passions. They thrashed the women and the children alike."[122] Yet another agent of suffering is the local landlord, whose "face glistened with the smile of the powerful."[123]

The new rulers of Africa cannot lead the people out of "a world drowning in poverty."[124] This conclusion is suggested not only in explicit references to politics and politicians, but also in symbolic representations in the text. Africa's politicians are represented in three different ways, beginning with Black Tyger and Madame Koto. The transformation of Azaro's homecoming joy into fear and disillusionment is produced by the growing hunger and violence of his father, the allegorical "founding father" of the country, who recreates himself as a boxer named Black Tyger. When Madame Koto joins the Party of the Rich, she is rewarded with electricity and a new car. As she gains in influence, Madame Koto's stomach becomes immense. Power is represented as a hunger that can never be satisfied, hence the prominent motif of food and eating in the novel.

The unreality and betrayal of formal politics is also reflected in the analogy of politicians to spirits who masquerade as humans.[125] Appearances are not what they seem; those who dance to the music of ascendant power are inhuman. In the novel, politicians double not only as spirits but also as rats. The vermin under the cupboard who devour the family food are like the "bad politicians and imperialists and rich people" who "eat up property."[126] The rats are poisoned eventually by the photographer. His capacity to expose lies makes him dangerous, and he has to flee temporarily. Upon return the photographer brings rat poison and "ghosts and memories."[127] Since the poisoned rats symbolize corrupt politicians, the photographer seems to represent an antidote to the repetitive suffering caused by political amnesia.

This is a novel of delegitimation, certainly. Women characters are particularly exploited and victimized, even if they have greater knowledge of politics than the men. Misery is attributed more to patriarchy and neocolonialism than to popular ignorance and superstition (which are suggested as well). Okri's fiction is an example of the type of literary politics that Appiah considers at odds with postmodernism.

Yet Okri neither absolves the sufferers of responsibility for a situation they have contributed to by forgetfulness, nor demands the eradication of nationalism and neocolonialism in the name of an ethically universal humanism. Reminiscent of Derrida's suspicion of both repetitive memory and the totally new, Okri suggests that hunger "for great transformations" is part of Africa's problem.[128] The road of life "cannot be finished" except by death.[129] But it can remain open: "A road that is open is never hungry."[130]

The Manufacture of Identity

Despite its title, Albert Memmi's *The Colonizer and the Colonized* is not a story of two autonomous polar opposites, characterized by goodness on one side and evil on the other. The theme of Memmi's book is colonial identity: what it is and how it is created. Consistent with Foucault's understanding of power as productive, Memmi states that "the colonial situation manufactures colonialists, just as it manufactures the colonized."[131]

The identities of all concerned are treated as the interdependent effects of relationships and are not independently given. This postmodern conception of the self is clear in the following passage: "The colonialist's existence is so closely aligned with that of the colonized that he will never be able to overcome the argument which states that misfortune is good for something. With all his power he must disown the colonized while their existence is indispensable to his own . . . He will persist in degrading them, using the darkest colors to depict them. If need be, he will act to devalue them, annihilate them. But he can never escape from this circle."[132]

Memmi argues that "the bond between colonizer and colonized is thus destructive and creative. It destroys and re-creates the two partners of colonization into colonizer and colonized."[133] Despite the reference to "two partners," a distinction is made early in the book between three identities on one side of the divide: colonial, colonizer, and colonialist. According to Memmi, "a colonial is a European living in a colony but having no privileges." Such a person exists in theory only.[134] A European who rejects colonialism is a colonizer; an apologist for empire is a colonialist.

A colonizer has two choices. He (they seem to be all men) can leave the colony and thereby resume his former identity as a European. Or he can become a "turncoat" and throw in his lot with the colonized. The obstacles to the second path — the one that Memmi describes as "moral heroism" — are threefold.[135] First, there is the colonizer's enjoyment of privilege, which would have to be relinquished. Second, there is the cultural difference of the colonized people, a revulsion of their food, music, and lifestyles produced by racist thought and reinforced by "the little strains of daily life."[136] And third, there are the significant tensions that divide the "abstract universality" of the one side from the methods and objectives (terrorism and national liberation, respectively) of the other.[137]

Unable to identify fully with either colonized peoples or colonialists, the colonizer, for Memmi, is doomed to political ineffectiveness. The best way to "put an end to his contradiction and uneasiness" is to get sent home to Europe.[138]

The European without guilt is a colonialist, an active participant in perpetuating the status quo. Supposedly conscious of inequality and injustice, the colonialist longs for "the disappearance of the usurped" even if that means his own self-destruction.[139] The situation of the colonialist must always, therefore, be paradoxical. To participate in oppression is to know oneself an oppressor, and yet to wish for the disappearance of the downtrodden is to will the death of one's own self.

In echo of Levinas, Memmi suggests that the colonialist cannot fail to connect his own existence to that of "the other man" whom he has helped to oppress when he asks: "How long could he fail to see the misery of the colonized and the relation of that misery to his own comfort?"[140] Self-consciousness and awareness of interdependence apparently "leads to a veritable ideal reconstruction of the two protagonists of the colonial drama."[141] But like Fanon's categories of white, Negro, and Jew, the terms *colonialist* and *colonized* are not true descriptions of autonomous people, but social categories manufactured in relations of power.

Memmi speaks of identities as "images" and "portraits." Confronted continually with the portrait of colonized man as an "animal or an object," the colonized eventually adopts the dehumanizing identity as his own: " 'Is he partially right?' he mutters. 'Are we not a little guilty after all? Lazy, because we have so many idlers? Timid, because we let ourselves be oppressed?' Willfully created and spread by the colonizer, this mythical and degrading portrait ends up by being accepted and lived with to a certain extent by the colonized. It thus acquires a certain amount of reality and contributes to the true portrait of the colonized."[142]

For Memmi as for Fanon, the colonial situation is legitimated through the circulation of dichotomous categories such as white/black, good/evil, colonizer/colonized. But these combine in different ways to create the identities of the people who actually live through the colonial experience. It has already been shown that the category of colonizer contains three different identities. On the other side (or in between), Memmi finds four groups of people: "resident aliens," such as Italian and Maltese citizens in Tunisia; candidates for racial assimilation, the majority of them Jewish; the recently assimilated, such as the Corsicans in Tunisia and the Spaniards in Algeria; and collaborators among the colonized.[143]

As a Tunisian Jew, Memmi was a hybrid combination of two categories. He cast further doubt on the comprehensiveness of his own classification scheme when he described himself as "a native in a colonial country, a Jew in an anti-Semitic universe, an African in a world dominated by Europe."[144] He suggests in the preface to his best-known work that he knows both "partners" well from being positioned in-between. As Sartre said of Memmi, he was "neither" colonizer nor colonized and yet he was "both."[145]

The question now is how Memmi's political thought (along with Fanon's and Head's, which does this more than Okri's) combines analyses of power with strategies for attaining human dignity, worth, and freedom.

Liberations

Freedom as Self-Recovery

For persons like himself, Memmi weighs the option of liberation through either racial assimilation or colonial revolt. The former strategy is Fanon's "turn white or disappear." Although Memmi does not say so, metamorphosis into a colonizer is actually a form of revolt—against assumptions of permanent racial difference in the colonial situation. Memmi speaks from personal experience (his wife was a blue-eyed Frenchwoman named Marie) when he describes interracial marriage as "the extreme expression of this audacious leap."[146]

The problem with individual assimilation as a strategy of liberation, for Memmi, is that it leaves colonial power relations untouched. If colonizer and colonized are "dynamically meshed one with another" then "it is useless to hope to act upon one or the other without affecting that relationship, and therefore, colonization." Although assimilation has its attractions, Memmi insists that "a collective drama will never be settled through individual solutions." Widespread revolt is the better option, indeed "the only way out of the colonial situation."[147]

In terms of Appiah's nativist/nationalist stage of African political thought (Darby and Paolini's second movement of postcolonialism), Memmi is nationalist if that means treating "a national and ethnic form of liberation" struggle as inevitable.[148] But the decolonized nation-state is *not* Memmi's ultimate political objective, which is why he is a postcolonial theorist in Appiah's terms as well as in Darby and Paolini's. Complete liberation is said to require freedom from the very conditions of struggle that made exit from colonialism possible. "A nationalist," says Memmi, "must conquer himself and be free in relation to that nation . . . But it is indispensable that he have a free choice and not that he exist only through his nation."[149]

Memmi's attitude to liberation is neither nationalist, nor (just as important) logocentric. The replacement of a negative myth with a positive one, whereby "suddenly, exactly to the reverse of the colonialist accusation, the colonized, his culture, his country, everything that belongs to him, everything he represents, become perfectly positive elements," may be understandable. But the mere inversion of moral judgments (whereby everything bad is recast as good, and vice versa) is no substitute for a more fundamental change in attitude toward conventional distinctions. As long as "the colonized continues to think, feel and live against and, therefore, in relation to the colonizer and colonization," Memmi suggests that he will suffer "from the pangs of bad faith" and take comfort only from "the intoxication of fury and violence."[150]

What Memmi calls "complete liberation" requires the demolition of *all* received identities, not just a reconception of the existing self as morally worthy. This is apparent in the concluding chapter, where he argues as follows: "To live, the colonized needs to do away with colonization. To become a man, he must do away with the colonized being that he has become. If the European must annihilate the colonizer within himself, the colonized must rise above his colonized being. The liquidation of colonization is nothing but a prelude to complete liberation, to self-recovery."[151]

Self-recovery means that the "former colonized will have become a man like any other."[152] The once-colonized person will not be fully human and free unless he ceases to define himself through invented categories. Human freedom, for Memmi, requires the decolonization of identity.

Freedom as Self-Scrutiny

> By calling on humanity, on the belief in dignity, on love, on charity, it would be easy to prove, or to win the admission, that the black is the equal of the white. But my purpose is quite different: What I want to do is to help the black man to free himself of the arsenal of complexes that has been developed by the colonial environment... For not only must the black man be black; he must be black in relation to the white man.[153]

Memmi's assessment of the inevitability of anticolonial violence is found as well in Fanon's *The Wretched of the Earth*, written in 1961. The need to counter violence with violence is the theme of this work, which takes the liberation struggle beyond the colonial relationship and into the realm of the Cold War, the postcolonial national bourgeoisie, and the dependence on foreign capital.[154] Reflecting active involvement with the Algerian resistance, the text engages issues not addressed by Fanon the practicing psychiatrist. Although it is important, I will leave a thorough assessment of that later scholarship to others. For it is in the earlier *Black Skin, White Masks* that Fanon's critical humanism is as apparent as "an existential humanism that is as banal as it is beatific."[155]

Fanon (like Pityana after him) placed little stock in calls for racial equality. He argued that the black man is not to be declared equal but set free, and that freedom requires "nothing short of the liberation of the man of color from himself."[156] As with Memmi, there is no unquestioned acceptance of conventional distinctions between Negro and white or colonized and colonizer; nor is there a mere inversion of moral judgments. Fanon did not insist, for example, that the Negro become master in Africa instead of the white man. He states that "when there are no longer slaves, there are no longer masters."[157]

Freedom, for Fanon, requires political consciousness and collective struggle: "What emerges then is the need for combined action on the individual and on the group. As a psychoanalyst, I should help my patient to become *conscious* and abandon his attempts at a hallucinatory whitening, but also to act in the direction of a change in the social structure."[158]

Fanon's black consciousness embraced Afrocentric education: "The establishment of children's magazines especially for Negroes, the creation of songs for Negro children, and ultimately, the publication of history texts especially for them."[159] Yet *Black Skin, White Masks* did not seek freedom in recovering a precolonial identity and common cultural past: "Let us be clearly understood. I am convinced that it would be of the greatest interest to be able to have contact with a Negro literature or architecture of the third century before Christ. I should be very happy to know that a correspondence had flourished between some Negro philosopher and Plato. But I can absolutely not see how this fact would change anything in the lives of the eight-year-old children who labor in the cane fields of Martinique or Guadeloupe."[160]

Instead of attempts to recover the past, Fanon wants "the effort to recapture the self and to scrutinize the self" so that "men will be able to create the ideal conditions of existence for a human world."[161] Only then, for Fanon, can former master and slave walk "hand in hand" together.[162]

Freedom through Love

In Head's *A Question of Power*, the personal liberation of Elizabeth from her mental tortures is inseparable from that of Sello the monk (the goodness of Africa), even as he warns her to retain her mental independence. Elizabeth's capacity to flourish in Botswana, like the Cape Gooseberry imported from South Africa, requires the unleashing of "African realism," a philosophy that is both humanist and African.[163] It entails an inclusive black power rooted in suffering and humility.[164] But sanity and freedom are ultimately tied more to deracialized love than to a solidarity based in racial difference or collective suffering.[165] This emphasis on love of Africa and all of its people as the basis for community distinguishes Head from both Memmi and Fanon.

In the Batswana society that becomes the independent state of Botswana, Elizabeth is finally liberated from mental suffering (her "soul-death") by her own struggles and by the love of an American friend named Tom.[166] The political problem of the novel, however, is African nationalism and not the Batswana people. The village where Elizabeth resides is actually a challenge to nationalist efforts to create homogeneous nation-states, because it is neither uniformly xenophobic, nor the home of "natives" only. Despite efforts by Dan and others, the village remains open (like Okri's "famished road" as well as Head's individual characters) to boundary crossings and self-redefinition.

The village is an African space that brings local people like Elizabeth's friend Kenosi together with settlers and visitors from elsewhere. The latter are represented (apart from Elizabeth herself) by a group of Danish development workers including the "half-mad" Camilla, by the schoolteacher Eugene and other refugees from South Africa, and by the American Tom. As well as being Elizabeth's friend, Tom is an advocate of "rapid economic development."[167]

The resultant community is not indicative of a revolutionary time and place beyond human struggle and hardship, for it is riddled with oddities and tensions. "How strange was the network of human relationships at the Motabeng Secondary project!" comments Elizabeth of the agricultural project where she works.[168] But the genuine efforts in the village to "establish the brotherhood of man"[169] are the "African realist" counterpoint to the evils inflicted by Dan, Medusa, and Sello of the brown suit. A local community with open boundaries, mutual responsibility, love of Africa, and no will to racial classification is the political key to human dignity, worth, and freedom.[170]

The Time and Place of Postmodernism

This paper has analyzed theories of power, identity, and liberation in four exemplary postcolonial texts. Its purpose was to reveal in these texts critical humanist affinities with postmodernism — as I understand it — where others have found only tensions or an absence of connection.

Two important points should be made by way of conclusion. First, the intention was not to suggest that the four authors reviewed here were or are "overtly deconstructionist" in the same way as Said, Spivak, Bhabha, or Gates. Young may be correct to suggest that "the relation of the enlightenment, its grand projects and universal truth-claims, to the history of European colonialism" has been "the special interest of the French."[171] But it does not follow that African or other "third world" political thought with more than a passing resemblance to contemporary French philosophy is merely derivative of it. Nor does it follow that the inverse is necessarily true; that if Fanon and others have theorized the identity of the self as an effect of power relations then postmodernism is derivative and novel only for its "jargon."

Echoing Fanon, it is important to situate self-consciously postmodern thought in its "proper time" and "proper place." The historical context of postmodernism is the time of decolonization and the globalization of capital, not post-1968 France. And its intellectual place is within a tradition of critical efforts to decolonize European thought and political practice.

The second important point concerns the nature of ethical politics. As the above discussion has shown, postcolonial theorists have not offered a single path to freedom; liberations are plural. But the absence of a Kantian injunction to universalize either judgments of power or assessments of change does not render scholarship morally savage. Human suffering, as Bessie Head's novel so poignantly shows, has operated through racial classification, inventions of racial "types," and constructions of inferiority. To deconstruct and try to think beyond racial/colonial categories is a moral and political project.

Notes

1. Kwame Anthony Appiah, *In My Father's House: Africa in the Philosophy of Culture* (New York: Oxford University Press, 1992), 155.

2. David Theo Goldberg, "Modernity, Race, and Morality," *Cultural Critique* (spring 1993): 197.

3. Ibid., 212–13.

4. Ibid., 222.

5. John L. Hodge, "Equality: Beyond Dualism and Oppression," in David Theo Goldberg, ed., *Anatomy of Racism* (Minneapolis: University of Minnesota Press, 1990), 96.

6. Ibid., 105.

7. Goldberg, "Modernity, Race, and Morality," 220.

8. See, in general, Paul Gordon Lauren, *Power and Prejudice: The Politics and Diplomacy of Racial Discrimination* (Boulder, Colo., and London: Westview Press, 1988).

9. Goldberg, "Modernity, Race, and Morality," 213.

10. Ibid., 220.

11. Rodolfo Stavenhagen, "Indigenous Peoples, the State and the UN System: Claims, Issues and Proposals," *The Thatched Patio* 2 (May 1989): 16.

12. Hodge, "Equality: Beyond Dualism and Oppression," 103.

13. Both quotes are from Donald Woods, *Biko* (New York and London: Paddington Press Ltd., 1978), 34, 107.

14. See, for example, "Black Consciousness and the Quest for a True Humanity," in Steve Biko, *I Write What I Like* (London: Heinemann, 1978), 87–98. On Black Consciousness philosophy more generally, see Kate Manzo, "Black Consciousness and the Quest for a Counter-Modernist Development," in Jonathan Crush, ed., *Power of Development* (New York and London: Routledge, 1995), 228–52.

15. See, for example, David Campbell, "The Deterritorialization of Responsibility: Levinas, Derrida, and Ethics after the End of Philosophy," this volume.

16. Quoted in ibid.

17. Quoted in Woods, *Biko*, 34.

18. Paul Gilroy, *The Black Atlantic: Modernity and Double Consciousness* (Cambridge: Harvard University Press, 1993), 54.

19. Appiah, *In My Father's House*, 152.

20. Ibid., 149–50.

21. Ibid., 18–19.

22. Ibid., 155, 143, 152.

23. Ibid., 155.

24. Fredric Jameson, *Postmodernism: or, The Cultural Logic of Late Capitalism* (Durham: Duke University Press, 1991), ix.

25. Robert Young, *White Mythologies: Writing History and the West* (London: Routledge, 1990), 19.

26. Michel Foucault, "What Is Enlightenment?" in Paul Rabinow, ed., *The Foucault Reader* (New York: Pantheon, 1984), 39.

27. Michel Foucault, *History of Sexuality* (New York: Pantheon, 1987), *Madness and Civilization: A History of Insanity in the Age of Reason* (London: Tavistock, 1967), *Discipline and Punish: The Birth of the Prison* (New York: Vintage Books, 1979).

28. See, for example, Kathryn A. Manzo, *Domination, Resistance, and Social Change in South Africa: The Local Effects of Global Power* (New York: Praeger, 1992).

29. Foucault, "What Is Enlightenment?" 39–40.

30. Jacques Derrida, *The Other Heading: Reflections on Today's Europe* (Bloomington: Indiana University Press, 1992), 19.

31. Ibid., 81.

32. Once an admirer of the Iranian revolution, Foucault had apparently concluded before publication of his most influential works that the spirit of revolution so favored by French intellectuals is inevitably undemocratic — a recipe for, and not an antidote to, human suffering and oppression. This point was made in a television documentary written and produced by philosopher Bernard-Henri Levy.

Entitled "The Spirit of Freedom," the four-part series was aired by the Australian Special Broadcasting Service (SBS) in January 1995.

33. See, for example, Jacques Derrida, *Writing and Difference* (London: Routledge and Kegan Paul, 1978).

34. Quoted in Woods, *Biko*, 124.

35. On other pitfalls see Anne McClintock, "The Angel of Progress: Pitfalls of the Term 'Postcolonialism,'" *Social Text* 31/32 (1992): 84–98.

36. Homi Bhabha, *The Location of Culture* (London and New York: Routledge, 1994), 4, 53.

37. Appiah, *In My Father's House*, 155.

38. Bhabha, *The Location of Culture*, 5–6.

39. Edward Said, "Intellectuals in the Postcolonial World," *Salmagundi* 70/71 (spring/summer 1986): 44–81.

40. Phillip Darby and A. J. Paolini, "Bridging International Relations and Postcolonialism," *Alternatives* 19, 3 (summer 1994): 371–72.

41. A collection of essays edited by Gates (one that includes works by Said, Spivak, Bhabha, Derrida, and Appiah) displays the influence of Derrida in its title. See Henry Louis Gates Jr., ed., *"Race," Writing, and Difference* (Chicago: University of Chicago Press, 1985).

42. Darby and Paolini, "Bridging International Relations and Postcolonialism," 378.

43. Ibid., 376–77.

44. See, for example, V. Y. Mudimbe, *The Invention of Africa: Gnosis, Philosophy, and the Order of Knowledge* (Bloomington: Indiana University Press, 1988); *The Rift*, trans. Marjolyn de Jager (Minneapolis: University of Minnesota Press, 1993); and his personal memories of Foucault in "Saint Paul-Michel Foucault," *Transition* 57, 122–27.

45. Appiah, *In My Father's House*, 155.

46. Young, *White Mythologies*, 19.

47. See Bhabha's chapter, "Interrogating Identity: Frantz Fanon and the Postcolonial Imperative," in *The Location of Culture*; and Gates's "Critical Fanonism," *Critical Inquiry* 17 (1991): 457–70.

48. Mudimbe, *The Invention of Africa*, 15.

49. Frantz Fanon, *Black Skin, White Masks* (New York: Grove Press, 1967), 183.

50. From Bessie Head, *A Question of Power* (Portsmouth, N.H.: Heinemann, 1974), 16.

51. Ibid., 19.

52. Head was arguably an anthropologist as well as a novelist. See also her nonfictional account of Botswana's *Serowe: Village of the Rain Wind* (London: Heinemann, 1981).

53. Head, *A Question of Power*, 52.

54. Ibid., 58.

55. Ibid., 41.

56. Ibid., 73–82.

57. Ibid., 137.

58. Fanon, *Black Skin, White Masks*, 104.

59. Ibid., 100, 47.

60. Ibid., 146.

61. Ibid., 100.
62. Ibid., 19.
63. Ibid., 37.
64. Ibid., 102–3.
65. Ibid., 93.
66. Ibid., 165.
67. Ibid., 180.
68. Ibid., 188.
69. Ibid., 190.
70. Ibid., 189–90.
71. Ibid., 231.
72. Ibid., 175.
73. Ibid., 160.
74. Ibid., 170.
75. Ibid., 72.
76. Ibid., 47.
77. Ibid., 177.
78. Ibid., 156.
79. Head, *A Question of Power*, 17, 19.
80. Ibid., 44.
81. Ibid., 46, 132.
82. Ibid., 15.
83. Ibid., 104.
84. Ibid., 137.
85. Ibid., 40, 21.
86. Ibid., 19.
87. Ibid., 87.
88. Ibid., 36, 40.
89. Ibid., 38, 40.
90. Ibid., 12–13.
91. Ibid., 38, 44, 64.
92. Ibid., 45.
93. Ibid., 159, 183.
94. Ibid., 104.
95. Ibid., 46, 53.
96. Ibid., 105.
97. Ibid., 45.
98. Fergal Keane, "Spiritual Damage," *The Guardian*, 27 October 1995.
99. Ben Okri, *The Famished Road* (London: Jonathan Cape, 1991), 342.
100. Ibid., 496.
101. Ibid., 494.
102. Kwame Nkrumah, *Ghana: The Autobiography of Kwame Nkrumah* (New York: International Publishers, 1971), 189–207.
103. Ibid., 9.
104. Ibid., 190.
105. Okri, *The Famished Road*, 448.
106. Ibid., 6.
107. Ibid., 330.

108. Ibid., 192–93.
109. Ibid., chapter five of book two.
110. Ibid., 387.
111. Ibid., 28.
112. Ibid., 33.
113. Ibid., 41.
114. Ibid., 455.
115. Ibid., 220, 269–70.
116. Ibid., 241.
117. Ibid., 167.
118. Ibid., 307.
119. Ibid., 382.
120. Ibid., 444.
121. Ibid., 174, 256.
122. Ibid., 451.
123. Ibid., 123.
124. Ibid., 308.
125. Ibid., 107, 111, 136.
126. Ibid., 233.
127. Ibid., 362.
128. Ibid., 180.
129. Ibid., 329.
130. Ibid., 497.
131. Albert Memmi, *The Colonizer and the Colonized,* 2nd ed. (Boston: Beacon Press, 1991), 56.
132. Ibid., 54.
133. Ibid., 89.
134. Ibid., 10.
135. Ibid., 23.
136. Ibid., 25.
137. Ibid., 26–30.
138. Ibid., 44.
139. Ibid., 53–54.
140. Ibid., 7.
141. Ibid., 55.
142. Ibid., 87–88.
143. Ibid., 13.
144. Ibid., 161.
145. Ibid., xxi.
146. Ibid., 121.
147. Ibid., 126–27.
148. Ibid., 39.
149. Ibid., 152.
150. Ibid., 138–39.
151. Ibid., 151.
152. Ibid., 153.
153. Fanon, *Black Skin, White Masks,* 30, 110.
154. Frantz Fanon, *The Wretched of the Earth* (New York: Grove Press, 1961).

155. Bhabha, *The Location of Culture*, 61.
156. Fanon, *Black Skin, White Masks*, 8–9.
157. Ibid., 219.
158. Ibid., 100.
159. Ibid., 148.
160. Ibid., 230.
161. Ibid., 231.
162. Ibid., 222.
163. Head, *A Question of Power*, 66.
164. Ibid., 134–35.
165. Ibid., 11–13, 54, 202.
166. Ibid., 188.
167. Ibid., 132.
168. Ibid., 80.
169. Ibid., 158.
170. Ibid., 203.
171. Young, *White Mythologies*, 9.

CHAPTER SEVEN

Ruth, the Model Emigré: Mourning and the Symbolic Politics of Immigration

Bonnie Honig

> And we Americans are the peculiar, chosen people — the Israelites of our time.[1]

Immigrants are one of the chief dangers against which Americans are trying to defend their home country these days. And yet, immigrants or foreigners have at other times provided some of the energy that has helped shape the character of the United States. How should we think about this ambivalence?

Some suggest that today's immigrants are less welcome and perceived to be more dangerous to the unity of the republic because they tend not to be white.[2] There is some truth to that. But it should also be noted that ethnics now thought of as white were not so identified when their grandparents first came to the United States as immigrants. Irish immigrants, southern Italians, and others were thought of as black.[3]

It is also said that the human capital of contemporary immigrants is lower than that of their predecessors. Recent arrivals tend to be less educated and less wealthy than those who entered the United States prior to the loosened 1965 Immigration Reform and Control Act.[4] Others stress the self-selection of immigrants: those who make the journey tend to be the boldest, most resourceful members of their communities.[5] Ample data support all sides of the human capital debate and so far there is no resolution in sight. That may say something about the inadequacy of the data or about the politics of its collectors and interpreters. Or it may say something about the power of the symbolic politics at work here: Would concerns about immigration simply disappear if it could be shown conclusively—as some claim it has been—that (for example) immigrants put more into the economy than they take out? Or that they tend to assimilate into the dominant culture by the third generation of residence in the United States, rather than form separatist enclaves in perpetuity?

Rational arguments about the costs and benefits of foreigners fail to settle (though they may inform) the politics of immigration because the issue has as much to do with identity as with interests.[6] Periodic politicizations of immigration are often occasioned by tensions in the economic or political order, but they are also always symptoms of a perpetual public anxiety about national identity and unity. The felt need (never wholly satisfied) for national identity frames the way regimes treat foreigners and gives rise to vastly different stories about them. Contemporary American newspapers are filled with both anxious reports of foreigners fragmenting domestic institutions and approving reviews of immigrant memoirs celebrating "hybridity," a non-assimilative, hyphenated, bilingual, and bicultural identity. This ambivalence about foreigners stems from the regime's determination to recuperate foreignness for a national project and not just from the nature of the immigrants or ethnics in question.

The political and cultural demand for a shared identity can be the ground of democracy (as Rousseau thought) or it can generate demands for social unity that are, particularly in multicultural settings, in tension with liberal democratic principles. In this essay, I explore the role of foreigners in fostering and hindering the development of shared identity and institutions. I argue that democratic principles are best realized at this moment in a commitment to a *politically engaged, democratic cosmopolitanism* in which the will to national unity or identity is attenuated and democratic actors have room to seek out political, cultural, and other forms of not just identity-based affiliation at the subnational, national, and international registers. Increasingly, democratic practice exceeds the states it seems to presuppose; democracy's demos is dispersed.

I approach these issues using the biblical Book of Ruth, a text deployed by Cynthia Ozick and Julia Kristeva in some recent reflections about identity, immigration, nationalism, and cosmopolitanism. I develop my account of cosmopolitanism by way of a critique of Kristeva's version of that ideal and by producing a new reading of Ruth that emerges out of an engagement with Ozick's and Kristeva's readings of that text. Like Ozick and Kristeva, I see Ruth as a generative, potentially very powerful source of new ethics and dispositions. My aim, then, is not to read Ruth in a contextualist fashion, but to intervene and partic-ipate in *contemporary redeployments* of the Book of Ruth as part of a symbolic politics of immigration.

Ruth

The Book of Ruth begins with a flashback. A man named Elimelech, his wife Naomi, and their two sons leave Bethlehem to escape famine. They move to Moab, having heard that Moab is flourishing while Beth-lehem suffers. The move to Moab is controversial. Elimelech has aban-doned his community in a time of need and, worse yet, has gone to live in Moab, the home of the historical enemies of the Israelites. This for-bidden move, and the famine that occasions it, suggest that the Israelites have fallen away from their fundamental moral principles.

The Moabites are lacking virtue as well, but theirs is no temporary corruption. They denied water to the Israelites as they wandered in the desert from Egypt to the Promised Land, and when the Israelites camped at Beth Peor, some Moabite women tried to seduce the Israelite men into illicit relations and idol worship. For this, Deuteronomy's prohibi-tion against intermarrying with Moabites is uncompromising: "None of the Moabites' descendants, even in the tenth generation, shall ever be admitted into the congregation of the Lord" (23:4).

Elimelech dies soon after settling in Moab. His sons marry two Moabite women but these men also die within ten years, leaving be-hind three childless widows, Naomi and her Moabite daughters-in-law, Ruth and Orpah. Naomi hears the famine in Bethlehem is over and de-cides to return home. Her daughters-in-law accompany her initially, but she soon tells them to "Turn back, each of you to her mother's house" in Moab (1:8). They refuse, Naomi insists, and finally Orpah, weeping, agrees to return to Moab, but Ruth remains. And when Naomi tells her again to leave ("See, your sister-in-law has returned to her people and her gods; return after your sister-in-law" [1:15]), Ruth responds poignantly:

> Whither thou goest, I will go
> Whither thou lodgest, I will lodge
> Thy people shall be my people
> Thy god shall be my god
> Whither thou diest, I will die, and there I will be buried. (1:16–17)

Naomi says nothing in response but she stops protesting and Ruth accompanies her on her journey.

In Bethlehem, Naomi is welcomed back by the women of the community. She announces her losses and declares her name changed from Naomi (which means "pleasant") to Mara (which means "bitter") (1:20). Naomi and Ruth establish a joint household. Ruth supports them by harvesting the remnants left in the field of a man named Boaz, who, as it turns out, is a relative of Naomi. Having heard of Ruth's remarkable loyalty to Naomi, Boaz welcomes Ruth to his field and sends her home with extra grain.

But Naomi and Ruth conspire together to achieve a more certain protection. Ruth seeks out (and perhaps seduces) Boaz one night on the threshing-room floor and calls on him to extend his protection to her through marriage while also redeeming a piece of land that was left to Naomi by Elimelech. Boaz notes that there is another male relative who has prior right or obligation to redeem the land, but he promises to do what he can for Ruth. He goes the next morning to find the next of kin and convenes a meeting of the town elders to resolve the question of Elimelech's land. The next of kin's interest in redeeming the land dwindles when he hears that Boaz intends to marry Ruth. Knowing that if they have a son, the child could claim the redeemed land as his own inheritance without recompense, the next of kin offers his option/obligation to Boaz.[7]

Boaz and Ruth marry and have a son who is given to Naomi to nurse. The women's community celebrates, proclaims the child Naomi's son and protector in old age; pays Ruth the highest compliment, declaring her to be of more value to Naomi than seven sons; and names the child Obed. Ruth never speaks again and she is, of course, absent from the Book of Ruth's closing patrilineal genealogy, which ends with David, later the King of Israel. Ruth's precarious position in the Israelite order is stabilized by a marriage and birth that provide the founding energy for a new monarchic regime. In turn, Ruth's migration seems to be the vehicle for this welcome change. The Book of Ruth opens "In the days when the judges ruled," a time of famine, barrenness, and corruption, and closes amidst plentiful harvest and a newly born son with a genealogy anticipating the coming monarchy.

But this regime founding leaves us nonetheless uncertain about Ruth's status as an immigrant. How should we read Ruth's closing silence? Has she been successfully assimilated or has she been left stranded? More generally, what connections between immigration and founding are presupposed and consolidated by this great short story? What is a Moabite woman — a forbidden foreigner — doing at the start of the line of David?

Immigration and Founding

According to two of Ruth's recent readers — Cynthia Ozick and Julia Kristeva — Ruth is a model immigrant. Ozick reads Ruth as a tale of reinvigoration by way of conversion or assimilation. (This is in line with the dominant, traditional reading of the story.) Ruth's conversion to Judaic monotheism from Moabite idolatry testifies to the worthiness of the Jewish God. Ruth's devotion to Naomi exemplifies Ruth's virtue, which is an example for everyone and a ground for the rule of David. Ruth, the model immigrant and convert, supplements the Israelite order and saves it from the wayward rule of judges by founding a new sovereign monarchy.

For Kristeva, by contrast, Ruth unsettles the order she joins. Israelite sovereignty is secured by Ruth, but it is also riven by her, by the moment of otherness she personifies as a Moabite. While Ozick's Ruth completes the Israelite order, Kristeva's Ruth makes it impossible for the order to ever attain completeness. And this, Kristeva argues, is Ruth's great service to the Israelites: she disabuses them of their fantasies of identity and makes them more open to difference and otherness. But Kristeva's Ruth does not only disrupt the order she joins; she also adopts its customs and rituals and tries to get along. From Kristeva's perspective, that makes Ruth a valuable model for those contemporary Muslim immigrants who tend to resist absorption into their receiving regimes.[8]

Ozick's and Kristeva's redeployments of Ruth combine two of the dominant and enduring responses we have to immigrants. Immigrants are either valued for what "they" bring to "us" — diversity, energy, talents, industry, and innovative cuisines, plus a renewed appreciation of our own regime, whose virtues draw immigrants to join us — or they are feared for what they will do to us — consume our welfare benefits, dilute our common heritage, fragment our politics, and undermine our democratic or cosmopolitan culture. Both responses judge the immigrant in terms of what she will do for or to us as a nation.

The first (welcoming) response models immigration as an occasion for citizens (who are perhaps jaded) to reexperience the fabulous wonder of founding, the moment in which the truth or power of their regime was revealed or enacted for all the world to see. Notably, Moab is (as President Clinton put it in a speech in the Middle East in the fall of 1994) "the land where Moses died and Ruth was born." Ruth is the vehicle through which the Law comes alive again, generations after the death of the lawgiver, Moses. Ruth's immigration and conversion reperform the social contract of Sinai and allow the Israelites to reexperience their own initial conversion, faith, or wonder before the Law. Ruth's choice of the Israelites re-marks the Israelites as the Chosen People, a people worthy of being chosen. Here, the immigrant's choice of "us" makes us feel good about who we are. (In the American context, the pleasure and reinvigoration of having been chosen is illustrated and produced, for example, by the *New York Times'* periodic publication of a photograph of new citizens taking the oath of citizenship. That pleasure is further protected by the failure to keep continuous official statistics on remigration or emigration.[9])

The second (wary) response to immigrants also suggests a reexperience of the founding. Highlighted here, though, is the impulse to secure a regime's identity by including some people, values, and ways of life and excluding others.[10] Here, the immigrant's choice of us endangers our sense of who we are. We might see the Book of Ruth as an effort to reinvigorate Israelite identity without also endangering it by combining the story of Ruth's immigration with the story of Orpah's decision not to emigrate. The contrast between Ruth and Orpah highlights the extraordinariness of Ruth's border crossing, as Cynthia Ozick points out.[11] But the contrast also has another effect: it suggests that Ruth's migration to Bethlehem does not mean that Israel is now a borderless community open to all foreigners, including even idolatrous Moabites. Israel is open only to the Moabite who is exceptionally virtuous, to Ruth but not Orpah.

Together, then, Ruth and Orpah personify the coupling of wonder *and* fear, opportunity *and* threat, the sense of supplementation *and* fragmentation that immigrants often excite in the orders that absorb or exclude them. (Is Orpah not threatening? Traditional interpreters express their fears when they claim that Goliath is her descendant.) Personified by the distinct characters of Ruth and Orpah, these impulses may seem to be attached to different objects, the good immigrant versus the bad, for example. But what if we read Orpah as part of Ruth, a personification of the part of Ruth that cannot help but remain a Moabite, even in Bethlehem? The story might then illustrate the deep and abiding ambivalence that (even democratic) regimes tend to have about the foreigners living in their midst.

Ruth's foreignness is what makes her fabulous conversion possible. Her conversion is really worth something because she is a Moabite. It is her foreignness that enables her to re-mark the choiceworthiness of the Israelites and to refurbish their identity as a Chosen People. But Ruth's foreignness also makes her threatening to the order she might otherwise reinvigorate. There is no way around it: a *Moabite* has come to live in Bethlehem!

In short, Ruth figures the deep undecidability of the immigrant whose foreignness simultaneously supplements and threatens the receiving regime. Kristeva looks to the Book of Ruth for an alternative, seeking a way to welcome the foreignness we find so threatening, but her cosmopolitanism ultimately succumbs to a kind of national Chosenness of its own. I, too, turn to the Book of Ruth seeking alternatives.

Ozick's Ruth: Convert or Migrant?

Ozick's reading of Ruth is indebted to the traditional rabbinical interpretations, but also departs from them significantly. "I mean for the rest of my sojourn in the text to go on more or less without (the rabbis),"" she says.[12] Where earlier readers interpreted Orpah in terms of her unfavorable comparison with Ruth, Ozick pauses to look at Orpah in her own right. "Let us check the tale, fashion a hiatus, and allow normality to flow in: let young stricken Orpah not be overlooked."[13] Orpah is noteworthy not just for her failure, by contrast with Ruth, to emigrate to Bethlehem for the sake of Naomi and monotheism. Orpah stands out for her own admirable action: she married an Israelite in Moab (not a popular thing to have done, certainly) and came to love Naomi. Orpah may not have been up to the tests of monotheism and emigration, but she is an "open-hearted" woman, beyond the confines of "narrow-minded," conventional prejudice.[14]

Ozick's Orpah is special, but ultimately, in the crucible of the decision to emigrate or not, the true principle of her character is revealed. She represents "normality," not "singularity." Her wants are mundane; her imagination does not soar. In returning to her mother's house, she returns also to her idols. Orpah "is never, never to be blamed" for her choice, Ozick says, but she suggests nonetheless that history has, indeed, judged Orpah ("Her mark is erased from history; there is no Book of Orpah").[15] Ozick resists the judgment of history by pausing to reflect on Orpah. But Ozick also consolidates history's judgment by depicting Moab's (and Orpah's) disappearance from the world stage as deserved rather than contingent, and by figuring Orpah's decision as ordinary and immature in contrast to Ruth's decision, which is "visionary": "Ruth leaves Moab because she intends to leave childish ideas behind."[16]

The contrast between Ruth and Orpah, though softened by Ozick's appreciative hiatus, instantiates Ozick's distinction between the normal and the singular. But Ozick's contrast between Ruth and Orpah also works to effectively undo the undecidability of the immigrant, who both supports and threatens to undermine the order that both depends on and is threatened by her. Ozick positions Ruth, the immigrant, to reinvigorate the Israelite order without threatening to corrupt it. The threat of corruption, along with the specter of unconvertible foreignness, is projected onto Orpah, whose failure to emigrate symbolizes a failure to convert (and vice versa). If by staying home, Orpah stayed with her gods, then by leaving home, Ruth left her gods behind. The contrast leaves no doubt about Ruth's conversion. There is no danger in her presence in Bethlehem. She is surely one of "us."

The unthreatening character of Ruth's reinvigorative immigration is further consolidated by another moment in Ozick's essay. In a lovely insight into Naomi, Ozick sees her instruction to Ruth to follow Orpah and return to "her people and to her gods" as evidence that Naomi "is a kind of pluralist," *avant la lettre*.[17] Naomi is not a zealot, Ozick says. Orpah has her gods, Naomi has hers, and Naomi knows and accepts that. But Naomi's acceptance of Moabite idolatry is tied to the fact that Moabite idol worship occurs in Moab; her pluralism is territorial. When Naomi says that Orpah has returned to her people and to her gods, Naomi implies (and Ruth surely picks up on this) that it is not possible to go to *her* people in Bethlehem with Moabite gods. In Naomi's pluralism, people and their gods are tied together and positioned in their proper territorial places. Ozick is right that this is a valuable pluralism by contrast with the forms of imperialism and zealotry that will tolerate difference nowhere on earth. Its limits are more evident, however, by contrast with forms of pluralism that demand a more difficult toleration, that of differences that live among us, in our neighborhoods, right next door, in our own homes.

Ozick's positioning of Ruth and Orpah as personifications of singularity and normality, combined with her territorialization of cultural difference, establishes a safe and secure distance between Ruth and Orpah. This distance (intentionally or not) enables Ruth to serve as a vehicle for the reinvigoration Ozick seeks without also jeopardizing the identity of the Israelites. Ozick's Ruth supplements the Israelite order without at the same time diluting or corrupting it because the undecidable figure of the (Moabite) immigrant, both necessary for renewal and dangerous to the community, has been split into two. Orpah, the practical, material Moabite who stays at home with her idols, in her "mother's house," figures the Other, whose absence keeps the community's boundaries and identity secure, while Ruth, loyal, devoted to Naomi, possessed of the mature, abstract imagination needed to be faithful to the one invisible God, refurbishes the order's boundaries through her conversion.[18] This splitting protects the Israelite order from Moabite corruption while allowing it to profit from the supplement of Ruth's migration. In short, Ozick does not see the undecidability of the immigrant and the lingering foreignness of Ruth, so taken is she with the inspiring supplement of Ruth's reinvigorating virtue.

Ozick's disambiguation of Ruth and Orpah follows from two contestable interpretive claims: first, that the sole object of Ruth's choice was monotheism and, second, that Ruth's exceptional virtue won for her an easy assimilation into the Israelite order which was, in turn, only improved (and not also threatened) by her supplement. Ozick's reading, she herself says, is "spotty and selective, a point here, a point there," less an interpretation than a retelling.[19] Her goal is not exhaustive analysis; rather she seeks to reinvigorate this ancient text, to deploy it for particular, inspirational purposes. Nonetheless, I want to trace the multiple possibilities borne by this text, but which are hidden by Ozick's particular treatment because such a tracing illustrates the complexity of the symbolic politics of immigration.

Emphasizing Ruth's famous speech to Naomi, Ozick says that Ruth acted not only out of an impressive love for Naomi, but also out of a deep monotheistic faith. Why would Ruth say "Thy god shall be my god" if she was not moved by faith? Why would she even move to Bethlehem? "Everything socially rational," says Ozick, "is on the side of Ruth's remaining in her own country."[20] But the social rationalities of the situation are unclear. It cannot have been easy to return to Moab as the childless widow of an Israelite. Contra Ozick, Orpah's course was courageous too.[21]

Was Ruth moved by faith alone? Ruth may infer from Naomi's instruction — "See, your sister-in-law has gone back to *her people* and to *her gods*" — that Naomi is concerned about Ruth's unacceptability and unassimilability in Bethlehem. Do not worry, Ruth responds. I may not know all the customs but I will go where you go, live where you live, *your people shall be my people* and *your god shall be my god.* Is Ruth converting disingenuously, then? Not necessarily. As far as the text is concerned, it is not clear that she is converting at all. She may simply be reassuring Naomi — as so many immigrants have reassured their hosts and sponsors before and since — that she will cause no trouble for her. Faith may also have played a role in Ruth's decision, but the text gives us no reason to think it was dispositive. Most likely, Ruth's motives were multiple and complex; this is clear if we see Orpah as personifying one dimension of Ruth's impossible conflict.[22]

Intent upon recuperating Ruth's potentially disturbing migration for a national project, Ozick reads Ruth as a fable of reinvigorative assimilation and overlooks the evidence that Ruth's presence within the Israelite order was never unproblematically supportive, but always also threatening at the same time. Where Ozick sees virtue, conversion, and assimilation, the text of Ruth also suggests complication, recalcitrant particularism, and prejudice. Ruth not only reinvigorates the order she joins, she also taints and troubles it. The Book of Ruth refers to her as "Ruth, the Moabitess" several times (1:22, 2:2, 2:6, 2:21, 4:5, 4:9), suggesting that she, in some sense, stays a Moabite, forbidden, surely noticed, and perhaps despised by her adopted culture, even while also celebrated for the virtue she brings to it.

And (contra Ozick) Ruth is not only a virtuous character, she is also transgressive. According to some commentators, she boldly seduces Boaz on the threshing-room floor.[23] The seduction, though dreamed up by Naomi, is compatible with Ruth's identity as a Moabite, from whom the Israelites expected seduction. For Ozick, this scene (in which Ruth lies down next to Boaz in the middle of the night and uncovers his "feet") depicts "a fatherly tenderness, not an erotic one — though such a scene might, in some other tale, burst with the erotic." But the text does not side with Ozick.[24] It leaves open the question of what happened that night.[25]

Finally, why does Ruth not mother Obed? Why does Naomi take her place? One commentator argues that this is because childbirth was never Ruth's desire, but Naomi's all along.[26] Alternatively, or additionally, an alertness to Ruth's status as an (undecidable and therefore potentially dangerous) immigrant suggests that Naomi may step in to inculcate Obed properly in the ways of the Israelites because his Moabite mother would not be able—or could not be trusted—to do so. As an immigrant, Ruth has the power to reinforce the order's sense of wonder and faith by effectively reperforming the social contract of Sinai. As an immigrant, she also has the power to unsettle, dilute, and perhaps even fragment the community's sense of identity. The community's appreciation of Ruth's reinforcement finds expression in the women's celebration of her. The community's fear of fragmentation may find expression in its transfer of Obed from Ruth to Naomi: Ruth may not mother Obed because she is a Moabite.[27]

These complications are absent from Ozick's reading because she sees the undecidable figure of the immigrant as two distinct figures: the one who supplements the order (Ruth) and the one who might dilute or corrupt it (Orpah). Ozick sees things this way because she counts on Ruth to perform a function not unlike that of the legislator in Rousseau's *Social Contract,* whose combination of foreignness (he comes from elsewhere) and exemplary virtue enables him to restore a wayward order to its forgotten first principles. Rousseau solves the problem of the stranger's dangerous undecidability by having him leave as soon as his restorative work is done. (There is no provision for the office of the legislator in the regime's constitution.) Ozick tries to solve this problem the same way many multicultural Western democracies have tried: by having the helpful (part of the) foreigner/stranger (Ruth) assimilate and by ensuring that the dangerous (part of the) foreigner (Orpah) leaves or stays behind.

Orpah's departure to Moab is not Ozick's doing. It is reported by the text. But the text does not tell us how to position ourselves in relation to Orpah's disappearance. We might mourn, regret, resist, or accept it. Nor does the text tell us how to conceive of the relationship between Ruth and Orpah. We might emphasize their commonalities and seek out their connections or stress the distances between them. Perhaps to attain closure and profit most from Ruth's supplement, Ozick does the latter, domesticating Ruth's absorption and occluding the Orpah-like differences that (according to the text, anyway) still touch Ruth's character.

Kristeva's Ruth: The Ideal Immigrant

Julia Kristeva tries to (re-)capture the undecidability of the immigrant in her own reading of Ruth as a potentially alternative model of a founding myth.[28] She points out that Ruth, "the outsider, the foreigner, the excluded," founds a monarchic line that is riven by difference from the beginning.[29] The rift is generative: "If David is also Ruth, if the sovereign is also a Moabite, peace of mind will never be his lot, but a constant quest for welcoming and going beyond the other in himself."[30]

There is, however, no trace of this idealized ("welcoming") relation to the other in David's lament (cited by Kristeva) that "the people often speak to him wrathfully, saying 'Is he not of unworthy lineage? Is he not a descendant of Ruth, the Moabite?' " nor in David's wish (also cited by Kristeva) to be rid of his Moabite ancestry so that the people might properly revere him.[31] David was more zealous than Kristeva suggests in dealing with Others. He certainly outdid Saul in his willingness to destroy his enemies. Later rabbinic interpreters imagine David complaining about being identified with Ruth because he thinks (certainly the later interpreters think) the foundation of his regime will be more stable and more secure without her. At the same time, however, David needs Ruth, not to "worry" his sovereignty (as Kristeva puts it), but to supplement his own well-known deficiencies with the story of her exceptional virtue and also to support his efforts to expand Israel's sphere of influence to Moab.[32]

Kristeva argues that Ruth's gift to the regime *is* her foreignness and its worrying of Israelite sovereignty. But this misses the fact that for the Israelites, as for Ozick, Ruth's virtue is in spite of her foreignness or apart from it. Her gift to the regime is her exemplary character and faith, manifested in her willingness to leave Moab for Naomi and to convert to monotheism. Ruth's foreignness, per se, is no gift.

Kristeva is right, however, to see some promise in the Judaic embrace of Ruth and in the various biblical requirements charging Israel with hospitality to strangers or foreigners.[33] But she reads Ruth without Orpah (who is barely mentioned), and so Kristeva's Ruth easily becomes (as in

Ozick's reading) a figure of virtue for her willingness to convert to Israelite monotheism while leaving all disruptive differences behind in Moab. Without Orpah and all she represents (e.g., the recalcitrance of difference, the home-yearning of immigrants, the forbiddenness of Moabites), Kristeva loses hold of the immigrant's undecidability.

Orpah's absence from Kristeva's retelling of the story is significant. Kristeva seems to count on the ethics-generating power of stories about strangers to move us out of our insistence on national or ethnic self-identity, but in the end her own acceptance of strangeness turns out to depend on the stranger's willingness to affirm the existence and worth of the order she supplements and disturbs. Ruth is the model immigrant, for Kristeva no less than Ozick, because of her willingness to swear fidelity to Naomi, her people, and her god. Indeed, Kristeva's cosmopolitanism depends on similar pledges of allegiance from French citizens and immigrants alike.[34]

Kristeva's Orpahs: Cosmopolitanism without Foreignness

In *Nations Without Nationalism,* Kristeva returns to Ruth, the border-crossing convert, to figure a cosmopolitanism that Kristeva directs at French nationalists and at recent immigrants to France, such as the Magrebi denizens and citizens who "wear the Muslim scarf to school."[35] These immigrants resemble Ruth in their willingness to emigrate from their original homes, but they also resemble Orpah insofar as they remain attached to the particular culture of their home countries.[36] Is there nothing French to which immigrants might feel allegiance?[37]

The enduring attachment of many Algerian immigrants to their culture and homeland and their option since 1963 of citizenship in an independent Algeria lead many of them to either reject French citizenship or relate to it in purely instrumental terms. In response, those on the French Right have in the last ten years called for tighter controls on immigration and demanded that citizenship be awarded only to those who relate to France affectively. Those on the French Left resist efforts to control immigration and reject attempts to inscribe citizenship as an affective practice.[38]

Charging that the first response is too "nationalist" and the second too "world-oriented" (the Left is too ready to "sell off French national values") Kristeva carves out a middle ground between them and offers a cosmopolitanism that is distinctively French in which the nation is still important, but not an all-encompassing site of identity, centered not on *Volk* but on compact.[39] Kristeva resignifies the nation from a final site of affiliation to, in psychoanalytic terms, a *transitional object*. (A transitional object is a device, such as a favorite blanket or stuffed animal, that empowers the child to separate from the mother(land) and eventually to move on to an independent — blanketless/postnationalist — existence.) Brilliantly cutting across the French Right-Left divide, Kristeva's cosmopolitanism is rooted and affective, but attached finally to a transnational, not a national, object.

Kristeva's cosmopolitanism secures and is secured by affective relations to a series of "sets" — specifically self, family, homeland, Europe, and mankind — in which each set operates as a transitional object for the next.[40] By locating the sets in a progressive, sequential, trajectory of transition, Kristeva avoids the issue of possible conflicts among them. She also avoids the question of a specifically French affiliation by using the abstract term *homeland* for that set. But her call for an identification with Europe positions French and Magrebi subjects asymmetrically in relation to her cosmopolitanism.[41] And because her cosmopolitanism (as she says repeatedly) "make[s] its way through France," specifically by way of Montesquieu, it works to shore up a uniquely French identity, even while claiming to overcome or transcend it.[42] "[T]here is no way for an identity to go beyond itself without first asserting itself in satisfactory fashion," she says.[43] (But this generous recognition of the need to affirm identity before overcoming it is not extended to France's immigrant communities.)

There is surely no way out of this paradox, in which cosmopolitanism must be striven for through the particular, albeit heterogeneous (national) cultures that shape us. But Kristeva does not explore the paradox and she tends to leave the heterogeneity of France behind in her embrace of one particular strand of French Enlightenment thought. She is right to say we must "pursue a critique of the national tradition without selling off its assets." But her account of French cosmopolitanism ultimately protects (what she sees as) the nation's assets from critique and from critical engagement with others: "Let us ask, for instance, where else one might find a theory and a policy more concerned with respect for the *other*, more watchful of citizens' rights (women and foreigners included, *in spite of blunders and crimes*), more concerned with individual strangeness, in the midst of national mobility?"[44]

The limits of Kristeva's cosmopolitanism emerge again when, echoing Ozick's preference for Ruth over Orpah, Kristeva suggests that the "'abstract' advantages of a French universalism may prove to be superior to the 'concrete' benefits of a muslim scarf," implying that the scarf, unlike the nation, is essentially a fetish and is therefore unable, as such, to serve as a healthy transitional object.[45] She seems to have those who wear the scarf in mind when she says there are "mothers (as well as 'motherlands' and 'fatherlands') who prevent the creation of a transitional object; there are children who are unable to use it."[46] Kristeva sees these veiled women much as Ozick sees Orpah: tethered to their idols, their mothers, and motherlands, capable of some bold mobility but ultimately incapable of proper and mature transition, they mark (what Kristeva calls) the "melancholy" of nationalism.[47]

Kristeva quite rightly sees a generative possibility in a differently conceived French nation.[48] Why not accord the same possibility to the Muslim scarf? In *Women and Gender in Islam*, Leila Ahmed highlights the transitional properties of veiling in a particular context, arguing that for Muslim women in contemporary Egypt, the veil, worn increasingly by professional and university women, operates as a kind of transitional object, enabling upwardly mobile women to move from the familiar settings of their rural homes "to emerge socially into a sexually integrated world" that is "still an alien, uncomfortable social reality for both women and men."[49] Ironically, if Ahmed is right and veiling *can* function as a healthy transitional object, then Kristeva's figuring of the veil as a concreteness that may have to give way to the welcome abstraction of cosmopolitanism puts her in the very position of those mothers she criticizes, those "mothers (as well as 'motherlands' and 'fatherlands') who prevent the creation of a transitional object."[50]

The pleasing irony of this insight should not, however, blind us to the fact that the problem with Kristeva is not simply her failure to explore the transitional properties of veiling while managing nonetheless to see the transitional possibilities of the nation. Were that the case, she could simply change her position on veiling and the problem would be solved.[51] Instead, the problem with Kristeva is her failure to engage Others in her deliberations about the project, goals, and instruments of a cosmopolitanism she values too much to risk by including it in the conversation as a question rather than as the answer. Kristeva ends up in this awkward position because she neglects what Judith Butler calls the "difficult labor of translation," an ongoing project of political work that always also involves a critical self-interrogation and courts the risk of transformation."[52] Without a commitment to such a labor, Kristeva's cosmopolitanism already knows what it is—and what it isn't—and so it risks becoming another form of domination, particularly when it confronts an Other that resists assimilation, an Other that is unwilling to repeat for "us" the wonder of our conversion to world (or French) citizenship.

When Kristeva does invite an exchange with "foreigners, [which] we all are (within ourselves and in relation to others)," she imagines it will "amplify and enrich the French idea of the nation."[53] But this imagined exchange, in which Others join to complete the French idea, calls attention to the need for a different cosmopolitanism in which cosmopolitans risk their cosmopolitan (and nationalist) principles by engaging Others in their particularities while *at the same time* defending and discovering located universalisms such as human rights and the equal dignity of persons. There is not enough evidence of such a risk in the questions put to immigrants by Kristeva: "What does each immigrant community contribute to the lay concept of *national spirit as esprit general* reached by the French Enlightenment? Do these communities recognize that *esprit general* or not?"[54]

A democratic cosmopolitanism may, together with Ozick and Kristeva, find ethical renewal in the engagement with foreigners, but the energy of that renewal will not come from the foreigner's affirmation of our existing categories and forgiveness of our past "blunders and crimes."[55] Instead, the renewal of cosmopolitanism, the site and source of its energies, will come from engagements with foreigners who seem to threaten but with whom joint action is nonetheless possible; not easy perhaps, but possible.

Mourning, Membership, Agency, and Loss: Ruth's Lessons for Politics

The Book of Ruth may inspire a democratic cosmopolitanism. I return to Ruth by way of a psychoanalytic account of transitional objects so as to explore the experience of loss and mourning in projects of transition and translation. I focus on transitional objects, in particular, because the issue here is transition to a future democratic cosmopolitanism and because that device plays a central role in both Kristeva's account of immigration and in Ozick's reading of Ruth, in which Naomi is in effect the transitional object that enables Ruth to make the (progressive) move from Moab to Israel.[56] I treat psychoanalysis not as a universal method, but as a particular cultural paradigm that explores experiences of compensation and loss in a way that resonates with certain communities and cultures, not just individuals. That the cultural-symbolic connections among nationalism, immigration, psychoanalysis, and transitional objects are well established was demonstrated by the *New York Times Book Review*'s (25 June 1995) use of a flag-stuffed baby bottle to illustrate its review of Michael Lind's *The Next American Nation* (summer 1995).

Modeling issues of separation and autonomy in terms of the child's developing independence from the mother, the object relations school of psychoanalysis emphasizes the role of transitional objects in the process of individuation. I borrow from one version of this account but I distance myself from its reliance on the model of an original maternal relation so as to affirm the permanence of issues of separation. Separation and transition are issues not just for children or immigrants, but for all of us throughout our lifetimes. I also seek to avoid the progressive trajectory of developmental accounts. That trajectory infantilizes the immigrants whose transitions are at issue here and it affirms Western receiving regimes' perceptions of sending regimes as a "past that the West has already lived out" and which can be left behind without loss.[57] (Kristeva's and Ozick's progressive accounts tend to feed these prejudices too.)

In a Winnicott-indebted analysis emphasizing the loss that attends and occasions individuation and separation, Eric Santner argues that transitional objects enable separation in a healthy way only if certain conditions are met. First, the separation must not be traumatic; it must be temporary. Second, there must be a healthy environment conducive to transitional object play. And third, that play must have an intersubjective dimension; that is, it must be witnessed periodically by the figure whose (temporary) absences are being borne. If these conditions are met, the space of object play can serve as a site of healthy mourning for the loss entailed by transition. At play with the transitional object, the subject acts out her bereavement and is thereby empowered for separation and individuation (as in the "fort-da" game — a kind of peekaboo — described by Freud). There is empowerment here, not just mourning; the play provides the subject not simply with a substitute (for the loss being mourned) but with a lesson in what Peter Sacks calls "the very means and *practice* of substitution." At best, the subject learns *agency* in the face of loss (perhaps even as a result of it, if the conditions are right for such a learning).[58]

If these conditions are not met, neither mourning nor empowerment will ensue. Instead, the subject will first make a fetish of the object, engaging it in a furious and hyperbolic play that signals her denial of her loss. Second, the object will ultimately lose all meaning for the subject and she will abandon the object entirely, leaving it stranded. The evacuation of the object's meaning can result in "signification trauma," which leaves the subject stranded, silent, and speechless, outside the world of language, play, and mourning. Emphasizing all three dimensions of transitional object play — mourning, empowerment, and intersubjectivity — Santner summarizes Winnicott's view with an aphorism: "Mourning without solidarity [i.e., transitional object play in the absence of intersubjectivity or an intersubjective witnessing] is the beginning of madness."[59]

How does this account apply to Ruth? By pointing out that successful transitions are determined not by the nature of the transitional object itself but by the context in which it operates, Santner calls attention to the role of institutions, culture, community, and politics in projects of transition and translation, something to which Kristeva does not adequately attend in her critique of immigrant particularism. And Santner's focus on mourning, empowerment, and intersubjectivity calls attention to the fact that none of these three components of successful transition is available in Ruth's case. Ruth's separation from Orpah (who, in my account, personifies Moab) is traumatic. There is no healthy space for transitional object play, no intersubjective witnessing, and no possibility of proper mourning because Ruth is not given cultural, juridical, or psychological permission to mourn Orpah-Moab. Nor are we. Ruth made the right choice. Ozick and Kristeva agree on that. What could there be to mourn?

Ozick and Kristeva both seem to assume that their affirmation of the rightness of Ruth's choice (and their marginalization of Orpah) secures Ruth's transition from Moab. But if Santner and Winnicott are correct, the opposite is true: the insistence on the rightness of Ruth's choice leaves her (and us) unable to mourn Orpah-Moab and, in the absence of the proper work of mourning, Ruth's transition is jeopardized, even subverted, not secured. Naomi's power as a transitional object for Ruth *de-*

pends upon the proper mourning of Orpah and upon a kind of continued (perhaps hyphenated?) relation with her. At least, it depends upon recognizing that Orpah (Moab) is part of Ruth. Cast in Ozick's and Kristeva's terms, we might say that Ruth's insight into a universality remains touched by a particularity with which it may be in tension, but by which Ruth and her insight are nonetheless also nourished.

Indeed, contra Ozick and Kristeva, the Book of Ruth can be read as a tale of incomplete mourning, a fable of failed transition. Through the lens provided by Santner, Ruth's famous loyalty to Naomi exceeds the idealist and pragmatic interpretations considered above. No longer can it signal simply the selfless devotion of a virtuous woman; nor can it be only a mark of Ruth's immigrant practicality (a possibility I myself raised earlier, along with Fewell and Gunn). It is now undeniably possible that this clinging is a symptom of Ruth's denial of her loss of Orpah-Moab, a sign of Santner's first stage, in which the subject's denial of her loss leads to a frenzied attachment in which the transitional object is fetishized.

And Ruth's closing silence can no longer be taken to signal merely successful and complete absorption. Another possibility presses itself upon us: that silence may be a mark of Santner's second stage, the stage in which the subject suffers from a "signification trauma." In Ruth's case, the trauma is produced by the separation from Orpah-Moab and the corresponding loss of any meaningful relationship to Naomi, Ruth's adopted (transitional) mother. That second loss is finally symbolized by Naomi's adoption of Obed in place of Ruth, but it is foreshadowed much earlier by, among other things, Naomi's failure to introduce or even mention Ruth to the women who welcome Naomi back to Bethlehem.

These two moments in Ruth's story mark two familiar moments of immigration dynamics as they are modeled in contemporary multicultural democracies. One, a furious and hyperbolic assimilationism (or assimilative cosmopolitanism) in which all connections to the motherland are disavowed. And two, a refusal of transition and a retreat into a separatist or nationalist enclave that leaves the immigrant stranded in relation to the receiving country *and* the lost homeland. The two moments are figured developmentally by Santner and Winnicott, but they actually make simultaneous claims upon immigrants and receiving regimes.

This binary of absorption versus enclavism is generated by efforts to recuperate foreignness for national(ist) projects. Is there a way out of this predicament? Two directions are suggested by this analysis: First, we must respond constructively to the invocations of the privileges of hosts over guests that are so popular today.[60] In the United States, at the moment these invocations find expression in the resurgence of the English-only movement, the scapegoating of immigrants for the failure of the domestic and international capitalist economy to reproduce the American Dream, the blaming of immigrants and ethnics for the fragmentation of high culture (perversely enough at a time when the homogenizing powers of American popular culture are at their height), and the identification of enclavism with immigrants and ethnics at a time when the propensity to withdraw from public services and public culture is most characteristic not of foreigners, but of the wealthy.

In response, we must vouchsafe spaces that were not there for Ruth, spaces that meet the need for a certain kind of, as it were, transitional object play. The term *play* should not mislead. These are spaces of serious political work and negotiation in which the proper work of mourning can be initiated while other needs of living together are pursued. Mourning is not the exclusive provenance of incoming immigrants. Successful democratic transitions and expansions depend on the willingness of *both* receiving populations and immigrants to risk mutual transformation, to engage and attenuate their home-yearning for each others' sakes and for the sake of their political life together. Such actions in concert may occur by way of secondary associations that do not require citizenship for membership, though citizens participate in them too; neighborhood groups, local school-board politics, immigrant advocacy organizations such as the Workplace Project on Long Island, even those renowned, supposedly withdrawalist, immigrant mutual assistance organizations can be sites of transformative, absorptive, democratic participation, solidarity, and de facto (if not de jure) citizenship.[61]

These secondary associations must be complemented by educating residents to be citizens of the diverse world that is replicated inside their nation's territorial borders, to acquire second and even third languages, to understand their own cultures and political arrangements as part of a larger network of democratic possibilities, to see those arrangements as platforms from which to form subnational and international coalitions, and to see their democratic institutions as unfinished and amenable, therefore, to the amendments that might result from immigrant (and even "foreign") participation in democratic practices and movements at subnational, national, and transnational levels. The United States has a long history of alien suffrage ("finally undone by the xenophobic nationalism attending World War I") in which democratic participation is linked not to the juridical status of citizenship, but to the fact of residence.[62] At present, several cities allow noncitizen residents to vote in local, schoolboard (Chicago and New York), or municipal (several Maryland localities, such as Takoma Park) elections.[63] Alien suffrage is an important symbolic and political resource for those involved in immigration politics and cosmopolitan projects seeking to attenuate the identification of democratic agency solely with the privileged, juridical status of citizenship.

A second direction suggested by this analysis is transnational rather than subnational, but it is also associational and affective. Ruth's severed sororal relation to Orpah calls to mind the sister-city movement, which in some ways exemplifies and may yet help build a future democratic cosmopolitanism. Sister cities, affective sites of located, institutional transnationalism, are usually founded by local civic energies and initiatives. Their transnationalism makes them an important and potentially energizing complement to the subnational solidarities noted above.[64] And the fact that sister-cities establish relationships not limited "to carrying out a single project" makes them an important complement to more temporary, issue-oriented forms of local and international solidarity that are coalitional.[65] Most important, sister-cities interrupt projects of (re-)nationalization by generating practices of affective citizenship that exceed state boundaries (and sometimes even violate state foreign policy).[66] Together, subnational and transnational associations enact a cosmopolitan practice. They provide sites of leverage in national(ist) politics, while also serving as settings in which mourning, empowerment, solidarity, and agency can develop and find expression.

Retold, the Book of Ruth is not only a fable of founding and immigration; it is also — appropriately — a parable of mourning and membership. It gives an account of the institutional and cultural conditions for the proper work of mourning and teaches the importance of a meaningful and empowered agency of intersubjective spaces, actions in concert, multiple solidarities, civic powers, and (always contested) connections to the past. Because such spaces, actions, powers, and connections are available to Naomi in Bethlehem, she is restored to plenitude and agency. Ruth's fate is different because Bethlehem positions her and Naomi asymmetrically in relation to their losses. The women's community provides Naomi with support and sympathy. They witness her ritually mournful name change to Mara (though they never call her by that name) and she is empowered for agency (symbolized by maternity).

"The homeopathic constitution and (reconstitution) of the self takes place not in a vacuum," Santner says, "but always in a particular social context."[67] Ruth is provided with no such resources and no such context because her losses are not seen as such and her transnational connections to Orpah-Moab (a potentially alternative site of support and power) are severed. Like Antigone's mourning of Polynices, Ruth's mourning of Orpah is forbidden for the sake of a regime's stability and identity. Thus, Ruth's mourning, like Antigone's, is endless, melancholic. Her losses get in the way of the closure this community seeks to attain through her *and* in spite of her. Indeed, the fact that Naomi's restoration to the community is finally marked by her occupation of Ruth's position as mother to Obed suggests that the reinvigoration of this community and the stabilization of David's monarchy depend not only on the supplement of Ruth's inspiring example, but also, and at the same time, upon her marginalization.

The lessons of Ruth exceed those of (Ozick's) assimilation and Kristeva's cosmopolitanism. This great short story calls upon us to move further toward a democratic cosmopolitanism that seeks to secure for both immigrants and receiving populations the cultural, institutional, ethical, and political conditions for the proper work of mourning — and living — together.

Notes

For their comments on earlier drafts of this paper, I am very grateful to Seyla Benhabib, Jane Bennet, William Connolly, Richard Flathman, Jill Frank, Marjorie Garber, Patchen Markell, Martha Minow, Hanna Pitkin, Michael Rogin, Michael Sandel, Tracy Strong, Michael Whinston, and, especially, Linda Zerilli. I also owe thanks to the many others in attendance when I presented this material at Rutgers, Princeton, Northwestern, Harvard, the Center for Advanced Study in the Behavioral Sciences, and the American Bar Foundation. For financial support, I am indebted to the National Science Foundation Grant # SES-9022102.

1. Herman Melville, *White-Jacket, or, The World in a Man-of-War* (New York: Oxford University Press, 1990).

2. Sanford Ungar, *Fresh Blood: The New American Immigrants* (New York: Simon and Schuster, 1995), 20–21.

3. Noel Ignatiev, *How the Irish Became White* (New York: Routledge, 1995), 2.

4. George Borjas, *Friends or Strangers: The Impact of Immigrants on the U.S. Economy* (New York: Basic Books, 1990).

5. Alejandro Portes and Ruben G. Rumbaut, *Immigrant America: A Portrait* (Berkeley: University of California Press, 1990).

6. As Alan Wolfe puts it: "A framework organized around a balance sheet approach in which the assets and liabilities are added up is too rooted in utilitarianism to address why immigration has such symbolic importance for most Americans." Wolfe, "The Return of the Melting Pot," *The New Republic,* 31 December 1990, 32.

7. There is some debate about the details of this scene: Is the next of kin being asked to redeem the land through purchase or to redeem Ruth through marriage? For a summary of the debate and the best reading of the scene, see Danna Fewell and David Gunn, *Compromising Redemption: Relating Characters in the Book of Ruth* (Louisville, Ky.: Westminster/John Knox Press, 1990).

8. Some doubt that Ruth can be a resource for an account of immigration politics because the text tells the story of a single migrant while the contemporary issue concerns hordes of people. My view is that the text's success at dramatizing enduring issues of immigration politics is due partly to its use of personification. Moreover, the story of Ruth has established connections to immigration politics that precede my analysis. Marjorie Garber (personal communication) recalls playing Ruth in the late 1940s in a series of fundraisers sponsored by Hadassah to help Jewish refugees make their way to Palestine after the war. Interestingly, given Kristeva's use of the headscarf to mark the recalcitrance of Muslim immigrants, Garber, as Ruth, wore a headscarf to mark her character's European (refugee) identity.

9. Estimates are that 195,000 U.S. residents emigrate annually. See Priscilla Labovitz, "Immigration — Just the Facts," *New York Times,* 25 March 1996. I discuss in detail the symbolic functions of the iconic new citizen photograph in "Immigrant America? How Foreign-ness 'Solves' Democracy's Problems," in *No Place Like Home: Democracy and the Politics of Foreignness,* chapter 4 (Princeton: Princeton University Press, forthcoming).

10. Toni Morrison calls particular attention to the exclusionary dimension of the (re)founding effect of American immigration in relation to American Blacks. See Nicolaus Mills, ed., *Arguing Immigration* (New York: Simon and Schuster, 1994).

11. Cynthia Ozick, "Ruth," in Judith A. Kates and Gail Twersky Reimer, eds., *Reading Ruth: Contemporary Women Reclaim a Sacred Story* (New York: Ballantine Books, 1994), 221.

12. Ibid., 219–20.

13. Ibid., 221.

14. Ibid., 224, 222.

15. Ibid., 220, 221.

16. Ibid., 224, 227.

17. Ibid., 223.

18. In psychoanalytic terms, Orpah's (over)attachment to her mother(land) — represented by the phrase her "mother's house" (an unusual locution for the Bible) —

prevents her, as it did Antigone (who clung to Polynices, the displaced site of her longing for her mother, Jocasta), from entering the (paternal or monotheistic) Law, the realm of the Symbolic. Luce Irigaray notes the displacement in *Antigone* but, moved by a sensibility more tragic than Ozick's, finds a subterranean location for Antigone, who eternally unsettles the dominant order. Ozick pauses to reflect momentarily on Orpah, but she does not look to Orpah as a source of eternal dissonance or (in Irigaray's appropriation of Hegel's term) irony. See Luce Irigaray, *Speculum of the Other Woman* (Ithaca, N.Y.: Cornell University Press, 1985).

19. Ibid., 219.

20. Ibid., 225.

21. The difficulties of such a return are occluded by Ozick, who comments on the unusualness of Orpah's exogamy but then assumes that Orpah's life in Moab will be unproblematic: "Soon she will marry a Moabite husband and have a Moabite child" (Ozick, "Ruth," 224). Fewell and Gunn have a better grasp of the situation: "What are Ruth's opportunities in Moab? Who would want to marry a barren widow, much less one that had been living with a foreigner? And would she be known as the 'Israelite-lover,' the one too good for her own people? . . . In the end, we might ask, what takes more courage, the staying or the leaving?" Fewell and Gunn, *Compromising Redemption*, 97–98; cf. Rosa Felsenburg Kaplan, "The Noah Syndrome," in Susanna Heschel, ed., *On Being a Jewish Feminist* (New York: Schocken Books, 1993), 167.

22. Jack M. Sasson notes this device of personification elsewhere in Ruth: "A didactic device frequently resorted to by Biblical writers is to limit the spectrum of choice to two alternatives, only one of which will prove to be correct. An obvious method of putting such a concept in effect is the creation of two brothers, only one of whom will ultimately fare well. Mahlon marries Ruth — he will live on" (through the posterity of Obed). Other biblical examples noted by Sasson are Cain and Abel, Jacob and Esau, Ishmael and Isaac, all male. Why does Sasson not include Ruth and Orpah in his list? Perhaps because of his Proppian assumption that Orpah is a merely marginal character, not central to the tale and not worthy, therefore, of further interpretive attention. Jack M. Sasson, *Ruth: A New Translation with a Philological Commentary and Formalist-Folklorist Interpretation* (Sheffield, U.K.: JSOT, 1989), 16–17.

23. Judith A. Kates, "Women at the Center: Ruth and Shavuoth" in Kates and Reimer, eds., *Reading Ruth*, 194–95.

24. Ozick, "Ruth," 229–30. Ozick's claim echoes Hegel's that the brother-sister relation, of which he takes Polynices and Antigone to be exemplars, is unerotic. As Jacques Derrida points out, the claim is astonishing given the incestuous origins of this pair: "Antigone's parents are not some parents among others." Derrida, *Glas* (Lincoln: University of Nebraska Press, 1986), 165.

25. The Hebrew term used here for "feet" is a pun for genitals.

Jack Sasson gives a wonderful reading of the scene in which Boaz is said to mistake Ruth for a "Lillith." A Lillith is a demonic woman/spirit thought to be responsible for nocturnal emissions and male impotence. "[U]pon awakening, Boaz discerns the figure of a woman. Fearing that it might be that of a Lillith, he shudders in fear. The storyteller's joke is that Ruth turns out to be equally as aggressive in her demands to be accepted as a mate. In this case, we shall be shortly reassured (if we do not know it already) that matters will turn out well for all concerned." Sasson, *Ruth*, 78.

The "joke" of the scene depends on Boaz's misidentification of Ruth as a Lillith. What Sasson does not note is that the error is overdetermined not simply by Ruth's sex-gender, but also by her Moabite identity. Moabite women were particularly feared by the Israelites as temptresses and seductresses. This scene, therefore, is much more (or less) than a joke. It allows Boaz to experience his worst fears about Ruth — that her conversion/immigration notwithstanding, she is truly a Moabite after all, a bearer of desire who will not respect the proper boundaries of male, Israelite subjectivity. Boaz experiences those fears precisely in the moment of his misidentification of Ruth (whom he already desires) because in that moment his fears are safely displaced onto a Lillith.

26. Gail Twersky Reimer, "Her Mother's House," in Kates and Reimer, eds., *Reading Ruth*, 105.

27. I am reminded here of the not-quite-analogous story of the "Pelasgian inhabitants of Lemnos, who carried off Athenian women from Brauron and had children by them. When their mothers brought them up in the Athenian way, the fathers became afraid and killed both the mothers and their children. Because of both these deeds, the word 'Lemnion' was associated with anything bad" (Gail Holst-Warhaft, *Dangerous Voices: Women's Laments in Greek Literature* (New York: Routledge, 1992), citing Herodotus, *Histories* VI, 6, 138; at 211 n.54.

28. Noting Ruth's love for Naomi, Kristeva calls attention to the woman-to-woman passion at the base of the Davidic line, a passion that flies in the face of structuralist assumptions about the order-constituting function of the male homosocial exchange of women. One might well add to this the observation that the order-constituting exchange in this text is that of a male — Obed — who is passed from one woman, Ruth, to another, Naomi.

29. Julia Kristeva, *Strangers to Ourselves*, trans. Leon S. Roudiez (New York: Columbia University Press, 1991), 75.

30. Ibid., 76.

31. Ibid., 74.

32. Ibid., 75.

33. Ibid., 65–69.

34. Ibid., 63.

35. Julia Kristeva, *Nations Without Nationalism*, trans. Leon S. Roudiez (New York: Columbia University Press, 1993), 36.

36. Kristeva, *Strangers to Ourselves*, 194.

37. Kristeva, *Nations Without Nationalism*, 60.

38. Rogers Brubaker, *Citizenship and Nationhood in France and Germany* (Cambridge: Harvard University Press, 1992), 138–64; James Hollifield, *Immigrants, Markets and States: The Political Economy of Postwar Europe* (Cambridge: Harvard University Press, 1992), chapters 6–7.

39. Kristeva, *Nations Without Nationalism*, 37, 40.

40. Ibid., 40.

41. Norma Moruzzi, "A Problem with Headscarves: Contemporary Complexities of Political and Social Identity," *Political Theory* 22 (1994): 665.

42. Kristeva, *Nations Without Nationalism*, 38.

43. Ibid., 59.

44. Ibid., 46–47; my emphasis.

45. Ibid., 47. Kristeva does note the tenuousness of the distinction between fetish and transitional object, though, when she concedes that the transitional object is "any child's indispensable fetish." Ibid., 41.

46. Ibid., 41–42.

47. Ibid., 43.

48. Ibid., 47.

49. Leila Ahmed, *Women and Gender in Islam* (New Haven: Yale University Press, 1992), 223–24.

50. Ahmed studies veiling in Egypt, not France, but her argument was recently echoed by France's Federation of Councils of Parents of Pupils in Public Schools (FCPE), which opposed the expulsions of over seventy girls who wore headscarves to their schools in Lille and the Paris region: "These expulsions carry with them 'the immense inconvenience of confining these young girls to within their family circle and of limiting any possibility of emancipation' " (*Migration News Sheet*, November 1994, 2). Kristeva never questions why she (like so many others) expresses her concerns about Muslim particularism through Muslim *women*. This is not a new question; it was posed by Fanon in "The Unveiling of Algeria." Winnifred Woodhull hazards an answer to it, albeit not with Kristeva in mind. Echoing Fanon, she says, "In the eyes of many French people, girls of Maghrebian descent are generally diligent students and compliant people — in short, the most assimilable element of the immigrant population; if they begin to defend their right to 'difference,' the whole project of integration seems to be jeopardized." Woodhull, *Transfigurations of the Maghreb: Feminism, Decolonization, and Literatures* (Minneapolis: University of Minnesota Press, 1993), 48.

51. Thanks to Pratap Mehta on this point.

52. Judith Butler, "Kantians in Every Culture?" *Boston Review* (October–November 1994): 18.

53. Kristeva, *Nations Without Nationalism*, 47.

54. Ibid., 60; italics in original.

55. Ibid., 46.

56. Ozick, "Ruth," 227–28.

57. Shiv Visvanthan, "From the Annals of the Laboratory State," *Alternatives* 12 (1987): 41.

58. Eric Santner, *Stranded Objects: Mourning, Memory and Film in Postwar Germany* (Ithaca: Cornell University Press, 1990), 19–26; Peter Sacks, *The English Elegy: Studies in Genre from Spenser to Yeats* (Baltimore: Johns Hopkins University Press, 1985), 8.

59. Santner, *Stranded Objects*, 26–27.

60. See, for example, Kristeva, *Nations Without Nationalism*, 60.

61. Jennifer Gordon, "We Make the Road by Walking: Immigrant Workers, the Workplace Project, and the Struggle for Social Change," 30 Harvard Civil Rights-Civil Liberties Law Review 407 (1995); and Camilo Perez-Bustillo, "What Happens When English-Only Comes to Town? A Case Study of Lowell, Massachusetts," *Language Loyalties: A Sourcebook on the Official English Controversy*, ed. James Crawford (Chicago: University of Chicago Press, 1992), 201.

62. James B. Raskin, "Legal Aliens, Local Citizens: The Historical, Constitutional and Theoretical Meanings of Alien Suffrage," 141 University of Pennsylvania Law Review 1397 (1993).

63. Ibid., 1429–30. It should be noted, however, that residency can be a restrictive rather than a permissive requirement. Some cities, such as Long Island, use stringent proof of residency requirements to keep immigrants out of public schools. See "Immigrants Fight Residency Rules Blocking Children in L.I. Schools," *New York Times*, 7 August 1995.

64. The potentially empowering if also controversial connections that may be forged by sub- and transnational groups in coalition are illustrated by the following case, which also militates against the impression that sister-cities are benign and unimportant associations: In late 1988, the Lion's Club International of Taipei donated 10,000 Chinese-language books to the Monterey Park public library in California, intending the gift to "reinforce the closeness they felt with their sister-city, which many [had] begun to call 'Little Taipei.'" Mayor Barry Hatch saw in this gift an assault on American values and fought to refuse it, though he ultimately lost to a coalition of local civic groups and Chinese-American community leaders. See James Crawford, *Hold Your Tongue: Bilingualism and the Politics of "English Only"* (Binghamton, N.Y.: Addison-Wesley, 1992), 1–3.

65. Wilbur Zelinsky, "The Twinning of the World: Sister Cities in Geographical and Historical Perspective," *Annals of the Association of American Geographers* 81 (1991): 1.

66. Liz Chilsen and Sheldon Rampton, *Friends in Deed: The Story of U.S. Nicaraguan Sister Cities.* (Madison: Wisconsin Co-ordinating Council on Nicaragua, 1988).

67. Santner, *Stranded Objects*, 24.

CHAPTER EIGHT

Face-to-Face with the Dead Man: Ethical Responsibility, State-Sanctioned Killing, and Empathetic Impossibility

Patricia Molloy

> The image of the death house with its polished tiles and gleaming oak chair is fading. I turn my attention to where life is. Although I have decided that I will not be going to death row again, I cannot bear to think that there are some men there now who are facing death alone.[1]

> The other man's death calls me into question, as if, by my possible future indifference, I had become the accomplice of the death of the other, who cannot see it, is exposed; and as if, even before vowing myself to him, I had to answer for this death of the other, and to accompany the Other in his mortal solitude. The Other becomes my neighbour precisely through the way the face summons me, calls for me, begs for me, and in so doing recalls my responsibility, and calls me into question.[2]

In a recent article entitled "Violence, Law, and Justice," Karen Slawner notes that while scholars of international relations are accustomed to studying acts of state terrorism, torture, and human rights abuses that occur in the international sphere, few U.S. international relations scholars turn the gaze inward toward the legitimacy of governmental practices, such as those of capital punishment, which violate the human rights of U.S. citizens. Part of this reluctance, Slawner says, can be attributed to a "trick of disciplinary boundary making," which imposes a distinction between the "domestic" and "the international." The result is that the focus of American international relations is directed predominantly toward foreign policy.[3] Through her readings of Benjamin and Derrida,

Slawner argues that the domestic and the international are mutually con-stituting insofar as law and violence are inextricably linked in both spheres. She concludes with a call for a justice based, in a Levinasian sense, on an obligation to the state's victim as Other — an obligation that, as John Caputo suggests, locates itself in human flesh.[4] So, as David Campbell and Michael Dillon ask in interrogating the "engineered blind spots" of international relations: "Where is the body in international relations?"[5]

With the release of the film *Dead Man Walking*, the legitimacy of the violence of law in the domestic sphere has come under intense public scrutiny. Directed by Tim Robbins and based on Sister Helen Prejean's autobiographical account of counseling death row inmates in Louisiana in the 1980s, the film sets out to blur the boundary between victim and victimizer and expose the limits of justice. To this end I consider *Dead Man Walking* as a deconstructive text.

The film's central narrative is constructed as a series of face-to-face encounters between an unrepentant killer awaiting execution and the Catholic nun he requests first to help him with his appeal to the pardon board and, following its denial, to serve as his spiritual adviser. The plot thickens, and the emotional intensity of the film heightens, as Sister He-len is drawn to, and finds herself face-to-face with, the suffering of the victims' families (including that of the condemned man). In this sense, the film perhaps lends itself to its representation in the mainstream media as a "balanced" account of the "pros and cons" of capital pun-ishment. My intention in this paper is not to rehearse the death penalty debate. I propose, rather, to examine the representations of justice and death in the film by way of two emergent and contrasting positions in post-positivist international relations theory: Christine Sylvester's theory of empathetic cooperation, and Emmanuel Levinas's ethical philosophy of alterity.

Like the film itself, this paper asks more questions than it can an-swer. Some of the key ethical questions that unfold in the viewing of *Dead Man Walking* are, how do we reconcile our desire to feel compas-sion for, to identify and/or empathize with, one who commits undesir-able and uncompassionate acts? Is "empathy" possible at all if it pre-sumes a shared understanding of/with that which is unknowable and ungraspable, like the Other, and like death itself? These questions are also inherently political, becoming a matter of responsibility: "Why should

I concern myself? Who is this other to me?" As I shall argue, framing the question of responsibility to the Other in terms of empathy is problematic. Whereas Sylvester makes a distinction between an empathetic negotiation with Others and a colonizing and appropriative sympathy, a growing body of literature on the "risks" of empathy suggests a more cautionary approach to the ethical relation with the Other. The paper then suggests how through a Levinasian frame we begin to see the relationship between the nun and the killer as one that reaches beyond empathy, grounded rather in the nun's "obligation" to the Other. The final two sections examine further ethical responsibility to and for the Other, in terms of justice and politics.

The Exclusionary Practices of International Relations and the Case for Empathetic Cooperation

In addition to noting the arbitrary construction of the domestic and the international, Karen Slawner suggests that the positing of the state as the "sole legal personality" within traditional international relations theory has contributed to the reluctance of U.S. scholars to scrutinize their own "ostensibly democratic, and legitimate, governmental system."[6] With the state as sole agent, "citizens or subjects are not holders of rights or duties and ... are consequently vulnerable to human rights abuses being labeled 'internal affairs.' "[7] Indeed, the actual lived realities "inside" political communities are, according to R. B. J. Walker, deemed "unproblematic and uninteresting, of peripheral importance to the serious business of capital and state. To engage with the local is to be sidetracked into the trivial; to aspire to some broader and more universal conception of humanity is to recede into the mists of utopia."[8]

That the state-centrism of political realism is central to the debating club that now characterizes much of international relations (re)theorizing cannot be overstated. As Walker puts it, "theories of international relations tell us less about the character and consequences of state sovereignty than the principle of state sovereignty tells us about the categorical structures of international relations theory."[9] And it is principally repetitions of identity and difference, universal and particular, inside and outside, space and time, that structure international relations' structures. As such, the principle of state sovereignty and its locus of articulation "expresses an ethics of absolute exclusion"[10] a logic which thus excludes political theory, and the possibility of world politics, from in-

ternational relations. Political space-time must therefore be rearticu-
lated as a politics "that challenges the modern framing of other as Other,"
the framing of which is "expressed, reproduced, and legitimized by the
very distinction between international relations and political theory,"[11]
but articulated in such a way as to avoid reducing the other to the Same.

If the political is "evacuated" from international relations, so too are
women, as brought to light in feminist struggles to redirect the "third
debate" — and as Walker concurs.[12] For Christine Sylvester, however,
Walker's ambivalence about the potential contributions of feminist
theory (what with its fractures, struggles, and contestations) is troubling. Taking issue with Walker's move to pit "politics" against "relations,"
Sylvester writes: "Feminist psychoanalytic writings, for example, tell us
that 'relations' are produced by the conventions of human birth and
caretaking and then downplayed as boys become gendered. Adult 'men'
routinely act in ways that deny human relations and that affirm polari-
ties in which some of us seek freedom and the women seek connections. In the feminist psychoanalytic school of thought, 'relations' con-
notes closer bonds of sociality than the interest-group manipulations,
rules, and competition of 'politics.' "[13]

Sylvester recognizes that cultivated political spaces are necessary sites
precisely for posing and arguing what is "good for" women. And relations are needed to negotiate these "cultivated" political spaces.[14] It is in
conjoining "politics" and "relations" that Sylvester sees what she calls
"empathetic cooperation" as a potential model for scripting a more inclusive international relations than the "first debate era" would allow.
We need, therefore, to introduce new standpoints "and create reciprocal
relationships of being knowing through processes of empathetic cooperation."[15] Indeed, empathetic cooperation renders any choice between
politics and relations beside the point. "Empathy," says Sylvester, "leads
to listening to the excluded, listening to their sense of the good, knowing that they will present a fractured and heavily contested discourse
because they have been simultaneously inside and outside a master narrative. Cooperation comes in rescripting agendas to reflect the subjectivities that have been etched into the identities of empathetic listeners."[16]

Drawing on Kathy Ferguson's idea of "mobile subjectivities,"[17] Sylvester
defines empathy as "a willingness to enter into the feeling or spirit of
something and appreciate it fully," to be able to "hear what the na-
tivized say" and thus to be "transformed" in that hearing.[18] In this sense,

empathy means a communication across equal *and* unequal subject positions so that, in effect, identities "slide and shift."[19] It is the unsettling of our identities, the "rescripting of ourselves" in our negotiations with "contentious others," that Sylvester identifies as the starting point of rescripting international relations itself. As such, rewriting international relations is based on an empathetic cooperation with *difference*. This is, then, not a politics of liberalism but, rather, of liminality.[20]

The Liminal Criminal and the Limits of Empathy

While there is much to be commended in Sylvester's efforts to return international relations to a more ethical relation with difference, there is also reason for caution. In this section I want to address some of the limits an empathetic possibility of "knowing" the Other, or "sharing" her feelings, poses. As Drucilla Cornell reminds us with regard to Levinas, "[k]nowledge, at least in the sense of representation, is always a violation of otherness."[21]

In outlining some of the pitfalls of empathetic identification, I turn first to Diana Tietjens Meyers's formulation of what she calls "empathic thought" as a corrective to Kantian impartial reason which, she argues, assumes a single model of personhood.[22] Like Sylvester, Meyers sees empathy as a response to a "dilemma of difference," the exploitation of others, and unjust social exclusion. Empathy, then, is part of a larger political struggle. And like Sylvester, Meyers looks to feminist theories of subjectivity, which refute the notion of a unitary self. "Whether the individual moral subject making choices at the interpersonal level or the social moral subject making policy at the political level, the moral subject of empathic thought is nonunitary. The unidimensional moral subject— the monistic impartial reasoner—is replaced by a pluralistic, heterogeneous moral subject—a subject whose perception may be structured by culturally normative prejudice and who needs dissident speech to overcome prejudice and empathize with different others."[23]

Impartial reason therefore needs empathy as a base for moral reflection and moral judgment. For "[e]mpathy not only enables people to discern situations that call for a moral response, but also it is needed to identify morally significant considerations." This, says Meyers, is relatively straightforward. One must be able to identify opportunities in order to act morally. And the spotting of such opportunities "requires grasping what other people are going through."[24]

Meyers is careful to point out, however, that shrewdly sizing people up or attempting to sympathetically "fuse" with another are not exemplary of an empathic basis for moral reflection. To be sure, one may, instead, have manipulation in mind. For instance: "Masterful torturers who inflict suffering tailored to each prisoner's distinctive vulnerabilities must be astute observers of human nature. But their insight into their victims does not stem from empathy, for empathizing with another presupposes some degree of concern for that person. With concern for the individual underlying the moral basis of empathy, empathy could however be equated with sympathy—in that 'to sympathize with another is to share that person's feelings.' "[25]

But it is, in part, with the disparate notions of the relationship between empathy and sympathy that moral waters get muddied. For instance, for Christine Sylvester, empathy and sympathy are quite distinct. Whereas the former demonstrates the ability to "participate in another's ideas and feelings," the latter runs the risk of lapsing into a form of pity. Indeed, sympathy, "is a more distanced, socially correct response mediated by a constant 'I,' an immobile subjectivity."[26] Drawing on Judith Butler, Sylvester argues that sympathy may well be an appropriative move, a substitution of oneself for another and a colonization of the Other's position as one's own.[27]

Meyers, on the other hand, sees empathy and sympathy as a more complex *relation*. In her view, some forms of sympathy (like feeling saddened by a death because someone else feels saddened by it) are empathetic, while others are not. And herein lies the problem. She explains: "Unfortunately, when one's sharing of another's subjective state is occasioned, as it often is, by intense emotional involvement with that person, one is likely to be carried along by one's sympathy and drawn into the other's projects regardless of the wisdom of doing so. Empathetic sympathy often preempts moral reflection."[28]

Meyers thus identifies an alternative form of empathy based on an *imaginative reconstruction* of another person's feelings: "To empathize with another in this sense is to construct in imagination an experience resembling that of the other person . . . Though the vividness of empathic imaginings is often moving, empathizers do not share the subjective states with whom they empathize. One can imagine another's grief without grieving oneself."[29] As Meyers reminds us, it is undeniably difficult to empathize with those with whom we have nothing in common. And for the intended "recipient," claims to "empathy" can be infuriatingly presumptuous.[30] Imaginatively experiencing another's state of mind, therefore, would (presumably) make empathizing with one from a different background or circumstances more possible and less problematic.

Important in this reformulation of empathy is the distinction between "incident-specific" and "broad" empathy. The latter is a more extensive and complex relationship than an incident-specific empathy, which occurs within a relatively demarcated time frame and in isolation from other aspects of the recipient's life experiences.[31] "To empathize with another's subjectivity," Meyers says, "is not only to draw on one's past emotional life to conjure up that person's experiences in one's own mind, but it is also *to grasp the circumstances of that person's life* ... Grounded in protomoral concern for the other, *broad empathy yields protomoral knowledge of the other*."[32]

While Meyers argues (via Maria Lugones and Elizabeth Spelman), that this form of empathy is *not* culturally imperialistic, we would do well to recall Drucilla Cornell's warning of the limits of representation: that claims of knowing the Other (as that which lies *beyond our grasp*) is but a violation of the Other's exteriority.[33] Indeed, as Levinas holds, the absolutely other cannot be reflected in consciousness.[34]

Given the misunderstandings and dangers of empathy, is it a concept worth holding on to? As Megan Boler asks in reference to multicultural education, just "[w]ho and what ... benefits from the production of sympathy and empathy?"[35] In other words, even if it were *possible* to empathize with "someone for whom one feels no affection,"[36] say, a rapist and killer, is it any less problematic than an appropriative sympathetic gesture? Perhaps, as educational philosopher Ron Glass suggests, "these 'others' whose lives we imagine do not want empathy, [but] justice."[37] To be sure, in *Dead Man Walking* what is clear is that the condemned man is not seeking sympathy, repeatedly claiming "I ain't no victim," but justice: "Do not let me die."

To return to Boler, one of the risks of empathy in reading and teaching textual representations of violence and historical trauma (such as the Holocaust) is that it is often accompanied by pity in the form of a moral judgment of the other's experiences. In this sense "pity encompasses a power relationship through which we estimate the extent of suffering — whether the person 'warrants' our pity, and whether or not the person is to blame and then does not deserve our pity."[38] Moving closer to a Levinasian position, Boler frames the problem of empathetic identification in terms of responsibility and obligation. Boler suggests, in fact, that empathy is an emotional construct that, in effect, *abdicates* responsibility.[39]

The considerations raised by Boler are especially significant for an ethical reading of a film such as *Dead Man Walking,* wherein the exteriority of the Other (the criminal's liminality *and* the liminality of "the Criminal") is what is at stake. As Foucault points out, capital punishment is maintained less by invoking the enormity of the crime itself, than the "monstrosity" of the criminal.[40]

It is precisely this exteriority of the killer/Other that is utterly "beyond" Sister Helen's and the viewer's, indeed beyond my and your, grasp. Furthermore, just as there is no knowing the Other, there is no knowing death.[41] What I want to suggest is that rather than being an act of sympathy or empathy, pity or compassion, the nun's relationship with the killer/to-be-killed stems from a responsibility that, in a Levinasian sense, is "beyond" empathy (if empathy is to be understood as knowing the Other). Responsibility, in other words, is not an altruism, but an obligation: "No one is good voluntarily."[42] In the next section I will look further at how this notion of responsibility issues from "the face" of the Other, as a response to one's fear *for* the Other, and for the Other's death. As we shall see, for Levinas, violence is aimed at *the face of the Other.* Murder, Levinas maintains, is a negation of alterity.[43]

A Face to Die For: Levinas and Ethical Responsibility

Recent years have seen a tremendous import given to Emmanuel Levinas's ethical philosophy of alterity, which, in identifying the inherent "violence" of ontology and challenging ontology's primacy in philosophy, posits *ethics,* rather, as "first philosophy."

Levinas explains in his first major work, *Totality and Infinity,* that the problem with the Western philosophical tradition *is* ontology. Ontology is a philosophy of power, a relation with Being that in "neutralizing the existent in order to comprehend or grasp it" cannot be but a reduction of the other to the Same, the self, the knowing subject.[44] The philosophy ontology commands is "a suppression of pluralism."[45] The Other, then, cannot be apprehended in an all-encompassing "totality," can never be thematized, conceptualized, brought into consciousness, or captured in representation without sacrificing her genuine alterity, or exteriority. In brief, the point of *Totality and Infinity* is to reverse the terms of ontology and to present subjectivity as a *welcoming* of the Other as neighbor in conversation, an ethical relation that then calls the self into question and to justice. "The effort of this book," Levinas says, "is directed toward apperceiving in discourse a non-allergic relation with alterity, toward apperceiving in Discourse — where power, by essence murderous of the other, becomes, faced with the other and 'against all good sense,' the impossibility of murder, the consideration of the other, or justice."[46]

What Levinas describes as ontological violence, the taking hold of and grasping of the Other, has its counterpart in the state-sanctioned violence of war. "The visage of being that shows itself in war," he says, "is fixed in the concept of totality, which dominates Western philosophy."[47] The violence of war, he maintains, is directed only toward a being that is both graspable and capable of escaping every hold: "Violence can aim only at a face."[48] Yet, paradoxically, the face is what forbids us to kill.[49] That the face does so is doubtless why it is covered in the execution process. What is interesting about the growing popularity of lethal injection, as a more "humane" method of killing, is that the first shot relaxes the muscles of the face so that any visible signs of bodily pain are effectively eliminated.[50]

The place of the nonviolent relation with radical alterity that is ethics, is, therefore, the "face," that is, the "apparition," the "trace" of the other,[51] "the way in which the other presents himself, exceeding *the idea of the other in me.*"[52] And this way-in-which-the-other-presents-himself to me is through "an irrecusable order, a command" which, in halting the "availability of consciousness," calls me into question. *Consciousness,* therefore, is put into question by a face. For the absolutely other is not reflected in consciousness.[53]

It is the *response* to the Other's command that Levinas understands as a "responsibility" that empties the "I" of its imperialism: "To be an I . . . signifies not to be able to slip away from responsibility."[54] One's own identity starts with the impossibility of escaping responsibility, from "taking charge" of the other.[55] Responsibility is in this sense paradoxical, according to Levinas, insofar "that I am obliged, without this obligation having begun in me, as though an order slipped into my consciousness."[56] Responsibility is therefore incumbent *on me exclusively* and is what I *humanly* cannot refuse.[57]

One of the most crucial aspects of Levinas's thought and its implications for our understanding of state-sanctioned practices of killing the liminal Other/others (i.e., the weak, the poor, the "widow and the orphan"), is this very "asymmetry" of the face-to-face relation and what that brings to bear on the role of the responsible self in the event of the other's death.[58] It is worth recalling here that for Christine Sylvester, an empathetic cooperation with difference rests upon *reciprocal* relationships of being and knowing. For Levinas, however, the ethical relation, though intersubjective, is explicitly nonreciprocal. He explains: "In this sense, I am responsible for the Other without waiting for reciprocity, were I to die for it. Reciprocity is *his* affair. It is precisely insofar as the relationship between the Other and me is not reciprocal that I am subjection to the Other; and I am 'subject' essentially in this sense. It is I who support all. You know that sentence in Dostoevsky: '*We are all guilty of all and for all men before all, and I more than the others.*'"[59]

The essential asymmetry of the ethical relation thus disallows any presumption of equality between self and Other and emphasizes the irreplaceability of moral subjects.[60] With subjectivity defined as subjection, as being before and for the Other, my being responsible means, as well, that as a unique and noninterchangeable "I," I am *substitutable* for another.[61]

One of the more complex themes in Levinas's thought, and central to *Otherwise Than Being: Or Beyond Essence*, substitution is not so much an act, but what he refers to as a "passivity" wherein the self is absolved of itself.[62] It is important to emphasize here that this idea of substitution, of putting oneself in the place of another, is not the move of ontology's imperial I. Nor is it a form of coresponsibility grounded in compassion, benevolence, or empathy.[63] As Alphonso Lingis puts it: "To acknowledge the imperative force of another is to put oneself in his place, not in order to appropriate one's own objectivity, but in order to answer to his need, to supply his want with one's own substance . . . To put oneself in the place of another is also to answer for his deeds and his misdeeds, for the trouble he causes and for his faults. It is even to be responsible for the very pain he causes me, at the limit for his persecution — the contestation he formulates against me for what I did not author or authorize."[64]

Levinas sees substitution therefore as a form of "disinterestedness," the state of being the Other's hostage, to have one degree of responsibility more. It is a being responsible even for the Other's responsibility.[65]

And in this condition of disinterestedness, being "undoes its condition of being."[66]

But how does this asymmetrical ethical relation of being responsible for the Other — to the point of substitution — hold the self as responsible for the Other in *death*? Indeed, as Levinas sees it, prior to any knowledge about it, mortality lies in the Other.[67] Responsibility for the Other, which goes even beyond whatever acts "I" may have committed, so much that I place the Other before myself, means that I am to answer for the Other's death even before *being*.[68] It is, as we know, the existence of the self, the very right to be, that is called into question by the approach of the Other's face. The epiphany of the face is what disrupts ontology's claim of a prior right to existence wherein subjectivity reduces everything to itself, where pluralism is reduced to unicity. In exposing myself to the "vulnerability" of the face, my ontological right to existence is thrown into question: "[M]y duty to respond to the other suspends my natural right to self-survival."[69] The face, then, in its vulnerability, in its nakedness, destitution, and suffering, "is the Other who asks me not to let him die alone, as if to do so were to become an accomplice in his death . . . In ethics, the other's right to exist has primacy over my own, a primacy epitomized in the ethical edict: you shall not kill, you shall not jeopardize the life of the other. The ethical rapport with the face is asymmetrical in that it subordinates my existence to the other."[70]

Moreover, that I am called to answer for the Other and the Other's death before I can "be" at all speaks of the *temporality* of the ethical relation with alterity. The condition of exteriority or alterity of otherness is precisely its ungraspability in the present (which then calls me, that is, my existence — the "here I am" — into question). The relationship with alterity, with the other, is consequently, a relationship with the *future* insofar as the future is that which is not grasped but, rather, what lays hold of us.[71]

The unknown of death is a relationship with mystery.[72] But the fact that death is never "a present," that it "deserts the present" has less to do with any attempts to evade death than the fact that *death as such* is ungraspable. As Levinas explains: "The now is the fact that I am master, master of the possible, master of grasping the possible. Death is never now. When death is here, I am no longer here, not just because I am nothingness, but because I am unable to grasp."[73] Our relationship with death, thus understood, is a unique relationship with the future.[74]

Levinas's position vis-à-vis death is therefore in stark contrast to a Heideggerian being-toward-death. This indeed is his major point in "Time and the Other." Whereas for Heidegger, death is a "supreme virility," an event of freedom understood within *"Dasein's* assumption of the uttermost possibility of existence, which precisely makes possible all other possibilities" including the "very feat of grasping a possibility," for Levinas death is the limit of possibility, the impossibility of graspability.[75] More exactly, death is "the impossibility of having a project." It marks the moment when we are "no longer *able to be able."* Death, then, for Levinas, means the *end* of virility.[76] What is more, in death the solitude of the subject is not confirmed, but broken: "Consequently only a being whose solitude has reached a crispation through suffering, and in relation with death, takes its place on a ground where the relationship with the other becomes possible."[77] As Ruben Berezdivin sums up:

> Obligation from the other and his phenomenal rupture with the temporality of my initiative, my projecting, can only take place because in trying to project my death I become impotent of possibilities and lose my virility, suffering (becoming open to) the destitution of the other, which is ultimate and absolute in his dying in my stead. *The obligation which the face-to-face incarnates, I before you where you claim priority over me in your mortal transcendence, comes from the place of death: it is only as dead and dying, already dead, that the destitution and suffering of the other obligates, the face-to-face as dual is a facing up to the image of the other's cadaver.*[78]

The Sister and the Brother's Keeper:
Reading Ethics and Justice in *Dead Man Walking*

Why should I concern myself with the other? asks Levinas. Am I my brother's keeper?[79] Levinas holds that I am ordered to heed the call of the primordial other, from the outside, *traumatically* even. Consequently, questions like "What then is it to me? Where does he get his right to command? What have I done to be from the start in debt?" are beside the point.[80] To be sure, the choice to opt out of relationship with the other is, to put it simply, just not there: "It is impossible to free myself by saying, 'It's not my concern.' There is no choice, for it is always and inescapably my concern. This is a unique 'no choice,' one that is not slavery."[81]

To return briefly to international relations, this lack of a choice of choice is especially significant for rethinking ethical responsibility in "foreign" policy affairs. It means, for example, that we cannot declare that situations like the Balkan crisis are not our concern.[82] I would also argue that insofar as " 'we' are always already ethically situated," "we" cannot ignore the annihilation of (even the most reprehensible) others within the "domestic" sphere.[83] Indeed, Prejean insists that capital punishment not be considered a marginal issue. "It involves all of us," she writes in *Dead Man Walking*. "We're all complicit. Government can only continue killing if we give it the power. It's time to take that power back."[84] I will discuss some of the problems that occur with the "passage" from ethics to justice and politics in Levinas's thought, but I want to turn first to how the film *Dead Man Walking* exposes the call of the primordial Other as being beyond choice and explanation, a call that emanates from the face of a (not quite yet) "dead man."

As Susan Handelman points out, Levinas's notion of the face is often ambiguous and subject to varying definitions.[85] While he maintains that the face of the Other is not originally founded on visual perception and that at each moment it "destroys and overflows the plastic image it leaves me," it nonetheless and at the same time bears an expressivity. The Other's face "*expresses itself*" and in that expression brings a notion of truth.[86] The face, then, is still "a thing among things" that nevertheless breaks through the very form that delimits it. In so doing, "the face speaks to me."[87] As discussed in the previous section, it is "the face" that says "Do not kill me, do not let me die alone, die for me."

As many film critics were quick to point out, the emotional intensity of *Dead Man Walking* owes as much to the drama of the "face-to-face" conversational scenes between nun and prisoner as to the actual politics of state-sanctioned killing. In these scenes the camera plays a particularly important role in articulating both the spatial and social relationships between the nun and the prisoner. There is scarcely a scene in which the two are not separated by a boundary of some sort. In the initial scenes they are separated by a wire mesh grate so thick that their ability to see one another is as strained as their attempts at communication. Once the prisoner is transferred to the "death house," the meetings take place through a Plexiglas window upon which the image of the other is reflected. The final encounter between Sister Helen and Poncelet, prior to his "death" walk when she is allowed to touch his shoulder, is through the bars of his cell. In an interview on the American television program, *Frontline,* Robbins explains that the major challenge in terms of cinematography was to make the conversational scenes different visually, and to "create a kind of metaphor to the distance between them breaking away to . . . to when that touch happens on the shoulder. That becomes an important moment." On the same television program, Prejean describes the film as a story of unconditional love and redemption. At its heart is "the encounter between this nun and this very unsympathetic, unremorseful, guilty-as-the-dickens killer, and . . . what's going to happen to the two of them in the process of encountering each other."[88]

As the film begins, Sister Helen is on her way to Louisiana's Angola Prison for her first meeting with Matthew Poncelet, who has been on death row for six years for his part in the brutal murder of a young man and a woman, whom he also raped.[89] Knowing that Sister Helen is an outspoken opponent of the death penalty, Poncelet had written to her asking her to visit. We soon discover that Sister Helen is a "novice," so to speak, in such matters, her prior prison record consisting solely of a "singing nun" type of gig for juveniles. When quizzed by a suspiciously suspicious prison chaplain about her motivation for visiting such a monstrous criminal ("So what is it Sister, morbid fascination, bleeding heart sympathy?"), Sister Helen replies, "He wrote me and asked me to come." No other explanation seems necessary.

The nun's "motivation" in her involvement with a brutal and unrepentant (Poncelet repeatedly claims he is innocent) rapist/killer is, in fact, called into question throughout the film: by her family, by the residents of the predominantly African-American housing project in which she lives and works, by the families of Poncelet's victims, by Poncelet's mother, and by Sister Helen herself. And she is consistently at a loss for explanation. For instance, when at the dinner table of her more-than-comfortably-middle-class family, Helen finds her mother dismayed by her preoccupation with such a hopeless cause when there are so many others/Others she could be helping who are more "deserving." "What has drawn you to this?" she asks. To this, Sister Helen replies: "Mama, I don't know. I feel caught more than drawn. The man's in trouble and for some reason I'm the only one he trusts." Sister Helen's own doubts about her responsibility toward Poncelet come to the fore later in the

film when, after an unsuccessful pardon board hearing to halt his execution, Poncelet expresses his admiration for Hitler in an interview with
the press, describing how he'd like to "come back" as a terrorist and blow
up government buildings. In the face of Poncelet's now certain death,
Sister Helen, though doubtful that she can "save his soul" and convince
him to accept responsibility for his part in the killings, knows that she
cannot let him face death alone.

The pardon board hearing is a pivotal moment in the film, marking
the point at which the nun's relationship with the killer shifts from helping him fight for his life to helping him prepare to die, the point at
which the Other's cry "do not let me die" becomes "do not let me die
alone." As the decision is announced, Poncelet turns to Sister Helen
and says that he is allowed a spiritual adviser of his choice and asks if
she would do it. She nods yes. This could also be considered a point at
which Sister Helen's attempts to sympathize with Poncelet in his plight
shifts to obligation (there is no going back now) and to love. In the final
encounter before his execution, Sister Helen says to Poncelet: "I want
the last thing you see in this world to be the face of love. I'll be the face
of love for you."

Yet while it is clear to Sister Helen that, as a human being, Poncelet is
deserving of love, he is a difficult person to like. His lack of remorse for
his crimes, his racism, and his general macho demeanor (to the point
of making a sexual overture to the nun) renders the killer one of the more
reprehensible Others a self could wish to encounter. And any attempts
on the *viewer's* part to sympathize/empathize with the condemned man
are effectively thwarted with Robbins's consistent use of flashbacks to
the crime scene, using horrific detail and eerie lighting. With empathetic identification rendered impossible, Sister Helen, like the responsible viewer, has "no choice" but obligation. Such is the passivity of
responsibility.

It is also at the pardon board hearing that Sister Helen first meets
the parents of the murdered teenagers. Here the nun's relationship with
the monstrous killer, her defense of his right to life, is again challenged.
In the face of *their* destitution and suffering, the pain of their enor-
mous loss and their retributive rage toward the man responsible, she
feels caught in a moral bind. Some of the film's most emotionally charged
scenes are the subsequent encounters between Sister Helen and the victims' families. And it is their inclusion that leads many of the film's

viewers and reviewers to conclude that in showing "both sides" of the capital punishment debate, Robbins's is a "balanced" view to the effect that he takes no stand at all. But any ambiguity concerning Robbins's political position on the issue of state-sanctioned killing could also be read as an indicator of both the difficulty of acting responsibly and the passivity of ethical action, the passivity of being "hostage" to the other's call.[90] In this state of being hostage, of always having one degree of responsibility more, the absolute asymmetry of the ethical relation between self and other, nun and killer, is pronounced. He may be the one who is facing death, but she is the one who must "bear the wretchedness and bankruptcy of the other."[91]

But does my bearing the burden of responsibility for the Other necessarily entail that I never judge or question the Other's actions? Simon Critchley acknowledges that, in the spirit of Levinas's nonreciprocity, "[e]thically, I cannot demand that the Other be good." Still, he advises that "the extremity of this position must be tempered by the thought that, at the level of politics and justice, at which I am a citizen of a community, I *am* entitled to judge, to call the Other to account, to raise Cain's question."[92] This is an important consideration in our reading of *Dead Man Walking*. For Sister Helen, notwithstanding her ethical obligation to Poncelet, relentlessly questions his actions, in particular his refusal to admit them.[93] Eventually Poncelet breaks down and confesses to the nun his role in the killing of the young man and expresses his remorse in the moment prior to being led to the execution chamber. Then, in the final moments of his life, when strapped to the gurney and turned upright with arms outstretched in a Christlike pose, he apologizes to his victims' families. Yet with an addendum he proclaims that "killing is wrong, no matter who does it, me, or y'all, or your government."

The fact that Poncelet's sudden "redemption" was brought about only by the reality of his impending death heightened the controversy surrounding the film, leading to conclusions that the death penalty "works," that execution leads to absolution. Read in this way, the film could be regarded as an endorsement of the death penalty.[94] Read differently, the apparent ambiguity, or "crisis of meaning" within the film, could suggest an ambiguity of *justice* and its distinction from law. The justice demanded by the victims' families is not the "justice" called for by the killer and, in her substitutive mode, Sister Helen. We could infer, then, that in troubling the idea of justice, *Dead Man Walking* is a deconstructive text. For it is in the realm of justice that Levinasian ethics meets Derrida's notion of deconstruction.

Justice on Trial

In defense of deconstruction's inherent relation to justice and politics and in defiance of claims that deconstruction does not "address" justice, Derrida argues in "Force of Law" that deconstruction has done nothing but address it, albeit obliquely, because it is *unable* to do so directly.[95] Writes Derrida:

> a deconstructive interrogation that starts ... by destabilizing, complicating, or bringing out the paradoxes of values like those of the proper and of property in all their registers, of the subject, and so of the responsible subject, of the subject of law (*droit*) and the subject of morality, of the juridical or moral person, of intentionality, etc., and of all that follows from these, such a deconstructive line of questioning is through and through a problematization of law and justice. A problematization of the foundations of morality and politics.[96]

It is in problematizing the "mystical authority" of law's foundations that Derrida is able to make a distinction between law and justice. Responding to Montaigne and Pascal, Derrida posits that justice as law is not justice: "Laws are not just *as* laws. One obeys them not because they are just but because they have authority."[97]

Derrida tells us that the foundations of law rest on nothing but themselves, silencing the very violence of the founding act.[98] This is not to say that laws are in themselves unjust. In their founding moment they are neither legal nor illegal. But in this founding moment laws are instituted in a performative and interpretive force. Law is therefore always an interpretive act. Law's deconstructibility (which sets it apart from justice) is therefore twofold: "Law is essentially deconstructible whether because it is founded, constructed on interpretable and transformable textual strata ... or because its ultimate foundation is by definition unfounded."[99] It is the deconstructible structure of law that ensures the possibility of deconstruction. Justice, on the other hand, insofar as it lies outside of or "beyond" law, is not deconstructible, any more than deconstruction itself is. Deconstruction, in other words, *is* justice. In sum, "deconstruction takes place in the interval that separates the undeconstructibility of justice from the deconstructibility of *droit* (authority, legitimacy, and so on)."[100]

What is particularly important for our purposes is that Derrida bases his distinction between *law* (as stabilizable, calculable, a system of regulated and coded prescriptions) and *justice* (as infinite, incalculable, rebellious to rule and foreign to symmetry) on Levinas's understanding of justice, because of the latter's understanding of infinity and "because of the heteronomic relation to others, to the faces of otherness that govern me, whose infinity I cannot thematize and whose hostage I remain." Because according to Levinas, justice is the relation with the Other, the equitable honoring of faces, wherein, of course, equity is not *equality*, but absolute dissymmetry.[101] The idea of justice is infinite because it is irreducible, and it is irreducible because it is owed to the Other, before any contract and without any recognition or gratitude.[102] The surplus of duties over rights, it is the forgetting of self in the proximity of the other that moves justice. Moreover, out of my "inequality" with the Other to whom I am hostage is borne the equality of all.[103]

Now, matters would be much simpler if the above distinction between law and justice were a *true* distinction. But as it turns out, law "claims to exercise itself in the name of justice and . . . justice is required to establish itself in the name of a law that must be 'enforced.' "[104] In fact, there is no such thing as a law *without* "enforceability," whether this application of force be direct or indirect, physical or symbolic.[105] What deconstruction thus exposes is, in Drucilla Cornell's terms, the violence that masquerades as the rule of law, or, "law dressed up as justice."[106] What we see in *Dead Man Walking,* in addition to (but not separate from) the exposure of the distinction between law and justice, is an unmasking of the violence of a law that uses violence under the guise of preventing violence. Sister Helen sums it up more neatly: "I don't see the sense in killing someone to say that killing someone is wrong."

But as is consistently emphasized throughout the film, it is not just *any* "man" who is killed in this masquerade. That *there are no rich men on death row* echoes throughout the film. The object of violence in the state's name is the liminal Other, "the poor and the stranger," as evidenced in the disproportionate number of African-Americans who "receive" the death penalty.[107] The retributive "justice" in the United States aims, then, not only at "the criminal" per se, but at a culturally constructed criminal element: the "disturbing alterity within."[108] Sarah Goodwin and Elisabeth Bronfen argue in *Death and Representation* that individual executions, like the collective violence of war, serve both to purge and to restabilize an unstable group. Communities thus *require* images of alterity and sacrifice to define and secure their own boundaries.[109] A community's idea of itself in history cannot, therefore, be disentangled from the ways it represents *death*. "At the extreme," write Goodwin and Bronfen, "this can be understood as referring to those it chooses to kill, literally and symbolically: scapegoats. Kings, revolutionaries, widows, prostitutes, soldiers — all help define the community with their sacrificial corpses."[110] We should recall here how for Levinas, murder is the negation of alterity. Violence is directed only at that which is truly exterior, that which exceeds and "paralyzes" one's power. We kill, therefore, not to dominate, but to *annihilate* alterity: "The Other is the sole being I can wish to kill."[111]

One of the more troubling paradoxes of modern politics, therefore, is that violence is "*both* the practice which constructs the refuge of the sovereign community, and the condition from which the citizens of that community must be protected."[112] Campbell and Dillon argue, via Foucault, that in fleeing from violence to secure "security," modernity's "man" employs techniques of bodily mutilation and policies of mass death as "mundane political instruments."[113] And as Allan Feldman points out, it is the surface of the body that becomes "the stage where the state is made to appear as an effective material force."[114]

We could conclude, therefore, that as a practice of annihilating radical alterity (that which is truly Other), aimed as it is at the face and enacted upon the body, state-sanctioned killing — whether in the "theater" of war or in the spectacle of the execution chamber — is inextricably linked to "security." But I would caution that violence in the name of the state is not just an *instrument* of security, but also an "effect" of its discourse. Baudrillard, for example, speaks of security as blackmail. Here security is understood as another form of social control, universally present and ranging in form from life insurance to advertising slogans for seatbelts.[115] Capitalism, he argues, lives off the production of death yet pretends to manufacture security: "We have successfully infected people with the virus of conservation and security, even though they will have to fight to the death to get it. In fact, it is more complicated, since they are fighting for the *right* to security, which is of a profoundly different order. As regards security itself, no-one gives a damn. They had to be infected over generations for them to end up believing that they 'needed' it, and this success is an essential aspect of 'social' domestication and colonization."[116]

So successful has been the manufacture of security "needs" in the American social imaginary that it is a fear of violent crime, quite independent of its likelihood, that fuels support for the death penalty.[117] Prejean cites a 1986 Gallup poll which revealed that while 70 percent of respondents initially favored the death penalty, when they were given data revealing that capital punishment does not in fact deter crime and then offered the alternative of life imprisonment without parole, support for the death penalty dropped to 43 percent.[118] Given that in the United States one is much more likely to die in an automobile accident, or that strokes cause eleven times more deaths than homicide, one has to wonder what "really" underlies the security threat emanating from the figure (and face) of the Criminal.

We therefore have to imagine a "justice" that operates not in fear *of* the Other, but in fear *for* the Other; that is, a justice that the response of responsibility brings when responsibility is, in Derrida's words, "without limits" and incalculable.[119] It bears emphasizing here that while Derrida holds that justice exceeds law and calculation, this in no way should be read as a reason for staying out of juridico-political battles, whether within or between institutions and states. Rather, "incalculable justice *requires* us to calculate ... Not only *must* we calculate, negotiate the relation between the calculable and the incalculable ... but we *must* take it as far as possible, beyond zones of morality or politics or law, beyond the distinction between national and international, public and private and so on."[120]

Therefore, in excess of calculation, rules, and programs, justice lies in the future, indeed, opens up *for* the future the possibility of "the transformation, the recasting, or refounding of law and politics."[121] As regards capital punishment, Karen Slawner notes that the current retributive mode in the United States does not represent anything close to an obligation to the Other.[122] But the very deconstructibility of law opens up the possibility for rewriting the legal narrative in the hope of justice that "consists in listening to the Other in the knowledge that the current order has not exhausted all possibilities."[123]

Postscript

Given Levinas's claim of the primacy of the interhuman (face-to-face) relation, the structure upon which all other structures rest,[124] ethical responsibility holds promise for a post-positivist international relations oriented to dissolving the arbitrary divide between the "domestic" and "the international" and its related juridico-legal distinction between state-sanctioned practices of killing Others "inside" and "outside" state borders.

But is there a limit to Levinas's own understanding of ethical responsibility and its relation to politics and justice? Are some Others more "other" than others? Although in *Otherwise Than Being* Levinas posits that justice is justice only in a society that doesn't distinguish between those close and those far off, David Campbell warns of something amiss in the "passage" from ethics to politics: the expansion of the one-to-one of the ethical relation to the "one-and-the-many" of community. Part of the difficulty lies in Levinas's sometimes vague and contrasting thoughts on the state, the "third party," and morality, which are the means by which that expansion takes place.[125] Although a full discussion is not possible here, a brief sketch is necessary.

Although the focus of Levinas's scholarship is the individual one-to-one relationship with the Other, he associates the totalizing politics that reduces difference to sameness essentially with war.[126] In outlining the problem of war, Levinas exposes morality and politics as inherently oppositional. In fact, he ponders whether we might be "duped" by morality given the permanent possibility of war. For the state of war, Levinas claims, "suspends morality." Reading Clausewitz against the grain, Levinas concludes that politics, as the art of foreseeing war and winning it by every means, must be opposed to morality.[127] If left to itself, politics bears a "tyranny within itself," thus "it is necessary to oppose the particular ethical relation with the Other to the panoramic vision of political life that views society only as a whole."[128] Politics must always, Levinas insists, be able to be checked and criticized starting from *the ethical.*[129] As Critchley concludes, ethics then leads back to politics, and responsibility to questioning.[130]

As Critchley also points out, the passage from ethics to politics as laid out in *Totality and Infinity* is traversed all too briefly, taken up again in greater detail in *Otherwise Than Being*. In the latter work, "Levinas attempts to build a bridge from ethics understood as a responsible, nontotalizing relation with the Other, to politics, conceived of as a relation to the third party (*le tiers*), to all the others, to the plurality of beings that make up the community. The passage from ethics to politics is approached by Levinas in terms of 'the latent birth of the *question* in responsibility.' "[131] In fact, as Levinas sees it, responsibility for the Other becomes troubled with the entry of the third party (the whole of humanity, which watches me in the eyes of the Other): "The third party is other than the neighbor, but also another neighbor, and also a neighbor of the other, and not simply his fellow. The other stands in a relationship with the third party, for whom I cannot entirely answer, even if I alone answer, before any question, for my neighbor. The other and the third party, my neighbors, contemporaries of one another, put distance between me and the other and the third party. 'Peace, peace to the neighbor and the one far-off.' "[132]

Perhaps even more troubling than the entry of the third party are the doubts it raises as to the universality of responsibility to the Other.[133] Campbell's concern is that Levinas's conception of "proximity" as not being reducible to any modality of distance denies the specifically spatial implications of the concept. The short of it is that, for Levinas, with the entry of the third party the ethical relationship with the other becomes political, thus requiring a need for the state. But, so approving is Levinas's view of the state that it often "has the capacity to overlook the restrictions upon the freedom of others the state's security requires."[134] Campbell is referring specifically to Levinas's disturbing remarks concerning the 1982 massacre of Palestinian refugees during the Israeli invasion of Lebanon. When asked of the otherness of the Palestinian to the Israeli, Levinas replied: "The other is the neighbor, who is not necessarily kin, but who can be. And in that sense, if you're for the other, you're for the neighbor. But if your neighbor attacks another neighbor or treats him unjustly, what can you do? Then alterity takes on another character, in alterity we can find an enemy, or at least then we are faced with the problem of knowing who is right and who is wrong, who is just and who is unjust. There are people who are wrong."[135] It would thus seem that whereas Levinas may indeed see justice *in* a society where there is no distinction between those close and those afar, the border *between* societies, if it enables the transformation of alterity into enmity, "permits the responsibility for the 'other' as neighbor to be diminished."[136]

Nonetheless, Levinas's contribution to returning ethics to politics is considerable. For Campbell, Levinas's contrasting assertion that "the political order of the state may have to be challenged in the name of our ethical responsibility to the other," however restricted to the *domestic* political order, does allow for the extension of political action beyond those bounds.[137]

Finally, then, although the "passage" from ethics to politics in Levinas's thought may be a bumpy one, it does not diminish its importance in building a better international relations. It is not a matter of finding a one-size-fits-all theory of state violence, but a question of questioning the legitimacy of a state-sanctioned use of violence toward the Other/others wherever it occurs, and to ask if it is just.

Notes

1. Helen Prejean, *Dead Man Walking: An Eyewitness Account of the Death Penalty in the United States* (New York: Random House, 1993), 111.

2. Emmanuel Levinas, "Ethics as First Philosophy," in Sean Hand, ed., *The Levinas Reader* (Oxford: Basil Blackwell, 1989), 83.

3. Karen Slawner, "Violence, Law, and Justice," *Alternatives* 20 (1995): 459–60.

4. Ibid., 472.

5. David Campbell and Michael Dillon, "The Political and the Ethical," in David Campbell and Michael Dillon, eds., *The Political Subject of Violence* (Manchester and New York: Manchester University Press, 1993), 162.

6. Slawner, "Violence, Law, and Justice," 459.

7. Ibid., 459–60.

8. R. B. J. Walker, *Inside/Outside: International Relations as Political Theory* (Cambridge: Cambridge University Press, 1993), 152–53.

9. Ibid., 23.

10. Ibid., 66.

11. Ibid., 183.

12. Christine Sylvester, *Feminist Theory and International Relations in a Postmodern Era* (Cambridge: Cambridge University Press, 1994), 163.

13. Ibid., 165.

14. Ibid.

15. Ibid., 96.

16. Ibid.

17. See Kathy E. Ferguson, *The Man Question: Visions of Subjectivity in Feminist Theory* (Berkeley and Los Angeles: University of California Press, 1993), especially chapter 6.

18. Sylvester, *Feminist Theory,* 96.

19. Ibid., 98.

20. Ibid., 99.

21. Drucilla Cornell, *The Philosophy of the Limit* (New York and London: Routledge, 1992), 68.

22. Diana Tietjens Meyers, *Subjection and Subjectivity: Psychoanalytic Feminism and Moral Philosophy* (London: Routledge, 1994), 26.

23. Ibid., 18.

24. Ibid., 26.

25. Ibid.

26. Sylvester, *Feminist Theory*, 166.

27. See Christine Sylvester, "Empathetic Cooperation: A Feminist Method for IR," *Millennium*, 23 (1995): 327.

28. Meyers, *Subjection and Subjectivity*, 32.

29. Ibid., 32–33.

30. Ibid., 33–34.

31. Ibid., 34–35.

32. Ibid., 35–37, emphasis added.

33. See note 20.

34. Emmanuel Levinas, "The Trace of the Other," in Mark C. Taylor, ed., *Deconstruction in Context: Literature and Philosophy* (Chicago and London: University of Chicago Press, 1986), 352.

35. Megan Boler, "The Risks of Empathy: Interrogating Multiculturalism's Gaze," in Michael Katz, ed., *Philosophy of Education 1994* (Urbana: University of Illinois Press, 1995), 211.

36. Meyers, *Subjection and Subjectivity*, 34.

37. Boler, "The Risks of Empathy," 211.

38. Ibid., 212.

39. Ibid., 210–11.

40. Michel Foucault, *The History of Sexuality: Volume I* (New York: Vintage Books, 1990), 138.

41. See Elisabeth Bronfen and Sarah Webster Goodwin, eds., *Death and Representation* (Baltimore and London: Johns Hopkins University Press, 1993).

42. Emmanuel Levinas, *Otherwise Than Being: Or Beyond Essence*, trans. Alphonso Lingis (Dordrecht: Kluwer Academic Publishers, 1981), 11.

43. Emmanuel Levinas, *Totality and Infinity: An Essay in Exteriority*, trans. Alphonso Lingis (The Hague: Martinus Nijhoff Publishers, 1979), 198.

44. Ibid., 45–46.

45. Ibid., 221.

46. Ibid., 47.

47. Ibid., 21.

48. Ibid., 223, 225.

49. Levinas, *Ethics and Infinity: Conversations with Philippe Nemo*, trans. Richard A. Cohen (Pittsburgh: Duquesne University Press, 1985), 86.

50. See Prejean, *Dead Man Walking*, 217.

51. Levinas, "The Trace of the Other," 351.

52. Levinas, *Totality and Infinity*, 50.

53. Levinas, "The Trace of the Other," 352.

54. Ibid., 353.

55. Emmanuel Levinas, *Otherwise Than Being: Or Beyond Essence*, 14.

56. Ibid., 13.

57. Emmanuel Levinas, *Ethics and Infinity*, 101.

58. Emmanuel Levinas, "Time and the Other," *The Levinas Reader*, 48.

59. Emmanuel Levinas, *Ethics and Infinity*, 98.

60. Zygmunt Bauman, *Postmodern Ethics* (Oxford: Blackwell Press, 1993), 48.

61. Levinas, *Otherwise Than Being*, 117.

62. Ibid., 115–17.

63. Bernhard Waldenfels, "Response and Responsibility in Levinas," Adriaan T. Peperzak, ed., *Ethics as First Philosophy: The Significance of Emmanuel Levinas for Philosophy, Literature and Religion* (New York and London: Routledge, 1995), 44.

64. Alphonso Lingis, "Introduction," in Emmanuel Levinas, *Otherwise Than Being*, xxii–xxiii.

65. Levinas, *Otherwise Than Being*, 117.

66. Levinas, *Ethics and Infinity*, 100.

67. Levinas, "Ethics as First Philosophy," 83.

68. Ibid.

69. Emmanuel Levinas and Richard Kearney, "Dialogue with Emmanuel Levinas," in Richard A. Cohen, ed., *Face to Face with Levinas* (New York: State University of New York Press, 1986), 24.

70. Ibid.

71. Levinas, "Time and the Other," 44.

72. Ibid., 40.

73. Ibid., 41.

74. Ibid.

75. Ibid., 40–41.

76. Ibid., 42.

77. Ibid., 43.

78. Ruben Berezdivin, "3 2 1 Contact: Textuality, the Other, Death," in Robert Bernasconi and Simon Critchley, eds., *Re-Reading Levinas* (Bloomington and Indianapolis: Indiana University Press, 1991), 197–98, emphasis added.

79. Levinas, *Otherwise Than Being*, 117.

80. Ibid., 87.

81. Levinas, "Ideology and Idealism," *The Levinas Reader*, 247.

82. David Campbell, "The Deterritorialization of Responsibility," this volume, chapter 2.

83. Ibid.

84. Prejean, *Dead Man Walking*, 130.

85. Susan A. Handelman, *Fragments of Redemption: Jewish Thought and Literary Theory in Benjamin, Scholem, and Levinas* (Bloomington and Indianapolis: Indiana University Press, 1991), 209.

86. Levinas, *Totality and Infinity*, 50–51.

87. Ibid., 198–99.

88. For interviews with Robbins and Prejean, see "Angel on Death Row" at http://www2.pbs.org/wgbh/pages/frontline/angel/. (Current as of 20 November 1998.)

89. The film is a composite of events and characters from Prejean's experiences with two death row inmates, Patrick Sonnier and Robert Lee Willie, both executed in the electric chair in 1984. Though the details of the crime in the film are mostly those committed by Sonnier, the character of Matthew Poncelet is based mostly on Willie.

90. As Alphonso Lingis writes, "Exceeded on all sides by responsibilities beyond its control and its capacity even to fulfill, the responsible subject is depicted by Levinas in distress." See his introduction in Levinas, *Otherwise Than Being*, xviii–xix.

91. Levinas, *Otherwise Than Being*, 117.

92. Simon Critchley, *The Ethics of Deconstruction: Derrida and Levinas* (Oxford: Blackwell Press, 1992), 232.

93. This refutes Baudrillard's claim that the "rational humanism" of death penalty abolitionists is an abdication of responsibility. His argument is that left liberal thinking merely follows the tendency of the penal system. Whereas the right calls for a death for a death, the left asks that the criminal be spared "for *he is not really responsible.*" Not only does Sister Helen contradict this assertion, but Baudrillard's general claim that responsibility has been dead for a long time anyway would probably not rest well with most Levinasians. See Jean Baudrillard, *Symbolic Exchange and Death,* trans. Iain Hamilton Grant (London: Sage Publications, 1993), 169–71.

94. Owen Gleiberman, "A View to Kill," *Entertainment Weekly,* 19 January 1996.

95. Jacques Derrida, "Force of Law: The 'Mystical Foundation of Authority,'" in Drucilla Cornell et al, eds., *Deconstruction and the Possibility of Justice* (New York: Routledge, 1992), 12.

96. Ibid., 8.

97. Ibid., 12.

98. Ibid., 14.

99. Ibid.

100. Ibid., 15.

101. Ibid., 22.

102. Ibid., 25.

103. Levinas, *Otherwise Than Being,* 159.

104. Derrida, "Force of Law," 28.

105. Ibid., 6.

106. Cornell, *Philosophy of the Limit,* 155.

107. One of the more unfortunate aspects of the story's transition from book to film is the erasure of race from Prejean's analysis of capital punishment in the United States. While the two men she counseled were white, the majority of death row inmates are black. Prejean also argues convincingly that had their victims been black, Patrick Sonnier and Robert Lee Willie would have been less likely to receive the death penalty. See Prejean, *Dead Man Walking,* 48–50.

108. Bronfen and Goodwin, *Death and Representation,* 16.

109. Ibid., 15–16. See also David Campbell, *Writing Security: United States Foreign Policy and the Politics of Identity* (Minneapolis: University of Minnesota Press, 1992).

110. Bronfen and Goodwin, *Death and Representation,* 16.

111. Levinas, *Totality and Infinity,* 198.

112. Campbell and Dillon, *The Political Subject of Violence,* 161.

113. Ibid., 162.

114. Allen Feldman, *Formations of Violence* (Chicago: Chicago University Press, 1991), 115, quoted in Campbell and Dillon, *The Political Subject of Violence,* 162.

115. Baudrillard, *Symbolic Exchange and Death,* 177.

116. Ibid., 179.

117. See Prejean, *Dead Man Walking,* 116–17, 128–29.

118. Ibid., 116.

119. Derrida, "Force of Law," 19.

120. Ibid., 28.

121. Ibid., 27.

122. Slawner, "Violence, Law, and Justice," 473.
123. Ibid., 469.
124. Levinas, *Totality and Infinity*, 79.
125. Campbell, "The Deterritorialization of Responsibility."
126. See also Critchley, *Ethics of Deconstruction*, 221.
127. Levinas, *Totality and Infinity*, 21.
128. Critchley, op. cit., 222.
129. Levinas, *Ethics and Infinity*, 80.
130. Critchley, *Ethics of Deconstruction*, 223.
131. Ibid., 220.
132. Levinas, *Otherwise Than Being*, 157.
133. Campbell, "The Deterritorialization of Responsibility."
134. Ibid.
135. Emmanuel Levinas, "Ethics and Politics," in *The Levinas Reader*, 294.
136. Campbell, "The Deterritorialization of Responsibility."
137. Ibid.

CHAPTER NINE

Ethics and Identity in Global Market Research

Richard Maxwell

O Lord, thou hast searched me, and known me!

Psalm 139

Identity\Difference

Market research's services would not be needed by its major clients—
transnational consumer goods manufacturers—were all people in agreement about the value and feel of every commodity and service on earth.
Differences in taste and interpretation constitute the basic conditions
on which market research thrives. Its business is knowing all there is to
know about personal and collective representations of value; its modus
operandi is the rational, bureaucratic extraction of this information, i.e.,
consumer surveillance. Few cultural industries claim to be in the identity-making business, yet market research provides an effective staging
ground for the elaboration of the grand narratives and moral geographies of identity and difference: class, nation, gender, race. While these
major axes of collective and personal identity divide who's in and who's
out in a big way, there are millions of stories of identity and difference
to which market research must devote its undivided attention. Market
research confronts and contains the cultural unknowns in these stories,
making sense of consumer biographies for its corporate clients through
categorical representations of the marketplace citizen: targets, audiences,
clusters, segments, and so on. An interpretation of people's identity in

these terms flows from a value system dominated by exchange, the preferred taste culture of the commercial enterprise.

Every enactment and representation of personal or collective identity is indissolubly tied to the construction of difference. Herein lies the ethical problematic I want to confront in this chapter. There's great potential for harm to ourselves and others in securing knowable and stable boundaries around self and collective identification. At the same time, no interpretation of this harm and security can avoid reiterating the paradox, that is, without avoiding the problem. In *Culture and Society* (1958), at the end of his famous (first) attack on the "formula" that sees people as "masses," Raymond Williams was concise on this point of ethics: "To the degree that we find the formula inadequate for ourselves, we can wish to extend to others the courtesy of acknowledging the unknown."[1] Williams's injunction to acknowledge the unknown, as opposed to forcing others to fit pregiven formulas, invokes a high regard for the inevitable, injurious inclusions and exclusions entailed by alter-definitions in identity making. Along with recent writing on the paradoxical "strife and interdependence" in identity\difference,[2] this perspective bids those of us working in cultural and communication studies to recognize ourselves within an ethics of respect for the unknown. Such an ethics would delight in difference and guard against the diminishment or banishment of others who cannot be placed within the moral cartographies associated with the marketplace citizen, be that in masses, audiences, consumers, clusters, and similar notions of life in the global marketplace.

In this chapter I tackle the ethics of market research by examining identity making in the encounter between interviewers working for market research firms and the people interviewed. As I've explained elsewhere, these encounters initiate a process of consumer surveillance, and the interviewers furnish a human front for cultural imperialism in its latest globalizing stage.[3] I'm not convinced, however, that protecting privacy against the interviewer is the moral opposite of consumer surveillance. This moral assumption about privacy can, of course, motivate a critique of market research's role within the informational-cultural complex, but it can also silence the interviewers in a rush of prejudgment that denies insights into the ethical dynamics of the marketing encounter. This chapter looks for ways to politicize thinking about consumer surveillance that are responsive to questions of personhood and identity. My discussion of ethics does not revisit celebrated controversies, nor does it propose codes of conduct to resolve ethical problems within market research. I'm concerned with moral thought implicit in the marketing encounter and with the micropolitics flowing from such tacit standards of judgment and interpretation.

With the interviewers' help, I describe surveillance as a practice that aims to know people while at the same time suppressing the ethical sources available in the encounter. Surveillance thus defined can be enacted by a person inside the boundaries of their own individual (soul-searching) identity, or it can come from the outside, with or without the endorsement of a collective value set. In contrast, I describe the ethical moment in the marketing encounter as one that shakes the ground under the "strategies of distinction," and opens up ways of living with the contingency of identity and difference in everyday encounters in the global marketplace.[4] In a time when the figure of the free market is cloned with liberal democracy and held up as a gain over the vexing problems of state legitimacy, when deterritorialized approaches to collective identity and action define new times for politics within territorial democracies, an ethical source in the marketing encounter keeps in view the promises and problems for freedom that identity making generates within a culture regulated by strategies of distinction. On these terms, readers are free to judge my own interview with interviewers as a harmful form of surveillance or as an ethical moment (or, if you've managed to transcend the ethical problematic altogether, as a waste of time) — I don't think you can do this kind of research without facing this sort of evaluation.

The Interview Encounter

It was January 27, 1995. We took a coffee break at the end of two and a half hours of conversation. I was talking with Valle, Enrique, Gabriel, and Teresa — interviewers for Alef, a market research firm in Spain, which is owned by Millward Brown International, which is part of the Kantar Group, which is a property of the global information-communication conglomerate, WPP.

Valle relaxed and lit the only cigarette she would smoke that day. She grinned, inhaled, and leaned back in her chair in the pose of a veteran. "Probably the most interesting thing about interviewing happened to me while we were conducting a survey of cat and dog owners," she said. "Do you know how to find cat and dog owners after you've talked to everyone with a cat or a dog on the street?" Valle was not speaking about a random survey, but one designed instead to meet the objective of profiling someone who'd be likely to purchase her employer's client's pet food. For the interviewer working the street, this means that there was a quota to be filled and a problem to be solved. Valle's companions had apparently recognized the problem: their smiles displayed what I imagined was the expectant pleasure that comes from puzzling out similar conundrums.

Valle said that she solved the problem by looking for children she could befriend, which she did by bestowing in them her trust and care. "Hey kids," she said, reenacting the way she'd hail the children, "you wouldn't happen to have a little dog at your home, would you?" Greeting strangers as she would a friend opened many doors for Valle; few methods initiated the extraction of personal information from pet owners as well. Valle followed this strategy until one evening she came across a little boy who delighted in her question. "Oh yes, my mom has a dog!" he said. "Really?" said Valle, "would you take me home with you so I can interview her?" Yes, of course, no question, he'd be very pleased to bring Valle to his mother. Valle reasoned that "it's a big deal for kids to bring someone home who wants to do an interview with their mother; after all, she's a Very Important Person, and the fact that someone wants to interview her proves it."

Valle paused to sip her coffee and finish her cigarette. When she resumed, she made a point of emphasizing the boy's elation: it was pure pride of place the way he walked with her through the streets of Madrid, as if he were leading a parade with a brass band in tow. "Then at the apartment," Valle said, "I met his mother."

She was deaf and dumb. At first I didn't know what to do. There was the expression on the kid's face, so full of anticipation and happiness; but there was also my shame in wanting to tell the kid that it's impossible for me to interview his mother, a deaf and dumb person. A long moment passed, and I got more upset and angry; I was losing my patience, and resented having to be there. I realized then that the mother and child had been talking to one another, though I couldn't say how. I gathered up my patience, composed myself, and began the interview with the help of her son's translation. "Ask your mom this, ask her that," I would say. They spoke in this mumbling way, gesticulating or something, I don't

know how, then he'd translate her answer. I wrote it all down, knowing
that the interview wasn't a valid one. I did it anyway, for the kid. I did it
for that boy, even though I knew I wasn't doing my job.

The Ethical Moment in Market Research

The kid and the mysterious "mumbling" and "gesticulating" in Valle's
story take us to the ethical limits of market research, to the interpretive
aporia experienced by interviewers who cannot place a person or object. Market researchers are in the unique position of mediating the encounter between the global sales effort and the practices, values, and
desires of local populations around the world. When a given encounter
resists the local rules or takes place beyond the horizon of correct conduct, market research loses its representational authority and floun-
ders, making waves in the commercial order of things. And yet, its con-
ceit as a business service rests precisely on its institutional security in
the presence of unruly values and desires.

Market research firms have stretched their networks around the world
chasing after their most lucrative clients, transnational consumer goods
manufacturers. In tandem with this globalizing project, market research's
contact with people has multiplied in a growing number of local settings — though understandably concentrated in the north Atlantic region, marketers are busily establishing outposts in Africa, Asia, the Middle East, and Latin America. In the always-local encounter, there are
many different kinds of people from whom market research extracts
information. There are also various forms of contact with people, the
putative information sources, from credit records and telemarketing to
copy-testing and work-study programs, though none are as directly con-
frontational as the interview.

As the go-between, market research is in a difficult structural bind: it
has to make a difference for commercial culture by identifying the friend
and the foe, the "consumer" and the stranger, among its information
sources. In a crucial sense, then, market researchers know that we're labeled somewhat erroneously as mere consumers, and prove it daily by
treating shoppers as information suppliers in the global marketplace.
Market research performs its role as information extractor by risking
an offer to bring everyone into the promised land of post-scarcity in
exchange for personal details. Signs inviting this exchange are all around,

though their idiom and legal status vary from country to country: "convenience" check cashing and "discount" cards at the supermarket, "warranty" contracts to protect household gadgets, credit "protection," and "special offers" over the telephone — all of these life-enhancing perks in return for answering a few questions with personal information. The problem for marketers is that we don't always conform to the plans of a marketing encounter, treating it as an updated version of snake-oil sales, resisting the forced-choice nature of survey questionnaires, avoiding the encounter because we resent not knowing the performative rules, or because we're shy or we're in a rush. There are many reasons why we are indifferent to or disquieted by market research.

Market research, among other cultural institutions, commoditizes categories of consumers and media audiences; it invents identities to which a value of exchange can be attached. These categories, or taxonomic collectives, provide a neatly ordered top-down version of who we are, but they are hard to endorse as an identity because they treat us as strangers to ourselves. We are estranged variously as targets, institutional audiences, an audience commodity, and masses of consumers. Market research works hard to eliminate this strangeness of commoditized categories: it extracts information from us about our tastes, our value assessments of goods and services, and then recombines the familiar identity we've bound up in these things with the imperious and strange exchange values of global merchandisers. The rational, institutional goal of marketing is to put signs of ourselves into commodities. We can derive pleasure from self-identity and alter-definition in and through commodities by artfully composing a lifestyle, and a popular aesthetic, with expressive elements adorning the goods and services. To this extent we can participate in commercial culture by adopting the identity of the marketplace citizen as our own.

The extraction of personal information, in this view, constitutes imperious measurement and representation of people, value, and desire. However, imperialism (in this context, the threat that privacy and sovereignty will be annexed to the global corporate good) recedes from view when the interview encounter, or the unobtrusive character of seemingly passive electronic forms of surveillance, are framed in close-up. The perceived innocuousness of the encounter doesn't eliminate domination, of course, it just distances and ex-nominates the political economy. Welcome to the world according to advertisers and marketers, where our endorsement of commercial culture can be eased from us using our own desire, our self-identification in commodities.

From the perspective of the market encounter, then, the dominant moral cartography of the nation-state appears weak in comparison to the space produced by the global infrastructure of consumption. In the promised land, information about local life flows through global networks across the porous boundaries of consumer markets, virtually reshaping modern landscapes and shifting the borders of political engagement. There the besieged (nationalizing) welfare state is forced to compete for the public's allegiance against the (globalizing) corporate myth of enchanted consumer sovereignty enjoyed by the transcendent figure of the marketplace citizen. The moral guideposts for evaluating the imperious marketing encounter are, in turn, reterritorialized without and within the nation-state. On the one hand, they are supranational, as in the European Union's Directive on Data Protection ("Directive 95/46/EC") and the various responses from transnational information extractors like the Federation of European Direct Marketing (FEDIM). On the other hand, they are infranational, ranging from the conduct handbooks for marketing associations (increasingly modeled on supranational regimes) to the face-to-face encounter of interviewers and people. In this version of informational imperialism, the splintering of the moral problematic along entwined global and local axes also reterritorializes the politics of identity making.

The interview encounter comes with a technique and remit that limits allowable and knowable definitions of self, collectivity, and modes of action. Who or what we end up allying ourselves with plays out in both existential and institutional registers in the encounter and the ensuing process. When we are called upon to identify ourselves as friend or foe of commerce, market research's identity-making discourse conflicts with other, more or less contestable, identities. Individual and collective identity exceeds what's confinable to the categories of consumerhood or other identity containers such as gender, nation, and class. The supervenient order of national identity is not immune to the spillover, and overlap, of competing versions of common cause; the political field of engagement is decentralized within territorial democracies and spreads beyond the reach of international conflict and negotiation.

In this situation of contested loyalties, the client of market research runs the risk of losing our allegiance (market share, in their terms), which deepens the commercial crisis of control over desire and value, keeping the cycle of research in perpetual motion. The demand to maintain people's bond with consumer goods and services, and even to some degree with market research's social function, forces the interviewer to act as a friend under conditions in which they're never told what the moral parameters of such a deception are — though, not surprisingly, most of their supervisors claim to enforce national and international rules of conduct, as stated, for example, in the ethics guidelines of professional marketing associations. Be that as it may, the interviewers only get formal instructions on following the proper technique for the survey they're conducting; and there are relatively few techniques, like quantitative random-route or quota-based surveys, focus groups, and so on.

On the ground, the interviewers — who phone us, knock on our doors, hail us in the streets and shops, or ask us to evaluate the latest espresso-flavored beverage — face the possibility of confronting the unknown, that which is radically incommensurable within the terms of the marketing formula. Nevertheless, the moral circuitry inside the statistical machine (information processing, in their terms) sorts the ineffable into a rational set of differences fit for the client's exchange-based interpretation of identity and value (e.g., in terms of market demographics, geo-demographics, segmentation, and so on). Of course, these parameters of judgment and interpretation are not expressed in oaths of higher purpose, but rather in the mundane jargon of "following procedure" and "enhancing efficiencies." As the market survey makes categories of shoppers virtually equivalent with one another (targets, clusters), transforming groups of people into informational commodities in the process, the bureaucratic assessment of identity\difference lets marketers off the hook of acknowledging the unknown inside or outside their institutional identity. Thus when market research is forced to face up to the ineffable at any point in its procedure, it tends to do one of two things: it invalidates a component of its procedure, to suppress internal discord, or it silences the mysterious other, to avoid external challenges to its authoritative representations of marketplace identities.

And yet there are stories, like the one I offered at the beginning of this chapter, that show the encounter working out of kilter, as it were, at the limits of market research's practical moral thought. Valle experienced an internal struggle that pitted her desire to care for the child's pride against the care for her own identity as a person and as an interviewer. The boy led Valle, according to her account, away from her impatience and anger, and away from the sense of bafflement upsetting her. Though she didn't understand what the mother and son were saying, for they spoke a mysterious language, Valle managed to reduce her discomfort by shifting the mother's difference, represented as "deaf and dumb," onto the survey technique, which Valle felt compelled to define as "invalid." It was an invalid (disabled) technique, because the questionnaire could not bear to hear the mother's voice or her son's translation.

In this encounter, Valle escaped from the secure identity scripted for her by the survey technique. Her defection came when she couldn't do her job while facing the job being done on her — a discomfort acknowledged as shame, impatience, resentment, and anger. She verged on insulting the mother's difference by identifying her as a woman disabled and sense-less. The mother's devalorization, predicated on the market standard of ranking people as information sources, would have remained beyond question had the boy not intervened as an ethical source during the shake-up in the foundation of Valle's institutional identity. Valle resolved her predicament by turning the questionnaire into the only deaf and dumb object in the house, and then destroying it.

Valle's companions echoed her story with verbal recognition of the "psychological difficulty" of the job, which I took to be a mark of familiarity with distancing, or alienation, from their work — the disheartening gap between who they are and what they do. The interviewers experience this distancing if, but not exclusively if, they're faced with the problem of conduct when they cannot place somebody. The gap between who they are and what they do is fundamental here: lacking coherent rationale to make sense of the predicament — caught unawares, like Valle, in the moment's ressentiment — the fixed constructions of identity and difference installed in market research slacken just enough to elicit the power of ethical sources. The child enacted this power by showing the interviewer the way to partake in the simplicity of being with others whom, because of the institutional codes of identity and difference, she initially found unintelligible. Valle insinuated into the encounter her (egoistic) moral identity as a kindhearted person when she "gathered up her patience" instead of turning away from the stranger she couldn't place. As the story goes, Valle abandoned the putative information source, the pet lover, when she found herself confronted with the force of the boy's bluster and idiom blowing apart the guidelines of the technique — and this before she could look to her self as a moral guide. She made a fleeting ethical move in the midst of an interpretive aporia to hold what she couldn't understand in herself and others with high regard, and higher in the end than at least one (the technique) of the two existing moral sources available to her (her kind self was the other).[5]

Meanwhile, it must be said, consumer market research continues to be a chronic universalizer of the capitalist interpretation of value, exchange value, and it works diligently across the globe as the hired censor of competing interpretations; perhaps it could do other things, but when it comes to consumer markets it doesn't. In the process of censoring competitors and coordinating relations among dissenters, market research sets up a rational order of taste cultures, creating oppositions and gulfs within and between collective identities — this setup is what Bourdieu calls "strategies of distinction." With the interviewers' help, I want to add to this argument a new complication: inside the market research encounter there are potential ethical sources from which flow a deterritorialized politics of identity. The political impact registers within and without territorial democracies, scrambling moral maps of nation-states and national cultures. This is important because such ethico-political disruptions can destabilize the "strategies of distinction" that make, sustain, and rank identity within the globally networked infrastructure of consumption.

In market research, the sources for an ethics of encounter are available, for example, in the moment when the interviewer's reaction cannot be contained by the moral order she has hitherto endorsed, either within her institutional role or outside in narratives through which she's elaborated her self identity.[6] The child in Valle's story appears as an ethical source, as does the impossible language spoken by the mother and child. These are ethical sources because they confront the limits of thought about common cause within the market economy's infrastructure of consumption, not because they free up our individual and collective freedom by proving privacy is good or by demonstrating democracy at work through consumer markets. The boy amplified the ethical moment, placing Valle, however briefly, beyond the temptation of disposing of the unknown with a formulaic representation.

Still, only a few of the million stories in the market economy play out the way Valle's did. In fact, at the end of the day, interviewers are more likely to have soothed the symptoms of alienation by falling back on pregiven notions of themselves and others. Valle, for instance, followed up her story of the boy with another tale about two "dwarf sisters who had these little squeaky voices." Valle's investment in being a good-hearted person, like most interviewers, encourages her not to ridicule others; indeed, most of the interviewers I interviewed seemed to enjoy the surprise that often comes when meeting strangers. But the imperative to make sense of those they cannot place puts interviewers under the pressure of categorical norms of personhood. "For me," said Valle, "these little dwarf sisters were really weird, at least at first, because I'd never met such tiny people and seen their tiny clothes and all that — it just seemed unbelievable that they could be so small."

At the Threshold between Friend and Stranger

The experience of mundane unfreedoms and resentments provokes interviewers like Valle to build a repertoire of intrinsic moral conduct into the marketing encounter. Strong intuitions about right and wrong make all difficult exchanges of information ultimately negotiable. For instance, interviewers reported that they successfully maneuvered into an interview by bestowing solidarity upon laboring people or upon women confined to domestic toil — that is, by elaborating sympathies for the laid-off worker, the always overworked housewife, and the exacerbated parent. Or they succeeded by graciously receiving the solidarity bestowed on them by others, reporting exchanges like "My nephew is an interviewer, please come in," "I know how hard this work must be," or "Can I get you anything?" As it turns out, in being a friend to strangers, interviewers bend the rules of technique and procedural conduct.

"The personality of the interviewer shouldn't play a role in the process of the interview; it could happen, but we give them guidelines." Manuel Almeijeiras is the boss, the technical director of survey research at Alef. As he explained, the interviewers "have to be very proficient in the methodology, and there's always a methodology (unless we send them out to find somebody with a Mercedes-Benz)." The reference here is to the fact that the rich are few and survey quotas of them are statistically absurd. But where methodology meets the majority of working- and middle-class homes, says Almeijeiras, the interviewers "have to read the survey questions word for word, and if they don't, we notice."

The interviewers I interviewed dissented gently from their boss's opinion. Despite the technical rules and the handbooks on proper technique, "personality" is probably the most decisive feature of the marketing encounter. Personality, however, holds many connotations within an interviewer's self and institutional identity: it means extroversion, quick wits, empathy, consoling affect, youthfulness, uplift, a validating persona, and humility, among other features. Whatever personality is, it works best at the door, on the threshold between inside and out, friend and stranger.

Consider the effort to overcome the anxiety of intruding into the daily routine of people's lives. "Not everybody is cut out for this kind of work," said Valle. "It's not just the legwork either; imagine going up to some stranger's door and it opens up, that's hard." "It's not that hard," Enrique said. "At least not to go up to a stranger's door one time; the anxiety comes from doing it all the time." Enrique is a tough guy, and he's been doing this job for a number of years; he has a brother who is also an interviewer. "It wears on you," he said, "because you never know when the person's going to be screwed up on drugs, booze, or who knows what. Anyway, most of the time you do the interview at the door."

Valle insisted again on the threat of the moment by adding an element of empathy to her story: "There's also the mutual risk involved in going up to a door," she said. "They don't know what to expect, you're waiting on the other side for them to answer, and you feel as much in the dark as they do."

Efficiency and disinterest are also allies working through this moment of anxiety, as Gabriel pointed out: "It's a lot faster if you keep the interview at the door," he said. Enrique added that "probably 80 percent of the people interviewed won't even consider letting you come in the house."

Yet the draw of the empathy works against efficient technique in unpredictable ways, for example, when the interviewer offers a safer haven for revealing intimate stories than does the neighbor next door. "Sometimes," said Valle, "when a neighbor passes by, snooping around, the person you're interviewing doesn't want them to know what they're saying and invites you in." Valle explained that the neighbor would be unsympathetic to the things the woman is talking about, "her husband, his salary, the kids—she feels she's saying stuff that can only shock the neighbor."

"If it's a woman," said Enrique, "at least in my case, they don't usually ask me in." He was sure of himself. "I don't think women have an easier time getting people to open up to them," he said. "Oh sure it's true that there are more women interviewers, but not because they're better at getting people to open up." Teresa interrupted: "I don't know about that," she said. "One time a young woman answered the door crying, and I made her feel better by saying how there's nothing to be so upset about at her age." For Teresa, consoling others seems to be a permanent part of the job. "The girl calmed down and I got the interview," she said. "I just think women being interviewed don't like to stop what they're doing for a male interviewer." But then Teresa reconsidered. "A lot depends on the theme of the interview, on the individual interviewer, on the day—there are really no fixed rules," she said. "I'd have to say advantages are based more on personality than on the sex of the interviewer."

Personality again. "If people are at ease it's easier to convince them," Gabriel said. People don't mind the initial moment of encounter if the interviewer offers encouraging words in exchange for information. "You can get a lot of interviews if you're able to convey a sense of uplift," Teresa added. "That is, if you can show enthusiasm, but sometimes it's hard to insist when people are gloomy." Encounters with the gloom of modern life is a fact of the interviewer's routine; they must confront unhappiness and persevere in their work. "After a while on this job you start to know neighborhoods where you can expect bad tempers," Enrique said. "If you're in San Blas, for example," a working-class area in Madrid, "you know you're not going to be talking to a lot of engineers, and there's a lot of unemployment. This makes people seriously upset about life."

"I smile a lot," said Gabriel. "I think that my smile is . . . um . . . captivating, especially with older women; at least that's what they tell me." Enrique laughed, "Poor baby," he said. "Hey, it works for me," said Gabriel. "They see how young I am and ask if I'm a student, what I'm doing, and I tell them that I'm working my way through college." He grinned impishly.

"It can be dangerous, too, and you have to think fast," said Valle. "Once a man answered the door wearing only a little towel around his waist.

He insisted I come in, so I had to look around quickly for signs that it was safe to go in." Nobody explained this aspect of the job to Valle; she learned to deal with it on her own. "I guess I don't have any tricks like Enrique or Gabriel. I just try to be nice, though it's not like I go all smiles or anything." Then she said: "I think it's important to be a bit intriguing, though. So I'll try to spice up the questions by saying things like: Now, I don't know how you'd respond to this next question.... Let's see, it's kind of...well...And then they'd say: Kind of what? What question? Tell me. So I play a little game with them."

The performative rules of being interviewed can also be daunting, for not everyone feels comfortable that they have the proper manner for the encounter. In that case, the interviewer must validate the person's sense of self-esteem, as Teresa explained: "Sometimes people feel unqualified to answer, so you assure them it's not a test of their knowledge. People have said to me: How would I know about that? and I just try to appreciate them as individuals and reassure them that they know a lot." Enrique wasn't convinced: "People can be embarrassed by their ignorance, lack of education, when you ask them questions," he said. "But that's really a limitation based on a lack of confidence," said Teresa. "So you insist that they're really smart, they have an opinion of their own, and that it's important." The personal touch versus the technical touch. "You're prohibited from helping them, of course," added Teresa, "though you might coach them on one or two questions to get them started."

Many times, in contrast, the snobbery of the interview subject shapes the tone of an interview — it's worth noting that only about a third of all people chosen by technical procedure for contact agree to be interviewed, so there are people who agree to be interviewed but then are rude or snooty to the interviewer. As Valle put it, "On top of everything else, we don't have what you might call social recognition." She said: "Our status in people's eyes is unclear, so sometimes people seem to look down on what we do. They think because we're lower than them that they can slam the door in our face or, and I'm not sure if this is worse, that we get something out of their boring life story, which they of course think is fascinating. And we have to listen. The point is that these people don't know us at all, and we have to give the impression that we're writing it all down and what they're saying is really important."

All successful market encounters rely upon the kindness of strangers, from the obvious case of the interviewer to the life-enhancing promises

of credit-reporting agencies, junk mailers, and the goodness of consumers in accepting these promises. This even goes for the abusive interview subject who nonetheless answers questions; the interviewer must
kindly (if not happily) listen. In other words, there's profit for market
research in cultivating the identity of empathy among its army of interviewers and, to a certain extent, among those interviewed or surveyed.
Yet empathy can also work to hide the blow that fixes identity: those
who don't match the identity projected by the survey or the personal
projections of interviewers are turned away from the marketplace, becoming dreadful creatures, strangers lacking recognizable qualities as
consumers, the invalid ones. Kindness outwardly masks the survey's
pre-scripted definitions of people's self and collective identity and at
the same time sweetens the interviewer's and interview subject's inward and outward loyalties to the market economy. As empathy and
kindness erase the threshold between friend and stranger, market research makes us friends of commerce and, in the process, strangers to
ourselves.

Confession in the Culture of Distinction

The practice of market research is designed to enhance our lives as consumers by getting to know us, inside and out. At the same time, however,
in its pre-scripted prejudgments of value and people, market research
performs a kind of triage that segregates and stratifies experience, creating its own version of human refuse out of groups it cannot account
for. Its "dirty little secret," the one we know already, is that in its very
design market research betrays the promise of giving people what they
want. Besides the morality of stratifying value and desire on ability-to-
pay criteria, market research also makes moral choices when representing what and who it cannot make sense of—unless, that is, it chooses
to acknowledge the unknown and to endorse a sense of delight in finding itself on shaky ground (a tough choice, as we've seen). Together,
these two moral failures—discrimination and suppression of ethical
sources—probably best explain why most critics construe market research as a merely harmful form of consumer surveillance.[7]

   An alternative to condemning market research as harmful surveillance is proposed by David Lyon. Lyon is one of the few writers who
has confronted the thinness of moral arguments in surveillance theory,
especially those that hold onto privacy as a moral framework for over-

coming the moral poverty of surveillance society—the latter term is best seen as the double for the liberal (and virtuous) information society. For Lyon, privacy offers a weak basis on which to develop an ethico-political countersurveillance, since privacy discourse is not free from the family of practices that have engendered and sustained patriarchy, private property, possessive individualism, and harmful surveillance itself.[8]

In his study, *The Electronic Eye: The Rise of Surveillance Society,* Lyon divides theories about information-gathering techniques for monitoring and controlling populations into two opposing moral visions: utopian and dystopian. Lyon refuses to entertain much of the utopian literature that contends that information technologies will free up more freedom—this literature is ineffective, he suggests, because it denies the increasing concentration of corporate, state, and military control over the means of generating information; the bureaucratization entailed by military-state-capital growth; and the widening social cleavages wrought by accumulation and monopoly. Blue-sky utopias, in short, aren't likely to arise out of the prevailing political economy. Lyon thus avoids the trite arguments of futurists who've failed to do their homework.

While the political economy squeezes out emancipatory possibilities, Lyon also challenges Orwell's Big Brother and Bentham-Foucault's panopticon, even though he argues that these dystopian visions offer the more accurate metaphors for the surveillance-information society. Lyon fully appreciates Michel Foucault's reading of Jeremy Bentham's plan for the panopticon, arguing that it created a powerful way to explain how a population's visibility, coupled with invisible surveillance machinery, induces in the social body a state of uncertainty that not only subjects people to a situation of power, but also makes them the bearer of that power. He is nevertheless dissatisfied by what he describes as the inability of Orwellian or Foucauldian perspectives to think about what can be done to achieve a "desirable state of affairs" once they've articulated the undesirable.[9]

Beyond the utopian-dystopian fix, says Lyon, there's a competing approach based on Augustinian principles that interprets surveillance in the framework of a confession. In Lyon's Augustinian vision, the ideal of the confession locates surveillance within a space modeled on the City of God, the *Civitate Dei,* where social participation is based on a "given" human solidarity, as opposed to "effort" or "market position." From the vantage point of this moral geography "personhood is understood..."

as the *imago dei,* which again accents solidarity, dignity and responsibility" contra the data-images in, for example, the marketer's discourse. This is not utopianism, Lyon argues, since the practical problems people experience are always already conditioned by the vagaries of the temporal world, the earthly city, the "*civitas terrena,*" where "self-possessing power and other-denying violence again reign."[10] In short, to challenge the normativity of surveillance society, and the harm and security in identity making, we must look to the City of God for guidance and resist contempt for what faces us in the present world. The City of God, "the other city," provides a counter "present reality which both exposes wrong in, and offers alternatives within, temporal society."[11]

Like all moral sources, Lyon's confessional metaphor, is predicated on "a (putative) command or design from which interpretation and judgment can proceed."[12] Obviously, Lyon anchors his critique of the dystopians to foundations of Christian thought, pitting the Augustinian vision against the utilitarian perspective of Bentham, for instance, in order to interrogate certain key premises that migrated into later (i.e., Foucauldian) insights about the panopticon. According to Lyon, Bentham developed his view of surveillance from a parody of Psalm 139, the basis for the "god's eye" metaphor at the center of the panopticon. Lyon argues that Bentham's parody was wrongheaded because it transformed the hopes put to the psalmist's god — for omnipotence, care, and salvation — into a design of "moral architecture" — for social control through fear, uncertainty, and the absence of love. Lyon argues that Foucault confronted Bentham's "moral architecture" without questioning the effect that might have flowed from a parody that eliminated the psalmist's imprecation for self-revelation in/through a personalized relation with God.

In contrast to the panopticon's anonymous inspector, knowledge of inner and outer identity is grasped in the confessional space by way of an encounter with the central presence: "O Lord, thou hast searched me and known me! . . . Do I not hate them that hate thee, O Lord? And do I not loathe them that rise up against thee? I hate them with perfect hatred; I count them mine enemies. Search me, O God, and know my heart! Try me, and know my thoughts! And see if there be any wicked way in me, and lead me in the way everlasting!"[13]

Consider the psalmist's emphasis on knowing one's true identity, the real "me," by reckoning how it's been constituted in surveillance: "thou hast searched me, and known *me!*" Note also how Psalm 139 invites a test of personal loyalty to a higher purpose, in this case identifying one-self as friend or foe of God, with "perfect hatred" cutting a clear moral division between who's in and who's out. And in the last line, alterity is fully exposed through the encounter, yet represented as threatening oth-erness, "any wicked way," inside the self.[14]

Denied the possibility of this encounter-in-domination, prisoners in the panopticon are understandably doomed to be seen without seeing, while the panopticon inspector, playing a cowardly god, hides in order to see prisoners without being seen. Since the central presence cannot be confronted or scrutinized in the metaphor of the panoptic gaze, the ethical dynamics of the confessional encounter cannot be appreciated. It's for this reason, Lyon surmises, that "today's actors in the surveil-lance drama" have focused their criticism on "control by inspection and impersonal categorization."[15] With the confession metaphor of personal encounter installed again, the possibility of "seeing while being seen" returns to the theory of surveillance.

The confession offers a compelling analogy in the context of market research, a business that sets up and regulates points of contact between its corporate clients — who must "see" and "know" people through per-sonal value assessments of goods and services — and the consuming public — whose bodies, desires, and values are "seen" and "known." Al-though the interview technique and the pseudoscientific criterion on which it's based demand depersonalized conduct in the field, the inter-viewers I interviewed betrayed the mechanical approach and demon-strated how crucial the personal touch is for extracting information. In this sense, the interviewer's identity as empathy and surveyor in the "earthly city" coincides with the moral space of the "City of God" — the interview enacts a secular confession, the interviewer plays a non-theist confessor.

The process of confession must be understood outside of priest-confessor domination, however, since it is the communal context that Lyon seeks to emphasize. "Mutual confession," he says, "represents the road to transparency, which is of course anathema to the paranoid." Pressed as we are by the violence of the political economy, a politics of transparency either destroys its own virtuous goals or becomes conta-minated by the vicissitudes of modernity with which it is fated to asso-ciate. "But surely," asks Lyon, "transparency in the context of trust and forgiveness is utterly different from transparency in the thrall of power?"[16]

The question is how to push past skepticism (beyond contempt for the earthly city) to find an emancipatory space for the transparency of mutual confession.

Enter Jürgen Habermas, with radical qualifications, into Lyon's confessional. In the Habermasian ideal speech situation, opponents can always establish a ground of coordinated action; in the ideal speech act, there's never a plan of liberation that enslaves planners. While Lyon commends the goal of "undistorted communication," he joins those who see Habermas's vision of political unity as inadequate, since it cannot be easily uprooted from the ground from which it seeks to break free. It's hard to avoid making egocentric calculations in communicative action that do not rest on pregiven representations of self and others — the ethico-political dilemma embodied by the empathy. It's hard to find a communication medium left undistorted by political economy — the problem that hired censors of competing interpretations of value work throughout the informational-cultural complex. Then there's the paradox that collective action inevitably limits individual freedom (related by Lyon as a problem of insufficient development of the metaphor of the convenant). "Such difficulties would have to be faced," says Lyon, "before 'communicative action' could form the basis for a non-dystopian surveillance theory."[17]

But instead of facing these difficulties, Lyon returns to Augustine to launch a new surveillance theory inspired by Christian teachings, "animated by a hope of peace, rather than power, of participation, rather than exclusion, of love, rather than fear."[18] We needn't be attached to the Christian faith to salute these values, but Lyon's demand for a moral source leads him to find ways of transcending the (earthly) limitations of existing surveillance theory — and he's already rejected privacy. So what remains?

A demand remains to find a vantage point outside of the interdependence of harm and security in identity\difference. It's in that impossible location that Lyon would transform the purpose of consumer surveillance by replacing personhood, in the *imago dei*, for the data image, and participation and solidarity, in the confession, for mechanized one-way surveillance. The problem with this, of course, is that, except in the moral landscape charted by Psalm 139, there's no outside identity from which to secure universal allegiance to confessional self-pursuit. It's obviously a politically ineffective position if solidarity, peace, and love have to be pregiven for the confessional to work. The making of identity, or personhood, is indissolubly linked to the construction of difference, and so the potential for alter-definition to cause injury is not resolved by Lyon's reverence for Augustinian principles — the snag of the paradox of identity\difference.

There's also a snag for Lyon's confessional in the political economy of consumer market research: the latter regulates the unruly preferences for goods and services within a regime of tastes dominated by transnational commercial preferences, the structured "strategies of distinction." He's aware of this, yet he can only appeal to the metaphysics of morals outside of the political economy. There's an additional obstacle, probably not the last, in the pragmatics of the encounter itself: the ideal speech situation in practice cannot avoid the clash of contents, interpretive struggles, distortion in channels, and the collision of taste cultures embedded in "strategies of distinction."

Ironically, in searching for the external moral vantage point from which to regulate mutual surveillance, Lyon assures that the confession is no place for cultivating care for the unknown. In wishing for an external moral source to care for identity and difference — a better policy protecting privacy, for instance — we're simply beautifying the panopticon instead of acknowledging the ethical problematic at the heart of the identity-making business. As examples from interview encounters suggest, symbolic "other-denying violence" is predicated on personhood accented by solidarity and kindness, the *imago dei,* the face of the kind stranger.

Beyond the Confession

William Connolly argues that most confessional scenarios have a moment of conversion in them. This is obvious in the Augustinian perspective offered by Lyon, for in its confession-conversion proposal lies the potential of an "ethical awakening."[19] Mutual surveillance, the encounter-in-domination, promises some form of enhanced awareness of the practice of information extraction at the heart of the marketing encounter; at the same time, it marks an end point in the pursuit of self-knowledge: reveal how you know me, O market researcher, and I'll come to know the real me. Hope emanates from Lyon's endorsement of transparency in a critical dialogue, a hope that he wants to amplify beyond Habermasian principles of communicative action. What actually happens to the actors in the transparent encounter is not, however, made quite clear in Lyon's account. Personhood and participation are seen as good causes, but the empowerment through representation (mirroring the *imago dei*) and mutual surveillance ("seeing while being seen") are not freed from power that harms others.

Absent the support of priests, transcendent normative theories, metaphysics of morals, and otherwise dogmatic sources, the critique of market surveillance in the global infrastructure of consumption awakens to the following dilemmas: the legitimacy crisis of political order within territorial democracies and the difficult question of how to make policies in terms adequate for deterritorialized politics, identity, and ethics. Can policy within and without the nation-state be organized around the "cultivation of agonistic care for strife and interdependence in identity\difference"?[20] Can laws, directives, policies, and statutes representing and regulating the informational-cultural complex effectively install the paradox of identity\difference, or any paradoxical relation of harm and security, without putting the proverbial spanner in the normative works?

I've focused on interviewers for global firms because they have many tales of conflicts between corporate and popular interpretations of value in the global marketplace — salutary, mundane, insightful, and disturbing (apart from the fact that they're invested in being good people, work for imperious cultural industries, and identify themselves as kind strangers and empaths). The marketing encounter thrives on this kind of interpretive struggle, but sustains it without agonistic respect for the contenders: it works without apology as the hired chronicler/censor of competing stories and recombines personal stories of desire and value with the narrower value of exchange. The interpretive struggle at the center of this encounter-in-domination enacts a paradoxical relation of harm and security in its version of identity-making; a paradox that won't go away because we wish it away with a beautiful external standard of conduct and judgment — unruly unknowns, if not suppressed in the encounter, will make that abundantly clear.

Many of the connections that information extractors like marketers set up between people and their corporate clients lack the participatory features of a face-to-face confrontation — cash machines and credit cards position their users in the panoptic (di)vision of consumption where people's tastes and values are seen-tracked-mapped-predicted. An entire generation of Americans has grown up under the controls of bar codes and computers. My friends tell me that they enjoy the absence of face-to-face encounters, for these are anxiety-producing confrontations; they prefer dealing with machines and other passive forms of consumer surveillance. By suppressing the potential for inciting anxiety or resentment in the participants, however, the experience of information extraction comes to include a key disavowal of the moral dimension of imperious measures. Nevertheless, this invisibility merely ex-nominates the objective force of the political economy rather than weakening it, and it's for this reason that invisible surveillance, the panopticon, eludes an ethico-political critique, that is, outside the circle fixed by utopian and dystopian perspectives.

Inside this normative circle, privacy protection and rules regulating mechanized, passive surveillance are frozen as the good that opposes evil in the marketplace of the information-surveillance society. As workers in the consumer surveillance sector, interviewers are easy targets for the charge of invading privacy, a transgression that for some constitutes an attack on one of the key characteristic values of individual freedom. Extended to the national scale, these privacy invasions are also threats to sovereignty, especially in the increasingly globalized circuits of market research. Market research maps the extent and depth of identity and difference in the global marketplace, and the craft knowledge possessed by its technicians, machines, designers, and interviewers is guided by explicit and tacit codes of conduct. Yet the ethical problematic associated with this commercial enterprise exceeds the prevailing moral frameworks of privacy and sovereignty. Privacy and sovereignty can only shadow the surveillance-information society; in other words, privacy and sovereignty are moral but not dialectical opposites of surveillance-information.

At the same time, the critique and interpretation of market research, including this one, is pressed hard by intrinsic moral codes and attendant pursuits of self-knowledge. Critics as well as enthusiasts of the transnational infrastructure of consumption have been making many unexamined moral claims — for example, in terms of resistance, cultural imperialism, pleasure, national sovereignty, identity — without too much explicit engagement with the limitations of ethical foundations in their writing. I include myself among those who've been silent, or cagey, about ethics, and offer this chapter as my first cut at a vexing paradox.

Notes

I wish to thank field interviewers at the Spanish market research firm, Alef-Millward Brown: Enrique Rodriguez, Valle Rodriguez, Teresa Ortega, and Gabriel Fernandez; Manuel Almeijeiras, director of survey research at Alef; and Perla Haimovich of Perla Haimovich and Associates in Madrid, who described the confessional character of interviewing to me while I interviewed her in London. David Morley encouraged me to dig deeper into the ethics of interviewing interviewers, and William E. Connolly and Michael J. Shapiro showed me ways to do it.

1. Raymond Williams, *Culture and Society* (London: Penguin, 1966), 289.

2. William E. Connolly, *Identity\Difference: Democratic Negotiations of Political Paradox* (Ithaca: Cornell University Press, 1991); *The Augustinian Imperative: A Reflection on the Politics of Morality* (Newbury Park, Calif.: Sage Publications, 1993); and *The Ethos of Pluralization* (Minneapolis: University of Minnesota Press, 1995).

3. Richard Maxwell, "Out of Kindness and Into Difference: The Value of Global Market Research," *Media, Culture and Society* 18, 1 (January 1996): 105.

4. Pierre Bourdieu, *Distinction: A Social Critique of the Judgement of Taste,* trans. R. Nice (Cambridge: Harvard University Press, 1984), chapter 5; and *Sociology in Question,* trans. R. Nice (London: Sage Publications, 1993), 1.

5. Cf. Connolly, *The Augustinian Imperative,* 38.

6. Cf. Michael J. Shapiro, *Violent Cartographies* (Minneapolis: University of Minnesota Press, 1997), chap. 6.

7. D. Lyon, *The Electronic Eye: The Rise of Surveillance Society* (Minneapolis: University of Minnesota Press, 1994).

8. Ibid., chap. 10; cf. Nancy Fraser, *Unruly Practices: Power, Discourse and Gender in Contemporary Social Theory* (Minneapolis: University of Minnesota Press, 1989), part 3.

9. Ibid., 201.

10. Ibid., 212.

11. Ibid., 213.

12. Connolly, *The Augustinian Imperative,* 38.

13. Psalms 139.1, 21–24. H. G. May and B. M. Metzger, *The New Oxford Annotated Bible with Apocrypha* (New York: Oxford University Press, 1977).

14. Cf. ibid., 762n.

15. Lyon, *The Electronic Eye,* 78.

16. Ibid., 210.

17. Lyon, *The Electronic Eye,* 211.

18. Ibid., 212.

19. Ibid., 120.

20. Connolly, *Identity\Difference,* 220–22.

Contributors

David Campbell is professor of international politics at the University of Newcastle. His most recent book is *National Deconstruction: Violence, Identity, and Justice in Bosnia* (Minnesota, 1998).

William E. Connolly is professor of political science at The Johns Hopkins University and author of *Why I Am Not a Secularist* (Minnesota, 1999) and *The Ethos of Pluralization* (Minnesota, 1995).

Michael Dillon is professor of politics at the University of Lancaster. His most recent book is *Politics of Security.*

Bonnie Honig is professor of political science at Northwestern University and senior research fellow at the American Bar Foundation. Her forthcoming book is *No Place Like Home: Democracy and the Politics of Foreignness.*

Kate Manzo is lecturer in international development in the departments of geography and politics at the University of Newcastle, and the author of *Creating Boundaries: The Politics of Race and Nation.*

Richard Maxwell is associate professor of media at Queens College, City University of New York. He is the author of *The Spectacle of Democracy: Spanish Television, Nationalism, and Political Transition* (Minnesota, 1995).

Patricia Molloy completed a doctoral dissertation entitled *From the Strategic Self to the Ethical Relation: Pedagogies of War and Peace* at the Ontario Institute for Studies in Education, University of Toronto. Her next project is on Bosnia war movies and the ethics of spectacle.

Michael J. Shapiro is professor of political science at the University of Hawai'i and author of *Violent Cartographies* (Minnesota, 1997).

Daniel Warner works at the Graduate Institute of International Studies in Geneva. He has edited a volume titled *Human Rights and Humanitarian Law: The Quest for Universality,* and is currently directing a project on ethical perspectives for new issues in international politics.

Permissions

Index